RETURNS TO EDUCATION

The Jossey-Bass / Elsevier
International Series

Elsevier Scientific Publishing Company
Amsterdam

Returns to Education

AN INTERNATIONAL COMPARISON

GEORGE PSACHAROPOULOS

Higher Education Research Unit,
London School of Economics and Political Science

assisted by

KEITH HINCHLIFFE

Ahmadu Bello University,
Zaria, Nigeria

 Jossey-Bass Inc., Publishers
San Francisco · Washington 1973

RETURNS TO EDUCATION
An International Comparison

by George Psacharopoulos
assisted by Keith Hinchliffe

For the United States of America and Canada:

Jossey-Bass, Inc., Publishers
615 Montgomery Street
San Francisco, California 94111

For all other areas:

Elsevier Scientific Publishing Company
335 Jan van Galenstraat
Amsterdam, The Netherlands

Library of Congress Catalogue Card Number LC 72-83210

International Standard Book Number ISBN 0-87589-154-3

Manufactured in The Netherlands

FIRST EDITION

Code 7239

The Jossey-Bass/Elsevier International Series

Studies on Education

To my parents

Foreword

This book comes from the LSE Higher Education Research Unit and is one of a series on problems related to the economics of education. The Unit, which now has some fifteen research staff working on half a dozen projects, has been seeking to fill gaps in our understanding of the relationship between education and the economy as a whole. We have been trying to answer questions such as these: What is the connection between the number of educated people and the productive efficiency of the economy? How can one effectively study the educational system as a whole rather than in separate sectors, as official inquiries normally do? How do different ways of financing and providing education affect the individual choices of individual people?

The present book relates essentially to the first of these questions, although it touches on all of them. The cornerstone of practically any analysis in the economics of education is the relationship between benefits and costs associated with different levels of schooling. Once empirical data are available on these variables the information can be summarized into estimates of the rate of return to investment in education. So far, the literature has not been very helpful in providing empirical estimates of the returns to education, and has been limited to generalizations based on findings from about half a dozen studies. This is one of the reasons why the rate of return concept has not been widely accepted.

Recently, however, the necessary data for estimating the profitability of investment in education have become available in a number of countries. In this book we have reviewed 53 case studies of the returns to education representing the experience of 32 countries. The data contained in these studies are used to throw light on some basic questions which have intrigued researchers in this field for a long time: How do the returns to education compare with the returns to alternative forms of investment? What is the relationship between the private and social profitability of investment in education? Can inter-country differences in human capital endowments help to explain differences in the level of per capita income? Which educational level is more profitable? How do the returns to education in developed countries compare with those in less developed countries? Can the returns to education in different countries help to explain the phenomenon of the brain drain?

The results have indicated that in fact education is a good investment. However, it is the lower educational levels that exhibit the highest returns. On these criteria, university education is only marginally a "good investment". Of course the private returns to all levels of education are much higher than the social ones. When the returns are viewed across countries the pattern is that less developed countries enjoy higher returns to educational investment than more advanced countries. The results also indicate that the difference between poor and rich countries lies more in the difference in human than in physical capital. And that differences in the returns to education can help in explaining the brain drain.

In addition to the basic analysis which is conducted in terms of rates of return, a separate analysis of costs and earnings was undertaken. This has indicated the magnitude of the relative cost of different levels of education in a number of countries. As expected, higher educational levels are *relatively* more expensive in less developed than in advanced countries. Finally, an analysis of relative earnings by educational level has helped us to throw some light on the thorny problem of the elasticity of substitution among different types of educated labour. The results show that the degree of substitution is considerable and this gives weight to the rate of return versus the manpower requirements methodology in educational planning.

The overall conclusion from the book is that it is helpful as part of any educational planning exercise to attempt to assess the economic returns to education. At the least these calculations can throw valuable light on questions of resource allocation within the educational sector, and between education and the rest of the economy.

C. A. Moser

Acknowledgements

I am greatly indebted to a number of persons who have contributed in one way or another to the completion of this book.

The first credit must go to Professor Mark Blaug who has followed closely the development of this project since the very beginning and offered ideas, criticisms and suggestions for improvement. Readers familiar with his ideas will be able to see through the pages how much this book owes to him. Another major credit must go to Mr Richard Layard who has continuously scrutinized dark corners in the book and discovered many pitfalls. And Mr Gareth Williams has not only offered valuable criticisms throughout the project but also created the right research atmosphere in the Unit which made this study possible.

Mr Keith Hinchliffe has been more than an assistant to me, and this is reflected in the title page. He was responsible for most of the statistical analysis in this volume and moreover he has written parts of Chapters 8 and 9.

Professors Mary Jean Bowman, W. Lee Hansen, Sherman Robinson, T. W. Schultz and Burton Weisbrod have commented on earlier drafts on this study. Their criticisms have been valuable in shaping the orientation of the final product. I am also indebted to Drs. Chris Dougherty and Reuben Gronau, Professor Jerry Miner and Mr Gavin Osmond for offering detailed comments on the final draft. Dr Dougherty has in addition read the proofs and helped me make some important last-minute corrections.

During the early stages of this project Professors Samuel Bowles and Martin Carnoy and Miss Maureen Woodhall helped me locate a number of rate of return studies which I would otherwise have missed. And I would like to extend my gratitude to all those who allowed their unpublished results to be used in this study. The secretarial burden of the project was mainly carried by Miss Anne Usher who has never complained about typing too many drafts.

This project is one of a series of manpower planning studies supported by a grant from the Social Science Research Council to the Higher Education Research Unit. Preliminary results of the research reported in this book have been published in *The Journal of Political Economy*, *The Comparative Education Review*, *Minerva* and *Higher Education*.

To all above I express my deep thanks. And of course I am the only one responsible for failing, sometimes, to adhere fully to their advice.

London School of Economics   GEORGE PSACHAROPOLOUS
and Political Science

Contents

Foreword

Acknowledgements

1. Introduction and Summary   1
2. Rate of Return Estimation Procedures   19
3. Documentation of Profitability Studies Around the World   35
4. Searching for Rate of Return Patterns   61
5. The Allocative Efficiency of Investment in Education   75
6. Human Versus Physical Capital Accumulation in Economic Development   87
7. The Contribution of Education to Economic Growth   111
8. Cost and Earnings Structures   125
9. Testing Some Behavioural Models   137

APPENDIXES

A. The Sensitivity of Rate of Return Estimates to the Shape of the Age-earnings Profile   155
B. Comparative Information on the Contents of Existing Profitability Studies   158
C. Sources of Rate of Return Estimates Used in This Study   166
D. Unit Social Costs by Educational Level   173
E. Estimation of Human and Physical Capital Per Member of the Labour Force   178
F. The Distribution of the Labour Force by Educational Level and Relative Wages   183
G. Rate of Return Patterns and Alternative Measures of Development   187
H. Additional Tables   191
I. Glossary of Symbols   197

References   199
List of Figures   208
List of Tables   209
Subject Index   211
Author Index   214
Index of Countries   216
Books from the Higher Education Research Unit   217

Chapter 1. Introduction and Summary

This book has both an informative and an analytical function. The informative function is served by providing evidence on the economic returns to investment in formal education in a large number of countries. The analytical function is served by an attempt to make empirical generalizations from this evidence and thereby to throw some light on the role of education in the process of economic growth and development.

Concern for education by economists started about fifteen years ago when empirical investigations in the United States revealed that output was growing much faster than inputs as conventionally measured. The part of the growth of output unaccounted for by conventional inputs came to be known as the "residual" or the "coefficient of our ignorance". Original explanations of the residual such as "technical change" or "shifts of the production function" were of little help analytically. How could a country shift its production function or induce technical change so as to achieve a higher level of output?[1]

This led researchers to try to open the black box of technical change and reduce the unexplained residual. The main initial development was the quantification of the increase in the quality of labour inputs and this led to the creation of a new field in economics known as the "economics of human capital", or more narrowly, the "economics of education".[2] Since then there has been an almost 180° shift of emphasis in development planning, the emphasis changing

---

[1] For the earlier classics see Abramovitz (1956), Solow (1957), Fabricant (1959) and Schultz (1961). For further discussions see Denison (1962 and 1967), Griliches (1963), OECD (1964) and Bowman (1971). For a critical view see Balogh and Streeten (1963).

[2] In fact it was a rediscovery, since people as far back as Adam Smith and as recent as Marshall had already written about the economic consequences of education. For the historical evolution of the field see Bowman (1966), Blandy (1967) and Kiker (1966 and 1968).

from physical to human capital as the major source of growth.[3]

Once education had been seen as an investment, the next question was: what is the monetary pay-off from this investment? For, if the objective is an efficient allocation of resources between different uses, the yield on investment in men has to be compared with that on investment in other forms of capital. Suppose, for the moment, that the returns to investment in human capital can be satisfactorily measured. Then, if the returns to investment in a particular educational level are higher than the returns to physical capital, we would conclude that there is under-investment at this level of education. Conversely, if the returns to human capital are lower than the returns to physical capital, then investment in the second form of capital should be given priority. Therefore, at the centre of any discussion of optimal resource allocation lies the concept of a profitability measure of investment in education.[4]

Casual observation and statistical data indicate that people with more education earn higher wages relative to people with less education. For example, the average earnings of a male college graduate in the United States in 1959 were $9,255 and the corresponding earnings of a high school graduate $6,132.[5] Therefore, a college graduate would expect to earn on the average during his working life a net $3,123 over what he would be earning as a secondary school graduate. But in order to enjoy this extra benefit he would have to invest a certain amount of money in higher education. The total private cost of four years at college in 1959 was estimated to be $14,768, which includes both direct expenses such as tuition fees and books as well as indirect costs in the form of foregone earnings while studying.[6] The investment equivalent of the above venture is that of buying a promise to receive annually $3,123 at a cost of $14,768 now. A simple calculation shows that the annual yield of this particular investment is about 20 per cent, and this is what is known as the internal rate of return to investment in higher education.[7] Rates of return to invest-

---

[3] The popularity of the field is witnessed by the increase in the items of Blaug's bibliography from 792 in the 1966 edition to 1358 in the 1970 one.

[4] On this matter see Solow (1963) and Schultz (1967).

[5] See Griliches (1970), Table 2.

[6] See Hines et al. (1970), Table A-1.

[7] The crude calculation is 3,123 : 14,768 = 0.21. Of course, this calculation assumes that the benefit will remain constant over time and that it will accrue for ever. A correction for a finite working-life horizon (equal to 43 years) reduced the above rate of return by 6 per cent of itself. The reader should bear in mind that this is just an illustration, and that actual calculations are much more complicated than the above example and involve many controversial assumptions (see Chapter 2).

2

ment in other levels of schooling can be computed in a similar fashion.

During the last decade, rate of return estimates to investment in education have become available for a large number of countries. What we have done in this book is to collect the scattered rate of return evidence for as many countries as possible and analyze these rates in relation to other economic characteristics of the countries involved. Our general aim in collecting and analyzing these data is to learn more about the role of education in the process of economic growth and development. In particular, we expect to answer the following major questions:

(a) How does the profitability of investment in education compare with the profitability of investment in physical capital? The policy implication of this comparison would be to throw some light on the question of whether a country should invest more in steel mills or in schools.

(b) Can intercountry differences in the stock of human capital help to explain differences in the level of per capita income? Alternatively, what contribution has investment in education made to economic growth in different countries? The policy implication of this analysis would be to clarify the issue of whether a country could expect to increase its per capita income or accelerate its rate of economic growth most by increasing its stock of human capital.

In addition we aim to provide information on:

(c) The structure of the rates of return by level of education. This comparison should help us to decide which levels of education should be promoted relative to the others within a given country.

(d) The degree of public subsidization education receives in different countries. This provides an answer to the question of the economic cost of political decisions regarding the provision of free education in different countries, and whether the subsidies can be reduced without impairing the incentives of people to receive the desired level of education.

(e) A new index of educational development based on costs. Such an index provides an alternative to the Harbison and Myers educational index which is based on enrolments weighted by more or less arbitrary figures.

(f) The earnings ratios of people with different levels of education within a given country. This information, when combined with the numbers of people with different educational levels, indicates the relationship between income distribution and education in different countries and gives estimates of the degree of substitution between

3

different types of educated labour. Such estimates have implications for the particular methodology to be used in educational planning.

(g) The economic returns of higher education graduates who emigrate to work in a foreign country. This information provides us with a partial explanation of the phenomenon of the brain drain.

The book is organized as follows: the rest of this chapter contains an impressionistic overall view of the main analytical procedures and findings. The next chapter introduces the reader to the rate of return types and to the multiplicity of computational adjustments that rate of return estimates may contain. Chapter 3 presents a summary of profitability estimates as found in the original studies, together with the particular assumptions used by individual authors. The taxonomy of the rates of return for the purpose of international comparisons is the subject of Chapter 4. Chapter 5 considers the allocative efficiency of investment in education by comparing the return to education with the return on alternative forms of investment. The subject of Chapter 6 is the relationship between physical and human capital in economic development, while Chapter 7 presents estimates of the part of the rate of economic growth attributed to education. In the last two chapters the rate of return is disaggregated into its separate cost and benefit components, and these data are used to test hypotheses centering around human capital in a number of countries.

Which rate of return?

In Chapter 2 we present a theoretical introduction to the concept of the internal rate of return to investment in education. Particular attention is paid to the different types and to the labels often attached to rate of return estimates; we also examine a host of adjustments performed on empirical profitability estimates, either as necessary compromises because of lack of data or in order to approximate the theoretical definition of a given rate of return type. Therefore, in this chapter we explain what is meant by an average, marginal, overall, total, private, social, adjusted or unadjusted rate of return, and how these adjustments are made. Appendix A presents a sensitivity test of an actual rate of return calculation under alternative popular computational assumptions. The result of this test is that shortcut calculation procedures may over-estimate the rate of return to investment in education by as much as 16 percentage points.

Chapter 2 serves as an introduction to Chapter 3 which presents all

4

the profitability evidence we have been able to discove
evidence covers 32 countries in all continents. As more t'
profitability study exists for some countries, the total nu
studies reviewed is 53. The profitability evidence presenved
Chapter 3 is as found in the original studies without any attempt to
match classifications or assumptions for comparative purposes.
Studies of methodological interest are discussed briefly. In Appendix B the reader will find a concise presentation of the features of each
particular study, for example: the sample size used, whether private
and/or social rates were computed, and the types of adjustments made.

In Chapter 4 we select from the set of case studies reviewed the ones
to be used in the international comparison. The comparability criteria
were the comprehensiveness of the study and the provision of both
private and social rates. Since matching different schooling categories
was very difficult, we have re-computed certain rates in a number of
cases so as to achieve comparability. The details of how we arrived at
a set of more or less comparable rates of return by educational level
in 32 countries are given in Appendix C. For example, in those cases
where only social rates of return were computed for a country study,
but where the original age—earnings profiles were provided, we have
computed the private rates. Further, the profitability evidence is
organized in that chapter by different classifications so as to ease the
search for any empirical regularities that might exist.

Which educational level is most profitable?

After having settled on a set of more or less comparable rates, a
search is begun for any obvious regularities that exist either in the
structure of rates within countries or when the rates of return are
viewed across countries.

The first pattern that we detect in our data is that rates of return
decline by the level of education. Looking first at the social rates of
return, the average for primary education is 19.4 per cent, for
secondary 13.5 per cent and for higher 11.3 per cent. This pattern
proved to be statistically significant when tested by means of the
individual country observations. Private rates show a similar pattern
between the primary and secondary level (23.7 per cent and 16.3 per
cent, respectively) while the rate of return to the university level is 17.5
per cent. The second pattern in our data shows that the private returns
to investment in education are about 3 to 6 percentage points higher
than the social returns. The difference between private and social rates

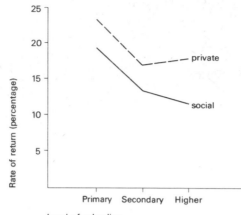

Figure 1.1. The private and social rate of return to investment in education by level of education (intercountry averages).

is even more pronounced in developing than in advanced countries, showing that the former group of countries subsidize their educational sector more heavily. The relationships between private and social rates of return by level of schooling are illustrated in Figure 1.1.

On the question of whether investment in the education of men is more profitable than in the education of women, the examination of 8 case studies where the returns for males and females are reported separately shows that, on the average, males show higher returns by about 2 percentage points at both the higher and secondary levels. The average return for males for primary schooling is 16.3 per cent while that for females is 9.8 per cent. Differences for secondary and higher education are much less pronounced (17.2 versus 15.5 per cent for secondary and 9.6 versus 7.2 per cent for higher, respectively).

The widely debated issue of whether a country should emphasize technical secondary rather than general education was not resolved, since it is very hard to draw any generalizations in view of the contradictory evidence we have on this particular point. For example, in Colombia the social return to technical education of males is substantially higher than the return to secondary general (35.4 versus 26.5 per cent, respectively) but this is not the case in the Philippines (11 versus 21 per cent) or Thailand where the return to secondary technical has a negative value (−6 versus 9 per cent, respectively).

Another debatable question concerns the return to postgraduate studies. Where evidence is available on postgraduate programmes, the figures show very modest returns. For example, according to some

6

studies the rate of return to a Master's degree in the United States and Great Britain has a negative value, and a Ph.D. only a very modest positive one. This is because of the high foregone earnings of students who study for advanced degrees. It should be noted, however, that the completion of a Ph.D. carries a premium over the completion of a Master's degree. Wherever rates of return are available for the Bachelor, M.A. and Ph.D. the order of ranking is B.A. > Ph.D. > M.A. For example, in Great Britain the social rate of return to a Bachelor's degree is 8.2 per cent, to a Master's degree negative and to a Ph.D. 5 per cent.

higher education by subject, but the pattern is too mixed to provide any generalization.

Investment in schools or investment in steel mills?

This question is concerned with the allocative efficiency of investment in education. This kind of efficiency can be looked at from two main points of view or any combination thereof: private versus social efficiency, and efficiency within the educational sector itself or between the educational sector as a whole and the rest of the economy. Social efficiency, for example, requires equality between rates of return to investment in education at all levels and also that these are equal to the social rate of return on physical capital. Private efficiency has a similar meaning. A glance at Figure 1.1 shows that within the educational sector social investments have been far from efficient, particularly between the primary and secondary levels. Of course, there is no reason why one should expect social efficiency. Regarding private efficiency, the near identity between private rates for secondary and higher education shows that from the individual point of view there has been, on the average, the correct distribution of resources between these two levels.

In order to test the allocative efficiency between investment in education as a whole and in the other sectors of the economy, we had two tasks: first, to construct a single profitability measure of investment in education in each country, and then to compare this measure with the yield on physical capital. In Chapter 5 we have constructed an overall rate of return to investment in education in each country as a cost-weighted average of the individual rates for each educational level. The cost weights are derived in Appendix D, based on enrolments at a given level times the annual social cost of investment for that level of schooling. This kind of comparison was only possible for the social

7

returns and in just over half of the cases examined the rate of return to investment in education is higher than the rate of return to physical capital as measured. However, this generalization is subject to a wide variation regarding the individual countries and levels of education. Breaking the sample into developed and less-developed countries the following pattern emerges. While in the less-developed-country group the average return to investment in education (19.9 per cent) is higher than the average return to physical capital (15.1 per cent), the opposite seems to be the case in advanced countries (returns of 8.3 and 10.5 per cent, respectively). This relationship between the return to the two forms of capital by level of development is illustrated in Figure 1.2.

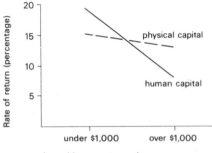

Figure 1.2. The social rate of return to physical and human capital by level of economic development (intercountry averages).

The returns to education and the level of per capita income

The above-suggested relationship between the level of development and the returns to investment in education is examined in a theoretical context in Chapter 6. Using an aggregate production function with human capital as a separate input, we see that the reason for the declining rates is simply a reflection of the law of diminishing returns to investment in this form of capital. That is, the more one country invests in education, keeping all other factors of production constant, the less will be the payoff to that investment at the margin. Our data confirm this expected negative relationship, although the slope of the curve is not statistically significant. The reason for this is that countries differ in other resources as well, such as physical capital, and this difference upsets the theoretical relationship.

The overall actual relationship between the returns to investment in education and per capita incomes is shown in Figure 1.3. Two patterns seem to emerge from this figure. First, by taking the sample of countries as whole, there is an overall negative relationship between the rates of return to investment in education and the level of economic development (broken line A—C). Second, by disaggregating the sample into developed and developing countries, a U-shaped pattern is obtained; i.e., the returns to education are declining at first until a certain level of development is reached, at which point the returns start to rise along with the level of development (solid line ABC). The first pattern and the first half of the second pattern are all consistent with our theoretical expectations, i.e., diminishing marginal returns to investment in education. Our explanation of the second part of the U-shaped pattern, the upward sloping BC curve in Figure 1.3, is that human capital is a complement to the high level of technology employed in rich countries.[8]

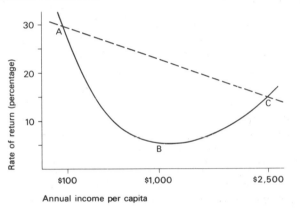

Figure 1.3. A rate of return to investment in education — level of economic development pattern.

Next, we attempted to find if there is any relationship between the rate of return and relative enrolments. Although no statistically significant relationship was found, the declining pattern repeated itself as illustrated in Figure 1.4. That is, the higher the enrolment in one educational level relative to the preceding one, the lower the rate of return to the former level.

---

[8] An alternative non-monetary index of economic development was tried, namely the percentage of agriculture in the composition of gross domestic product, but this measure did not result in a better fit than per capita income.

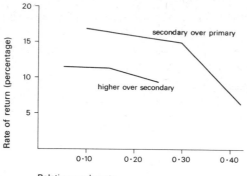

Figure 1.4. A rate of return to investment in higher and secondary education — relative enrolments pattern (intercountry averages).

Human versus physical capital in economic development

In the second half of Chapter 6 we investigate to what extent differences in physical or human capital endowments help in explaining differences in per capita incomes between the countries of the sample. For this purpose two indices are constructed. First, the value of physical capital per member of the labour force; and second, the value of human capital per member of the labour force. In rich countries with per capita incomes around $2,000, the physical capital measure averages around $19,000 and the human capital measure around $7,000. In countries with per capita incomes around the $300 mark, the value of physical capital per member of the labour force is about $4,000 and the value of human capital $600. Countries with per capita income below $100 have corresponding values of $800 and $80. The value of human capital is always less in absolute terms than physical capital within a given country, but whereas in rich countries human capital represents 38 per cent of the value of the physical capital stock, this proportion drops to 10 to 15 per cent for the lower-income-group countries. Stated in another way, the inequality between countries in terms of human capital endowments is greater than the inequality of per capita income or physical capital. These relationships are illustrated in Figure 1.5.

A cross-country aggregate production function was fitted to these data on human and physical capital stocks in an attempt to explain income differences. The production function was run in two alternative specifications. In the first formulation of the function there were three inputs: physical capital, human capital, and total number

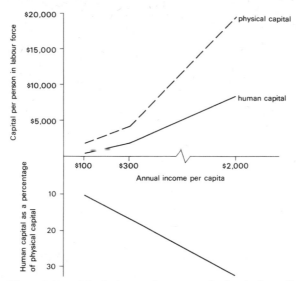

Figure 1.5. The relationship between human and physical capital by level of economic development (intercountry averages).

of persons employed. In the second formulation, physical capital was used along with three non-homogeneous labour inputs based on level of educational attainment as the explanatory variables. The results of these regressions indicate that human capital explains income differences better than does physical capital.

When the production function was run in terms of two distinct capital inputs, human capital showed a higher output elasticity (0.47) than physical capital (0.26), with crude labour showing the lowest elasticity (0.19). When the function was fitted using three distinct labour inputs, the elasticity of labour with secondary qualifications was the highest (0.37) followed by that of primary school graduates (0.14) and finally, higher education graduates (0.03).

The fitting of these functions permitted us to estimate shadow prices for the different inputs. The results seem to confirm earlier findings, that labour with secondary schooling has the highest marginal product, but it should be emphasized that the regression coefficients had large standard errors and hence little significance ought be attached to them. The shadow marginal productivity of physical capital was found to be not very different from observed profit rates (7 to 13 per cent depending upon the function specification), while the productivity of human capital was equal to 32 per cent. Regarding shadow and actual wages, secondary school graduates seem to receive about half of what they contribute to production,

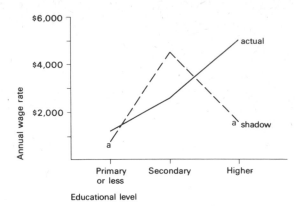

Figure 1.6. The relationship between actual and shadow wages by educational level of labour force (intercountry averages).

primary graduates appear to be slightly overpaid. Figure 1.6 illustrates the relationships as found in these calculations between shadow and actual wages for three categories of educated labour.

In the last section of Chapter 6 a generalized physical-human capital accumulation model is presented in an attempt to put together the bits and pieces of the partial relationships presented above.

The contribution of educatiqnal investment to economic growth

In Chapter 7 we put the rate of return to another use namely to account for differences in the rates of economic growth of the countries in the sample. This was done by means of two computational variants of a growth accounting equation. First, a Schultz-type growth accounting framework was used, where the rate of return to a given educational level is multiplied by the investment in that level so as to arrive at a rental, which is then related to the increase in national income. Next, we used a cross-sectional Denison-type growth accounting framework where individual countries are treated as temporal states in the process of growth. Finally, the results of these exercises are compared with those obtained by orthodox (time-series) Denison-type growth accounting.

The results of this growth exercise show that the contribution of education as a percentage of the rate of economic growth ranges between 4 and 23 per cent. Advanced countries such as Great Britain, Norway and The Netherlands show the lowest contributions.

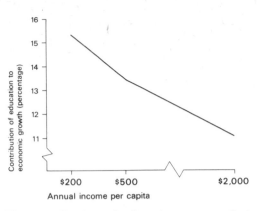

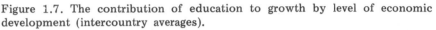

Figure 1.7. The contribution of education to growth by level of economic development (intercountry averages).

Aggregating countries into three groups we observe that although the returns to investment in education differ greatly between countries this is not the case for the contribution of education to growth. As Figure 1.7 illustrates, rich countries centering around the $2,000 per capita income mark show a contribution of education to growth of 11.2 per cent; countries in the $500 income group 13.7 per cent; and countries below the $200 per capita income mark 15.5 per cent.

When the contribution of education to growth is disaggregated by level of education, the primary and secondary levels average 46 and 40 per cent respectively of the total educational contribution for the sample as a whole, while the contribution of higher education amounts to the remaining 14 per cent.

On relative costs and earnings

In the last two chapters of the book we have disaggregated the rate of return statistic into its two separate components, costs and benefits. Looking at the costs first, we observe that many countries in the sample still devote most of their educational resources to primary schooling, about half the countries to secondary and only three to higher education.

Next, we were able to derive some comparative relative annual cost data to illustrate how expensive higher education is in terms of the cost of primary education in different countries. The result of this exercise is illustrated in Figure 1.8, which shows that the cost of one year of higher education in poor countries is 88 times the cost of primary

13

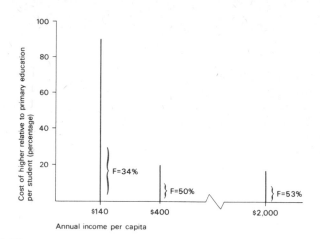

Figure 1.8. The cost of higher education relative to primary by level of economic development (intercountry averages) (F = percentage of earnings foregone in total cost).

education, whereas in rich countries the relative cost is only 18.

On the question of the composition of costs, 53 per cent of the total cost of higher education in rich countries is composed of foregone earnings, whereas the corresponding figure for poor countries is 34 per cent.

Turning to the relative earnings, the differentials decrease as the level of development rises. For example, higher education graduates seem to receive almost six-and-a-half times as much as primary school graduates in poor countries, while this proportion drops to around two-and-a-half in rich countries. Figure 1.9 illustrates the relationship between earnings differentials and the level of development.

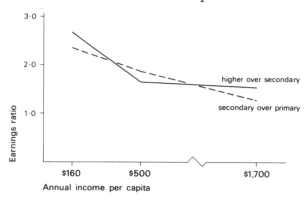

Figure 1.9. Earnings differentials between educated labour by level of economic development (intercountry averages).

14

The degree of substitution between different types of educated labour

When the proportions of persons employed with different educational qualifications are related to the wages they receive, it is possible to arrive at an estimate of the ease of substitution between different kinds of labour in production. This was done in Chapter 9 of this study and the results show that the degree of substitution between all categories of educated labour is substantial but that persons with lower educational qualifications are more easily substitutable than those with higher educational qualifications. The different values of the elasticity of substitution (σ) between pairs of educated labour are illustrated in Figure 1.10.

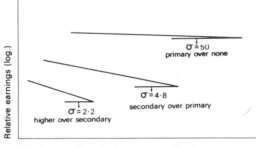

Relative quantities of educated labour (log.)

Figure 1.10. The elasticity of substitution between different kinds of educated labour.

Another result from this analysis is that physical capital is positively related to earnings differentials in developed countries. This is interpreted as evidence of the complementarity between physical and human capital.

And on some hypotheses about international migration

We have started this book by looking into rates of return at different educational levels and have then disaggregated the rate of return into its components of costs and benefits. In the final section of the book we again synthethize costs and benefits but into a new profitability measure. This is named the cross-rate of return to investment in education, and is a profitability measure which refers to the combined investment activity of university graduation at home and subsequent emigration to the United States.

15

The result of this exercise is twofold. First, in the historical sense, the cross-rates of return appear to be in all cases substantially higher than the returns to alternative investments, such as those in physical capital or even investment in higher education when the graduate is domestically employed. If we split the sample into two groups, the upper-income countries show an average cross-rate of return of 31 per cent and a domestic rate of return to higher education of 14 per cent. In lower-income countries the cross-rates of return have values of over 50 per cent, whereas the domestic rate is 25 per cent. Second, in the behavioural sense, the cross-rates of return seem to "explain" the brain drain better than do conventional standard-of-living measures. Using data on immigration to the United States, we tested the hypothesis that relative flows are a positive function of the cross-rate of return and a negative function of the domestic rate. On both counts this hypothesis could not be statistically rejected.

Synopsis

It is customary, at the end of a study like this to print two statements. First, that because of data limitations, coverage and the like, too generalized implications should not be drawn from it. Second, that further research on the subject is needed in order to provide conclusive answers to the questions asked.

In this respect this study does not depart from custom. Before any conclusive statements are made on the relationships between education and economic development, more solid evidence on the returns to education in some of the countries we have covered, and of course in additional countries, is needed. Moreover, the usual word of caution is particularly relevant in our case, for the first thing we have learned is that one should be very cautious in adopting profitability evidence in view of the adjustments that the estimate may contain and the differences in data reliability. In this study every effort has been made to remove the various adjustments but a great deal of unmatched data must still remain. It must also be remembered that some people go so far as to reject completely cost-benefit considerations as applied to education. As this issue has become more or less a matter of religion (i.e. either you believe in it or not) the agnostic or uncommitted reader should study the facts carefully before he adheres to a particular dogma. It is my hope that Chapter 2 will be of help in this respect.

Bearing in mind these qualifications, the results presented in this study seem to indicate the following:

16

(a) Whether one approves or disapproves of economic analysis applied to education, it is a statistical fact that education has both a private and a social monetary payoff and that this payoff is substantially higher in less-developed than in advanced countries. This statement does not deny that education has other than monetary effects. All it says is that by treating education as a form of investment we can quantify *at least one* of its multiple effects.

(b) The most profitable educational level in most countries is the primary one, while higher education shows a modest payoff, particularly in advanced countries. This suggests that arguments for universal primary education based on human rights are also supported by good economic sense.

(c) Returns to investment in human capital are well above the returns to physical capital in less-developed countries, while the two types of return are of almost equal magnitude in advanced countries. What this suggests is that less-developed countries should give greater emphasis to investing in human as against physical capital, while in advanced countries considerations other than economic payoff (for example, equal opportunity) must be invoked to justify the further expansion of the educational system.

(d) Per capita income differences can be better explained by differences in the endowments of human rather than physical capital.

(e) Furthermore, looked at from another point of view, investment in education contributes substantially to the rate of growth of output in most countries, particularly in the less-developed group.

(f) Labour with secondary educational qualifications seems to contribute in effect more to output than it is paid for.

(g) Higher education is very expensive in relation to the other levels of education, particularly in less-developed countries. This suggests that planners should be particularly careful to assess the benefits from this level of education before proposing expansion.

(h) Earnings inequality by educational level decreases as the level of development rises, but the growth of physical capital in the developed countries appears to work against further movements towards earnings equality.

(i) There is a high degree of substitution in production between different types of educated labour. What this suggests is that future expansion of the educational system should be based on calculations of relative costs and benefits rather than on "manpower needs".

(j) There is a very handsome return for those who graduate in the home country and subsequently emigrate to the United States. This economic payoff explains the phenomenon of the brain drain better than more conventional measures such as differences in the standard of living.

One of the major points shown by this study is the weak position of higher education in terms of economic payoff in advanced countries. The following quotation is for those who believe that everything has been said before by Marshall:

> "The growth of general enlightenment . . . has turned a great deal of the increasing wealth of the nation from investment as material capital to investment as personal capital. There has resulted a largely increased supply of trained abilities which has much increased the national dividend, and raised the average income of the whole people: but it has taken away from these trained abilities much of that scarcity value which they used to possess, and has lowered their earnings . . ., and it has caused many occupations, which not long ago were accounted skilled . . . to rank with unskilled labour as regards wages."[9]

---

[9] Marshall (1920), pp. 681—2.

Chapter 2. Rate of Return Estimation Procedures

In this chapter we will describe the theoretical and empirical aspects underlying rate of return analysis and in particular we will deal with the various assumptions and methodologies used in the calculation of estimates. The different theoretical rate of return types are discussed first and then we consider types of earnings data used in the actual calculations. Finally we discuss the multiplicity of adjustments performed on the earnings or cost side mostly as a compromise towards a theoretically correct profitability measure.

But first we should explain why we deal with rates of return rather than with present values. It is well known that these two profitability measures of investment compete with each other and moreover that the present value is allegedly a more correct measure.[1] We will not enter here into a discussion of the pros and cons of the two approaches but the reader is referred to the rich literature on the subject.[2] Suffice it to mention that 28 out of 53 profitability studies we have reviewed were only in terms of rates of return, fifteen of them presented both present values and rates of return, and only five of them were exclusively in terms of present values. If by nothing else, the rate of return measure has won the race by popular demand! Of course, all authors have been aware of the weakness of the approach, but they have not considered that these weaknesses were enough to invalidate their results.[3] For example, one of the objections to rate of return analysis is that the relevant equation might have more than one solution or yield imaginary numbers. But age—earnings profiles that cross more than once are rare. Certainly, the popularity of the rate of return lies in the fact that it can be readily compared with similarly calculated yields on other investment projects.

---

[1] Provided, of course, that total funds available for investment are unlimited. But with a restricted budget the rate of return provides a correct investment criterion.

[2] See in particular Hirshleifer (1958), Bailey (1959) and Ramsey (1970).

[3] For a collection of every conceivable objection to cost-benefit analysis applied to education, see Leite et al. (1969), Volume IIIA.

Rate of return types

According to investment theory, the rate of return on a project is a summary statistic describing the relationship between the costs and benefits associated with the project. It is defined as that rate of interest which will equate to zero the discounted net benefits. Thus, if the project's expected net benefits are B_t per year, extending over a period of n years, the internal rate of return (r) of this project is defined by solving equation (2.1) for r.

$$\sum_{t=1}^{n} \frac{B_t}{(1+r)^t} = 0 \qquad (2.1)$$

By analogy, the rate of return to a given educational level can be defined by comparing the costs and benefits associated with it. To clarify this further, a project called "higher education" will be considered. The costs during, say, four years' study consist of direct outlays (C_h) and foregone earnings (W_s) while the benefits reflect the differential between wages earned by a higher education graduate (W_h) and those earned by a secondary school graduate (W_s). On the assumption that the length of study will be four years and that the higher education graduate will have a working life of 43 years, the rate of return to investment in higher education may be found by solving equation (2.2) for r. Although this equation seems a little awkward

$$\sum_{t=-3}^{0} (C_h + W_s)_t (1+r)^{-t} = \sum_{t=1}^{43} (W_h - W_s)_t (1+r)^{-t} \qquad (2.2)$$

symbolically, it has the advantage of breaking the net benefits explicitly into a cost part (left-hand side) and a benefits part (right-hand side). All costs are cumulated *forward* to year 0 and all benefits are discounted back to the same point in time. Graphically, the calculation is summed up in Figure 2.1. This type of calculation can result in a series of rates of return associated with different educational levels.

The above definition was given in general terms. Depending on the exact variables entering the equation, we can distinguish several rate of return types.

Private versus social rates of return

One of the first distinctions made in the literature of rate of return analysis is that between the private and social rate. The private rate

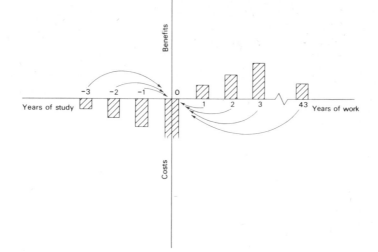

Figure 2.1. A cost-benefit comparison.

relates the costs of education as incurred by the individual to the benefits of education as realized by the same individual. Thus, if in equation (2.2) W_s and W_h refer to earnings after tax and C_h to the tuition fees and other schooling costs that the individual (not the institution) pays, then the resulting r is a private rate. In order to calculate the social rate of return to higher education we have to add taxes to the net earnings and we now define

$$W_s' = W_s + T_s \text{ and } W_h' = W_h + T_h, \tag{2.3}$$

where T_s and T_h are the income tax paid by the two kinds of graduates, and $C_h' = C_h + S_h$, where S_h is the amount of resources the society devotes to higher education per student, over and above the part borne by the student himself.[4] Substituting the values of W'_h, W'_s and C'_h in equation (2.2), we have

$$\sum_{t=-3}^{0} (C_h' + W_s')_t (1 + r')^{-t} = \sum_{t=1}^{43} (W_h' - W_s')_t (1 + r')^{-t} \tag{2.4}$$

the solution to which gives the social rate of return (r') to higher education.

It should be noted that in most cases students pay only a part of

---

[4] What we would like to have ideally as W'_s is the social marginal product of secondary school graduates (see p. 30).

21

the full costs of their education (namely $C'_h > C_h$) and that people with higher incomes pay more taxes than people with lower incomes (namely $T_h > T_s$). But since it is usual for

$$C'_h - C_h > T_h - T_s \tag{2-5}$$

a social rate of return will as a rule be lower than the corresponding private one. However, it is possible that in some cases the educational subsidy is low and income taxes are very high so that inequality (2.5) changes its sign, resulting in the social rate being above the private one.

The problems to which these two types of rates are directed are usually very different. In terms of public educational planning, where the authorities are concerned with rational resource allocation on the basis of profitability, the relevant rates are the social ones. Private rates are usually given prominence in discussions on private decision making and also in problems of educational finance.

Average versus marginal rates

Another distinction often made in rate of return calculations is between average and marginal. This distinction is often confusing as it is not always clear to what the margin refers: to the marginal student, the marginal year of schooling, or the marginal level of schooling?

Rates of return to education, as traditionally estimated, refer to the marginal level of schooling, where the age—earnings profile of people having schooling level S is compared with the profile of people having schooling level $S-1$. Equation (2.2), above, was an example of a marginal rate of return calculation to the university cycle. It is also possible, however, to compare the age—earnings profile of people having S level of schooling with those who have not been to school at all. In this case the estimated rate of return will refer to the whole schooling period of the individual up to the completion of the S level. In this sense the rate is called an "average" rate. For example, the following equation sets out an average rate of return calculation to higher education, (meaning in reality the returns to primary, secondary and higher) where the whole education cycle is fifteen years in length.

$$\sum_{t=-15}^{0} (C + W)_t (1 + r)^{-t} = \sum_{t=1}^{43} (W_h - W_o)_t (1 + r)^{-t} \tag{2.6}$$

where C and W are the direct costs and foregone earnings at each year of the schooling period and W_o is the wage rate of people without any schooling.

It should also be noted here that in countries where one level of schooling is a pre-requisite for another, for instance sixth form and higher education, calculations have often been made not only between higher education and sixth form but also between the two levels taken together and the level immediately preceding.

There is, however, one sense in which every estimated rate of return is marginal since all rates are valid only for one or for a small number of individuals. If enrolments and graduates at a particular educational level are rapidly expanded, the resulting shift of the supply curve to the right may alter the wage rate and consequently the rate of return. Ideally, a marginal rate should be marginal in all of the above senses. But this is never practically true. A marginal rate means, in practice, one to a whole educational cycle, and this is how we will use it in this book. Marginal rates to one extra year of schooling do exist but it is very difficult to make any useful international comparisons on this basis.

Where the marginal rate of return is most relevant is for decisions at the margin, as its name indicates. For example, it is relevant for a decision on whether to expand the compulsory schooling period by one year, or in the case where the returns to terminal qualifications (above some minimum schooling already obtained) are the purpose of the analysis. On the other hand, average rates of return to investment in education are useful on an informational basis, in the same way as a firm wants to know its average cost.

Ex post versus ex ante rates

A further distinction one must make in rate of return estimates is whether they are the result of an *ex post* or *ex ante* calculation. This distinction has not often been made explicit in the literature and confusion has resulted.

An *ex post* rate of return refers to the profitability of investment in education in the historical sense, i.e. as it has been recorded in the past. This type of rate is helpful to the extent that it presents evidence of the efficiency of past investment decisions but it allows very little analysis about the behaviour of individuals. All it says is whether their investment decision has been a good one or a bad one in terms of the monetary payoff. On the other hand, an *ex ante* rate of return contains a dynamic element and therefore could be looked upon as being the expected (future) rate for investments that take place today. This kind of rate is useful in a behavioural analysis of educational decisions. One could test if and how people react to the level of changes of the expected rate of return to investment in education.

So far so good in terms of theory, but when we come to empirical estimation things are very different. Practically all of the estimated rates of return to investment in education are neither *ex ante* nor *ex post*. They are simply cross-sectional rates used either in an *ex post* or *ex ante* sense according to the author's convenience or in order to solve the problem at hand! It is not difficult to understand why this is so. Ideally, an *ex post* rate of return should be derived by following a given cohort through time. But this is extremely difficult due to the lack of time series data on earnings by educational level. On the other hand, an ideal *ex ante* rate of return should be computed on the basis of future earnings of graduates by educational level. Therefore, in view of these empirical difficulties, rates of return are estimated on the basis of *today's* cross-sectional data which are extrapolated either backwards or forwards in time in order to obtain *ex post* or *ex ante* profitability measures. We will discuss how this is done in the following sections.

Males versus females

One of the distinctions rarely referred to in rate of return studies is whether the calculated rates are for all men, all women, employed men and women, or all men and women in the labour force. In fact, most empirical calculations have been for men only or for working men and women, but a few studies have calculated rates separately for women. At first sight it might be expected that the rates for women would be below those for the male population because of their generally shorter working life. In fact, this is not necessarily the case, for instance in professions where secondary-educated women are discriminated against but university-educated women are not. Since the rate of return calculations compare university-educated women with secondary-educated women, and university-educated men with secondary-educated men, it is possible that the latter rate will be below the former.

On-the-job training

Formal education is but one aspect of the whole "education

24

complex" which is associated with earnings. Other important aspects include the firms' training and apprenticeship schemes and the gaining of experience while actually being employed. Specific attention by way of quantitative estimation has been given by Mincer (1962) to the last two of these categories, encompassed under the term "on-the-job training". Attributing all earnings differentials to formal education will inflate the conventional measure of the rate of return, if the returns over cost to on-the-job training are above those to formal education, and vice versa. Thus, another sense in which a rate of return to investment in education can be characterized as "average" is that it refers to formal education and on-the-job training. In other words, every rate of return should be construed as a mixture of returns to formal education and on-the-job training.

Types of earnings data

The examination of 53 rate of return studies in 32 countries leads easily to the conclusion that the earnings data used vary widely in their form and comprehensiveness and hence in their quality. The type of earnings data necessary for rate of return calculations is in the form of age—education—earnings relationships for the total populations, but this is available in only a very few countries where these data are collected as part of the national census. In other countries, more approximate information has to be used and this takes several different forms. Some studies have been able to utilize sample surveys of the total population, or more often the urban population, while others have used samples of specific groups, for instance employees in particular industries or members of particular occupations or professions. In cases where this information is not available and is difficult to collect, earnings data have been taken from pay scales in occupations which demand particular educational requirements (usually the government or public sector) and then adjusted where deviations from the private sector are obvious. This is made more permissible in countries where these scales are frequently altered so as to mirror the changing supply and demand situations.

Income versus earnings data

The first rate of return estimates used income differentials as the basis for the calculation. However, a rate of return to investment in education should be based on earnings rather than income differentials since the latter will distort the required measure inasmuch as individuals differ in wealth. For example, the use of income differentials would lead to an overestimation of the rate of return to higher education in cases where these graduates have accumulated a greater stock of wealth relative to secondary school graduates for reasons independent of whether or not they have completed higher education.

Mean versus median incomes

In the early days of rate of return calculations, it was argued by some (e.g., Renshaw 1960) that the benefits attributable to education should be based on the median earnings of the particular age—education population rather than on the mean. The chief argument for this procedure, was in relation to earnings-related factors other than education. Median differentials are smaller than mean differentials owing to the skewness in the distribution of income but, it was argued, it is those factors which create this skewness, such as ability and social background, which rate of return calculations should attempt to eliminate. Most authors, however, continue to view mean income (or earnings) differentials as being the correct measure for rate of return studies, believing that if earnings factors other than education are to be accounted for then this should be done separately.

Marginal products versus market wages

For social rate of return calculations to have any meaning for public investment decisions, the assumption has to be made that employed persons are paid a wage equal to the value of their marginal product. In other words, earnings differentials are being used as a proxy for an individual's increased productivity which results from an increase in his education. For countries where conditions may prevail which create a distortion between the market wage and the marginal product of labour, it has been suggested that cost-benefit analysis should take place on a shadow or true marginal productivity basis rather than on the basis of observed market wages. Several models have been developed for this purpose in the literature of the economics of education.[5]

---

[5] For empirical applications of shadow pricing see Psacharopoulos (1970), Selowsky (1968) and Dougherty (1971a).

Cross-sectional versus longitudinal data

Rates of return are usually estimated on the basis of cross-sectional data. But how good is this measure for investment decisions that will last over the lifetime of the individual? Two solutions have been proposed to solve this problem: (a) to use longitudinal data, i.e. follow a cohort through time and obtain real age—earnings profiles. Rogers (1969) has made an attempt towards this end; and (b) to estimate rates of return at different points in time so as to have an idea of their trend over time. The last point is very important for educational planning.[6]

Horizontal versus true age—earnings profiles

In some cases the age—earnings profiles have been assumed to be horizontal at the level of the average wage. Obviously, the rate of return estimated from these profiles would be a good approximation of the true rate of return only to the extent that the horizontal profile accurately reflects the life cycle of earnings.

In Appendix A we have performed sensitivity tests of the effect of different age—earnings profiles on the rate of return. The results of these tests showed that the assumption of horizontal age—earnings profiles seriously over-estimates the true rate of return. Another short-cut method to calculate rates of return is to assume horizontal *and* infinite age—earnings profiles. The infinity assumption is rationalized by the fact that distant benefits (say 40 or more years ahead) do not alter significantly the rate return estimate due to discounting. Utilizing both these assumptions, the rate of return formula in equation (2.2) becomes

$$r = \frac{W_h - W_s}{4\,(C_h + W_s)}$$

But application of this formula to the data in Appendix A resulted in a rate of return half as large again as its true value.

Annual versus hourly earnings

It has been suggested that *hourly* earnings, rather than annual

---

[6] For the projection of rates of return over time see Layard (1971), Selowsky (1968), Dougherty (1971a) and Psacharopoulos (1968).

earnings, are a better measure of benefits for the purpose of rate of return calculations. The reasons given for this view are that annual earnings contain the result of periods of unemployment, over-time within the year, or possible substitution of income and leisure. Certainly, the above factors will not work in the same way for all educational groups compared and consequently the estimated rates of return based on annual earnings will be distorted.[7]

An omnibus of adjustments

Rates of return to investment in education are sometimes labelled "adjusted" or "unadjusted". In the following pages we examine what the usual adjustments are and how they are made.

The quality and relevance of empirical calculations of rates of return to education depend to a large extent on the quality of the data utilized. None of the studies outlined in Chapter 3 has had access to *all* the ideal types of data and therefore proxy measures and arbitrary assumptions have had to be used to varying degrees. The rest of this chapter, therefore, is devoted to a brief consideration of the problems involved and the different methods which have been used in attempts to overcome them. In this sense then, it will serve as a reference when presenting the profitability estimates in the following chapter.

Earnings standardization

It would be naïve to believe that earnings differentials are totally dependent on the level of education received. At least part of the earnings differential must be attributed to factors like ability, social class, sex, motivation, origin and the like. Two methods have been used to deal with "other than education" factors in rate of return analysis. The first one has been to apply an adjustment factor to the earnings — what Mark Blaug has baptized the "alpha coefficient" (α), (Blaug, 1965). That is, the earnings differential in the benefits side of a rate of return calculation now becomes $\alpha \Delta W$. Early studies in the United States led to the earnings differential being adjusted downwards by 40 per cent, the remaining 60 per cent reflecting differ-

---

[7] On this matter see Morgan and David (1963) and Schultz (1968). See also Schwartzman (1968) for a Denison-type growth exercise using average hourly earnings.

ences in earnings due to differences in education,[8] and consequently an α coefficient equal to 0.6 has been used in a great number of studies.

The second (and better) method for dealing with earnings-related variables other than education is the process of earnings standardization through regression analysis. When data on earnings and other characteristics of individuals are known, it is possible to estimate a so-called "earnings function" by multiple regression, accounting for the variance of earnings in terms of education, age, social class, father's occupation, region and all other relevant variables. Once these earnings functions have been estimated (possibly within an education—age group) all other variables are set at their means and expected age—earnings profiles are constructed. In this way, the difference in earnings between any two schooling levels is "standardized" for factors other than education.[9] Obviously, this procedure can be applied only in cases where large numbers of individual observations are available.

It should be noted that in view of recent evidence the ability factor may have been overemphasized in the literature. Rogers (1969), using a well controlled sample, has shown that ability differences are unlikely to have significant effects on the calculated rates of return.[10]

Unemployment

Age-earnings profiles often need a downward adjustment because of the probability of unemployment. If earnings data have been collected from a census of the total population, or from a sample of the total population, then such an adjustment is not necessary since unemployment effects will be reflected in the sample. This would not be the case, however, if the level of unemployment in the year of the census were extremely unusual. Data collected from samples referring to the employed persons or pay scales do need an unemployment adjustment. The unemployment correction usually takes place as a downwards adjustment of an age—earnings profile by the probability of the person being unemployed at a given age. That is, if W_{St} is the uncorrected annual earnings of a person with S years of

---

[8] See Becker (1964), Denison (1964) and references cited there.

[9] As examples of this approach see Carnoy (1964 and 1967a), Hanoch (1965 and 1967), Hunt (1963), Blaug (1971) and Thias and Carnoy (1969).

[10] For other efforts to separate the effect of income determining variables see Weisbrod and Karpoff (1968), Carrole and Ihnen (1967), Morgan and Sirageldin (1968) and Ashenfelter and Mooney (1969).

schooling at age t, the earnings corrected for unemployment are

$$U_St \ W_St$$

where U_St is the probability of unemployment of a given person at a given age. It is not possible to say what the resulting overall effect on the rate of return will be, since this depends on the relative amounts of unemployment for graduates of each educational level.

Probability of survival

Lifetime earnings profiles assume that each individual will live to a given age in order to enjoy the earnings associated with that age. A more realistic assumption demands that these earnings are adjusted downwards, so allowing for the probability of survival at each age. This is a very similar adjustment to the unemployment one, the earnings now being

$$S_t \ W_St$$

where S_t is the survival rate for a person of age t. The adjustment factors are usually readily taken from the country's life-expectancy tables. These tables, however, relate to the average for all education groups rather than a differentiation by groups which is the ideal form of data needed.

Labour force participation

The rate of return as estimated from cross-sectional data refers to members of the labour force. But if an individual or society contemplates investment in education one should allow that, in spite of present intentions, the individual may not after all become a member of the labour force. The typical example of this is women's education. Therefore, a further adjustment could be made by multiplying the earnings of a given individual in the labour force by the labour force participation rate (P_St) of the relevant group. In this case the expected earnings at age t would become equal to

$$P_St \ W_St$$

Productivity growth

Age—earnings profiles derived from cross-sectional data are

stationary in the sense that the effect of economic growth on earnings is not taken into account. There are two ways of rectifying this. First, future increases in productivity can be compensated for by multiplying the earnings of an individual at a given age by a factor reflecting the productivity change. For example, if the productivity of university graduates is expected to rise at a rate equal to γ per year, then the earnings at age t as implied by the cross-sectional profile should be multiplied by a factor equal to $(1 + \gamma)^{t-a}$, where a is the age at which the university graduate enters the labour force. The second way to adjust for productivity change is simply to add the expected rate of productivity growth to the estimated rate of return. That is, if the estimated rate of return on the basis of the unadjusted age—earnings profile is r, then the expected rate of return adjusted for productivity change is equal to $r + \gamma$.[11]

This adjustment is a very crucial one and should be kept in mind when interpreting the rates of return to be presented in Chapter 3. For if the actual rate of return is relatively low and of the same order of magnitude as the rate of productivity growth, the adjustment will have a very strong effect. This means that a negative rate of return may become positive or a low rate may be increased so as to pass the alternative rate test. Thus, when comparing rates of return from different sources one should be careful to see that all rates are either before the growth adjustment, or after it.

Private rates of return and taxation

The income streams associated with different levels of education should, for private rate of return calculations, be net of income tax. In most private rate of return studies it has been possible to apply tax rates to different earnings profiles, but in a few cases this has not been possible and the returns have therefore been inflated.

Consumption benefits of education

Rate of return studies to investment in education conventionally measure the benefits solely by consideration of the earnings streams. This is not to say that workers in this field of economics have ignored other benefits to the individual which flow from education,

---

[11] For a mathematical explanation of this method see Blaug *et al.* (1969) p. 215.

31

but rather it points to the theoretical and practical difficulties of handling these so-called consumption, or psychic, benefits. Without having quantitative information of their magnitude there are three ways in which they can be contained in rate of returns calculations. First, an arbitrary estimate of their size may be made and added on to the direct earnings stream; secondly, a proportion of the costs can be laid aside; or finally, and perhaps most legitimately, the statement can be made that the rates of return based on earnings alone are underestimated, and refer only to the investment component of education.[12]

External benefits

The external or indirect benefits of education to society or to the individual have proved to be the greatest stumbling block to the acceptability of rate of return analysis to many people. This is not surprising when the list of such benefits contains such diverse elements as the inter-generational effects, the creation of an informed electorate, the provision of a flexible labour market, the socialization of the younger members of society and the value of mothers' earnings which are only made possible by the provision of school places for their children. Fuller presentations of these and other items have been covered in depth elsewhere, with various implicit and explicit assumptions as to their size.[13]

In general, there are two ways in which to view the external benefits to education. First, they can be named and presented alongside the rates of return conventionally calculated using earnings data, with the statement that the economic effects of education as measured do not provide a complete basis for decision making although they do present a reasonable picture of the direct benefits. Secondly, an arbitrary estimate may be made of the magnitude of the external benefits, but such an estimate necessarily involves highly subjective weighting.

[12] This has been strongly suggested by Schultz (1963). For a different view see Blaug (1970, pp. 16—22) who argues that education is always both investment and consumption, "not only in the sense that education of one type in one country may act to increase further output while another type of education in the same country does not, but that the very same quantum of education, say a year's schooling for someone, invariably shares both consumption and investment aspects."

[13] See in particular Blaug (1965), Vaizey (1962), Weisbrod (1964) and again, especially Blaug (1970), chapter 4.

Risk and uncertainty

Although no actual calculations of rates of return have included the quantitative effects of income variance associated with each educational level, it may be that for private rate calculations this is an omission. The degree of variance should ideally refer to the differentials between two earnings streams, but a reliable estimate could be obtained by comparing the standard deviation of the incomes received by an age—education category with the mean.[14] For the private investor, a high degree of income variance would add to the risk of not receiving the expected income associated with his particular age—education category and it would be meaningful, therefore, to include risk discounts based on the degree of variation of earnings by educational level.

Timing assumptions

The particular length of study, entrance to the labour force and retirement assumptions obviously affect the numerical value of the rate of return. The less influential of these two concerns the retirement age, since benefits discounted over forty or fifty years represent a very small amount in terms of present value.

Of course the sensitivity of the rate of return to the timing assumption will depend upon the size of the rate of return itself. For example, a high rate of return will be little affected by the infinity assumption, but a low rate will be more affected by it; likewise, a present discounted value calculation will be little affected by the retirement assumption if the discount rate used is high, or greatly affected by it if it is low.[15]

Wastage

It may be the case that the typical graduate of a particular type of school may have stayed in school more than the official number of years for the length of the cycle. In this case, costs have to be increased according to the number of repeaters. In the same way, if

---

[14] For the earnings variance of qualified manpower in the British electrical engineering industry see Layard *et al.* (1971).
[15] For a sensitivity test in this respect see Appendix A.

50 per cent of the entrants into a particular level of education fail to complete the cycle, then to produce one graduate at this educational level requires that two persons must enter and therefore the cost of producing one graduate must include the cost incurred by the dropout. This will obviously lower the rate of return.

Foregone earnings

The universal assumption concerning foregone earnings is that they are equal to the earnings observed of the relevant age group that terminated its education at the level preceding the one in question (or at the base level for average rate of return calculations). Those foregone earnings are sometimes lowered by deducting the student's part-time earnings, while other authors have used the convenient assumption that these part-time earnings are equal to the direct costs of schooling, thus enabling them to work solely with earnings data for the rate of return calculation, (e.g. Hanoch, 1967).[16]

The age at which foregone earnings start deserves a different assumption in developed and under-developed countries. This age is certainly greater the more developed the country since, although a developing country may have a minimum schooling age of 15, farm employment may draw labour below this age.

The above presentation of rate of return types and the discussion of adjustments made, serves as a reference and introduction to the next chapter which is a presentation of the actual rate of return studies used in the analyses in this book.

---

[16] For an analysis of earnings foregone in the United States see Schultz (1971).

Chapter 3. Documentation of Profitability Studies around the World

Rate of return studies exist for countries in all five continents and in this chapter we review the studies which we have been able to discover for 32 countries.[1] For a more detailed comparison of the assumptions, data and methodology used in the different case-studies the reader is referred to Appendix B. We will begin our review with the countries of North and South America and then proceed to those in Europe, Asia, Africa and Australasia.

America

Profitability studies of investment in education have been conducted for the United States and Canada as well as for several Latin American countries including Puerto Rico, Mexico, Venezuela, Colombia, Chile and Brazil. Studies for the United States and Canada are the only ones in our sample which are based on Census of population data, most of the rest using sample surveys of the incomes of persons with different levels of education.

United States

Due to Census data availability on income by years of schooling, rate of return studies have flourished in the United States. One can find profitability evidence in this country for particular groups of people, for particular regions, for given subjects and for different points in time. In general, two types of studies can be distinguished for the U.S. First, there are studies that are based on country-wide samples and which are appropriate for international comparisons;

---

[1] Hawaii is treated as a separate country in this study. The reason is that the rate of return evidence refers to 1959 which corresponds to the year it became the 50th State of the United States.

and second, there are case studies that have used smaller samples and have contributed to the methodology of rate of return analysis.[2] We have dealt briefly with some of the second type of studies in the previous chapter, where the various assumptions were presented in calculating rates of return. Here we will only present studies of historical or international comparability interest.

The first landmark in empirical profitability studies in the United States is the study by Glick and Miller (1956) who, after analyzing 1949 Census data of median income by age, race, sex, education and adjusting the income data by the probability of survival, penned the phrase that a college education is worth $100,000. However, no discounting was used. A few years later, Houthakker (1959) used the same source of data and derived present values of lifetime incomes of persons with different amounts of schooling. His approach was more sophisticated than Glick and Miller's in that he discounted mean incomes and took income tax into account. The main conclusion from Houthakker's study was that the $100,000 value of college education could only be regarded as an upper boundary. Miller (1960) extended his earlier work with Glick by estimating the lifetime incomes of people with different years of schooling in 1939, 1946, 1949, 1956 and 1958. His main finding was that the relative income position of highly educated workers did not change in the period studied, which he interpreted as meaning that the demand for this kind of labour in fact kept pace with the increased supply.

The first rate of return estimates *per se* appeared in an early work of Becker (1960) and were later presented more fully by him in 1964. Becker's initial concern seemed to be whether there was under- or over-investment in college education in the United States. Based on the censuses of the population, he computed a private rate of return to college education of 12.5 per cent in 1940 and 10 per cent in 1950. These rates refer to urban white males only, and are adjusted for ability, unemployment and mortality. The corresponding social rate of return was equal to 9 per cent in both years. A direct comparison of the above estimates with the rate of return on physical capital led him to the conclusion that there was no evidence of under-investment in college education, at least on the basis of the direct economic benefits. In his later study, he produced some additional evidence of the returns to college education in 1956, 1958 and 1961. The whole set of estimates showed that the profitability of investment in college education in the United States did

---

[2] Obviously, studies in the above two categories are not mutually exclusive.

not change appreciably between 1939 and 1961.[3] Becker has also produced rate of return evidence for high school graduates. In contrast to the returns for college education, those for high school education have shown an ascending pattern over time.[4]

T. W. Schultz, the pioneer and conceptual instigator of much of the work in this particular field, has also produced some rate of return estimates for the three educational levels in the U.S. in 1958. These were 35 per cent for elementary, 10 per cent for high school and 11 per cent for college education (Schultz, 1961). But one has to go to the work of Hansen (1963) for a comparative landmark. This study gave private and social rates of return for a variety of schooling combinations in 1949. The income data source was the Census of Population. Concentrating on the completed schooling cycles, the social rates of return were found to be 15 per cent for elementary (eight versus zero years of schooling), 11.4 per cent for four years of high school, and 10.2 per cent for the four years of college. The corresponding private rates of return were infinity,[5] 14.5 per cent and 10.1 per cent. Because of the 1950 Census data limitations, Hansen used income data in his study instead of, ideally, earnings by level of education completed. It took the 1960 Census to fill in this data gap.

Hanoch (1967) introduced another milestone in rate of return studies, in terms of both methodology and reliability of the estimates produced. Based on a 1/1000 sample of the 1960 Census, which reported the earnings and other characteristics of more than 57,000 males in 1959, he was able to estimate earnings functions which included a large number (23) of explanatory variables. The sample was divided into 24 groups defined by race, region and age, and earnings functions were estimated within each group. Beyond schooling and age, the explanatory variables referred to the type of

---

[3] The private returns for white male college graduates unadjusted for ability differences were 14.5 per cent in 1939, a little over 13 per cent in 1949, 12.4 per cent in 1956, and around 15.0 per cent in 1958, and 1961. (Becker, 1964, p. 128).

[4] The private rates of return to white male high school graduates unadjusted for ability were 16 per cent in 1939, 20 per cent in 1949, 25 per cent in 1956 and 28 per cent in 1958. (Becker, 1964, p. 128).

[5] Many rate of return studies have produced infinite or very high private profitability estimates for primary education. This figure has a mathematical rather than an economic meaning. It simply reflects the fact that elementary school children have zero or very low foregone earnings and when this is combined with free tuition it can easily produce an infinite private internal rate of return.

residence, the origin of the individual, mobility, marital status, size of family and number of children. By means of multiple regressions, expected age—earnings profiles by years of schooling were estimated. No adjustments were performed on the benefits side, other than the ones reflected by the explanatory variables of the earnings functions. Although private rates of return were estimated, no tax adjustments were made. On the cost side it was assumed that part-time student earnings and direct costs of schooling were equal.

The results of Hanoch's analysis for the Whites/North sub-group, i.e. the one which according to Hanoch is the most reliable in terms of data, were as follows: when the elementary school graduates were compared with persons with zero to four years of schooling, the private rate of return was above 100 per cent; four years of high school yielded a rate of return equal to 16.1 per cent; and the extra four years of college gave a profitability estimate of 9.6 per cent. Hanoch also estimated the rate of return on seventeen plus versus sixteen years of schooling, and this was equal to 7.0 per cent. This figure corresponds to an average rate of return to postgraduate programmes in the United States.[6]

Another study which was carried out simultaneously and was very similar to Hanoch's was made by Lassiter (1965). Using a 5 per cent sample of the 1960 Census of Population he computed the following type of earnings function

$$Y = a + bS$$

where Y is income, S is years of schooling completed and a and b are the estimated parameters. The fitting of the above equation allowed him to compute private rates of return based only on opportunity costs (i.e. assuming zero direct costs of schooling). In a later work (1966) he reported similar rates of return for 1949. A comparison of the 1949 and 1959 rates of return shows a small increase over time.[7]

Lassiter has also analyzed the returns by race/region groups. One of his findings was that the return to non-white college graduates in central cities was only one-half the return to white graduates (4 per cent as against 8 per cent). But non-whites in rural farm areas enjoy almost the same returns as whites in the same areas.

The latest global study of the returns to education in the United

[6] This figure refers to both the completion of Master and Doctorate, as well as to drop-outs one year or more after the Bachelors degree.

[7] For example, the return to sixteen years of schooling for white males in the North was 8 per cent in 1949 and 9 per cent in 1959. And the returns for non-whites in the South were 4 per cent and 6 per cent in the respective years.

States is by Hines *et al.* (1970). This study used the same basic earnings data as Hanoch (1/1000 sample of the 1960 Census), but there is an explicit consideration of educational costs which enabled the authors to estimate social as well as private rates of return for 1959. The social rates of return for white males were found to be equal to 17.8 per cent for elementary school graduates, 14 per cent for high school graduates and 9.7 per cent for college graduates. On the private side, the corresponding rates were 155.1 per cent, 19.5 per cent and 13.6 per cent. These rates are before adjustments for secular growth in incomes, mortality, ability or taxes; but one of the things this study demonstrates is that, after all adjustments are made, it is possible that the final rate of return figure will be very similar to the unadjusted one, since many of the adjustments act in opposite directions and therefore cancel out.

Canada

We have been able to find two studies of the returns to education in Canada, by Wilkinson (1966) and Podoluk (1965). In both studies, data from the 1961 Census of Population have been used. Wilkinson's estimates are in the form of (private) net present values of lifetime earnings for different occupations. Podoluk, on the other hand, computed private rates of return to investment in education based on pre-tax incomes. The rates were equal to 16.3 per cent for high school graduates (as compared with persons with five to eight years of elementary schooling) and 19.7 per cent for university graduates (relative to high school graduates).

Puerto Rico

The rate of return study for Puerto Rico is by Carnoy (1970). Using special tabulations from the 1960 Population Census, he produced rate of return estimates for males and females in urban and rural areas. The private rates unadjusted for labour force participation for males are over 100 per cent for primary, 26.4 per cent for secondary and 23 per cent for higher education. The corresponding social rates are 19.8 per cent, 20.1 per cent and 11.9 per cent, respectively.

Mexico

The study of the rates of return for Mexico is also by Carnoy

39

(1964). Abstracts of his original work have appeared elsewhere (Carnoy, 1967a) and (Carnoy, 1967b). The Mexican study is unique in that a pioneering attempt was made to standardize rates of return for factors other than education. Carnoy's study was based on a cross-sectional sample of 4,000 male wage-earners in 1963. The questionnaire provided data on the wage or salary of the employee, the number of years of schooling he had completed, his age, his father's occupation, the type of industry he was employed in and the city in which he was located. This sample permitted the estimation of earnings functions, as discussed in the previous chapter. The results of the regressions were that, when schooling alone was used as an explanatory variable of income, 43 per cent of income variance was explained; when age was added as an independent variable the schooling explanatory power dropped to 36 per cent; and when other variables such as age, city, father's occupation, industry and attendance were added, schooling explained only 29 per cent of the income variance. Yet schooling was found to be the largest single determinant of income differences. These earnings functions permitted the construction of age—earnings profiles with or without standardization for the variables mentioned.

Both private and social rates of return were estimated. In terms of unstandardized rates, the private returns range from 21.1 per cent for three years of schooling to 36.7 per cent for fifteen years of schooling. The corresponding social rates of return range from 17.3 per cent to 29.5 per cent. What is of extreme importance is that standardization for factors other than education reduced the returns for the lower educational levels by about 15 percentage points, whereas the returns for the higher levels were reduced by only 2 to 3 percentage points. This suggests that a single value of α should not be used for all educational levels but rather a range of values which increases up the educational ladder. In other words, the lower the educational levels compared, the lower that part of the earnings which is strictly due to education.

This finding may seem strange, as one would expect *a priori* the inverse relationship to be true; that is, the higher the educational levels compared, the lower the part of the earnings differential strictly due to education. This common illusion is based on the fact that the ability factor has been overemphasized regarding the α coefficient. The fact that the α coefficient is the result of two opposing forces is frequently ignored and these forces are ability *and* socio-economic background. Whereas ability screens the flow of students to the higher educational levels, the socio-economic background screens the flow of students from the earliest educational levels. What empirical evidence shows, is that the socio-economic background at the early stages is much more important than the ability factor later on.[8]

Venezuela

The rate of return study for Venezuela was made by Shoup (1959) and is one of the earliest of its kind. Although few details are known of the sources of the data, sample size and adjustments performed, Carnoy (1967b) notes that the post-primary rates probably refer to urban males only. It is also probable that they contain a growth adjustment. This study has always been regarded as giving rather extreme results particularly at the primary level where, using illiterate agricultural workers as the base group, the rate of return was estimated at 130 per cent. When the earnings of the illiterate *urban* workers were used as the control group, the rate dropped to 82 per cent, which is still a very high figure by any standard. The rate of return for secondary education was equal to 17 per cent (eleven versus seven years of schooling) and the rate for university graduates was equal to 23 per cent (fifteen versus twelve years of schooling).

Colombia

There have been four rate of return studies of investment in education in Colombia. The first one was by Franco (1964), as reported in Carnoy (1967b). Private rates of return were estimated for urban male workers and these were found to be 20 per cent for primary education (one to five years of schooling), 19 per cent for secondary technical schooling (six to eleven years of schooling), 30 per cent for general secondary (six to eleven years of schooling), and 19 per cent for university (twelve to seventeen years of schooling). The other three studies deserve some lengthier discussion because of the particular methodologies that were used.

Schultz's (1968) study is based on a rather small sample of the urban labour force in Bogota, in 1965. The sample included 684 men and 316 women, ten years old or over. Earnings functions were estimated separately for men and women. The independent variables of these earnings functions were schooling, age, years of residence in

---

[8] On this matter see also Thias and Carnoy (1969).

Bogota, and other sources of family income. The third variable was included in order to catch the effect on earnings of the number of years of residence in the urban setting. The inclusion of the fourth variable rests on the hypothesis that the more income is available in the family from other sources, the less the effort of the person in the sample to earn more income himself. In addition to these two new independent variables in earnings function estimations, Schultz stressed the importance of hourly earnings as the dependent variable — the reason for this being that annual or 'even weekly earnings over-state the real income effect associated with increased schooling, as they include a substitution effect. That is, the fact that a person earns more per hour after an increase in his schooling may alter his allocation of time between work and leisure. If this is the case then the hourly earnings may provide a better measure of the returns to schooling than the weekly or annual earnings.[9] Schultz adjusted his data on the benefits side for under-employment by dividing the person's weekly earnings by 48. The earnings of domestic servants were increased by a factor equal to 3, to take into account fringe benefits in kind. (Another set of rates of return was also calculated without using this assumption.) Taxes were not deducted from earnings in estimating the private rates of return.

In estimating the earnings functions, independent variables were excluded when found not to be associated with earnings. The adjustment of hourly earnings for under-employment and fringe benefits was not important for men but very important in estimating women's earnings. "Other income of the household" was not associated with men's earnings but it was associated with women's earnings. The "duration of residence in Bogota" variable was in no case significantly associated with earnings. The costs of schooling were based on Franco's earlier study. Schultz estimated separate rates of return for men and women. His private estimates based on adjusted earnings for men were 18.4 per cent for primary schooling, 34.4 per cent for secondary schooling and 4.4 per cent for university. The corresponding social rates of return were 15.3 per cent, 26.5 per cent and 2.9 per cent. The highest rates of return calculated by Schultz were for vocational secondary schooling (52.5 per cent, private and 35.4 social).

A final highlight of Schultz's results is that the rates of return are higher for women than for men for vocational secondary and

---

[9] The way in which annual or weekly earnings are affected will depend upon whether leisure is a superior or inferior good, see Schultz (1968) p. 7.

university education, but lower for primary and general secondary.[10]

Selowsky's (1968) study of Colombia consists of a thorough exercise showing how different assumptions can affect a rate of return estimate. Using a sample of 10,715 male and female urban workers in Bogota in the 1963—6 period, he estimated a variety of social rates of return using various assumptions. For example, the completely unadjusted rates of return to the three educational cycles were 40 per cent for primary, 24 per cent for secondary and 8 per cent for university. The labour force participation adjustment reduced these rates to 33 per cent, 21 per cent and 6 per cent respectively. Further adjustment for unemployment reduced the rate of return to primary education to 28 per cent, but left the other two rates unaffected. The combined effect of a labour-force participation adjustment and differences between shadow and market wages reduced the primary rate of return by only 1 percentage point.[11] This latter correction consisted of dynamizing the rates of return by making earnings a function of time. Future real wages were obtained by projecting the demand and supply for each category of labour through time. On the assumption that the annual rate of growth of each labour category will be the same in the future as it was in the past, this adjustment did not lead to any significant change of the rate of return estimates.[12]

On the basis of his results Selowsky concluded that today's rates of return are rather insensitive to different patterns of expansion of the educational system. This is a very optimistic conclusion for the use of rates of return in educational planning.

The final profitability study for Colombia is from Dougherty (1971a). Using the same wage-data sources as Selowsky and more or less the same shadow-pricing procedure, he derived social rates of return for 1969. These rates were equal to 21.1 per cent for primary education, 20.7 per cent for secondary and 7.4 per cent for higher. Dougherty has also calculated rates of return referring to the future, based on alternative expansion paths of the educational system. An interesting finding of his study (particularly in relation to Selowsky's

---

[10] For a detailed comparison of the returns for men and women in several countries, see Chapter 4 below.
[11] The shadow wages on which this correction was based were derived from an hybrid (two-level) CES—Cobb—Douglas production function and some values of the elasticity of substitution between different kinds of educated labour. For the specification of this production function see Bowles (1969), or Bowles (1970).
[12] Only the rate of return to secondary schooling was reduced by one percentage point.

conclusions) was that if higher education continues its present expansion in Colombia the social rate of return to that level of education will virtually be zero by 1985.

Chile

There are two variants of rate of return estimates for Chile. The first one is by Harberger and Selowsky (1966). Using case studies for the income of the urban labour force by years of schooling and for the costs of education, they computed social rates of return for 1959. These were 24 per cent for the primary level, 16.9 per cent for the secondary and 12.2 per cent for university. The "special" option of secondary education (eight-and-a-half versus six years of schooling) yielded a rate of return equal to 29 per cent. According to Carnoy (1967b) these rates appear to be over-estimated as Harberger and Selowsky used constant age—earnings profiles over the lifetime of the individual.[13]

The second variant is by Selowsky (1967) who used the same cost data as the previous study but a different earnings source. This led to social rates of return to primary and secondary education equal to 24.8 and 22.9 per cent, respectively.

One should also mention the existence of another study which, although not containing any rate of return estimates, did give some insight into the relationship between education and earnings in Chile. Valdes (1971), using a sample of 328 wage and salary workers employed in 48 farms in 1965, showed by multiple-regression analysis that about half of the wage differentials could be explained by differences in schooling.

Brazil

We have been able to discover four rate of return studies for Brazil, all Ph.D work. The first one is by Hewlett (1970) in which the earnings data were from a survey of 1,200 male and female employees in urban and rural areas. Both private and social rates were estimated for 1962. The private rates which were based on the assumption of zero direct costs of schooling were as follows: 11.3 per cent for primary, 22.2 per cent for the first cycle of secondary,

---

[13] Carnoy (1967b) has recomputed the rates of return for the primary and secondary level and found them to equal to 11.6 per cent and 12.3 per cent, respectively.

20.5 per cent for the second cycle of secondary and 38.1 per cent for higher education. The corresponding social rates were 10.7 per cent, 17.3 per cent, 17 per cent and 14.5 per cent. Hewlett also estimated the returns to teacher training for females only, and these were found to be negative, both on the social and private counts.

The second study is by Castro (1970) who produced social rate of return estimates for Bello Horizonte and Itabirito, based on a combination of assumptions about costs and length of study. His basic rates for Itabirito were 21 per cent for elementary, 20 per cent for the first cycle of secondary, 107 per cent for teacher training college and 14 per cent for university.

In another study, Lerner (1970) used data from the Brazilian Demographic Census. The sample size from which age—earnings data were used, was 4,700. Regression analysis yielded estimates of earnings by level of formal education. Exogenous variables other than education included sex, colour and place of residence. Lerner's estimate of the private rate of return to elementary schooling (four plus over zero years of schooling) for females was more than double (38.6 per cent) the one for males (17.9 per cent).

Lastly, Rogers III (1969) estimated social and private rates of return to a number of subjects within higher education. His overall social rate to higher education in the Northern region of Brazil is 15 per cent, whereas the corresponding private rate is 20.7 per cent.

Europe

Rate of return studies for European countries were non-existent until a few years ago because of the lack of appropriate earnings data for such calculations. Today, however, we have been able to discover profitability evidence for eight European countries: Great Britain, Norway, Sweden, Denmark, Netherlands, Belgium, Germany and Greece.

Great Britain

There have been several studies of the returns to education in Great Britain based on sample surveys. The first attempt was by D. Henderson-Stewart, published as an appendix in Blaug (1965) and reported again in Blaug (1967). The study was based on a random sample of 6,500 male heads of households aged 20 years or more in Great Britain. Although median income was originally tabulated,

45

subsequent adjustments provided mean earnings by terminal education age. An α coefficient of 0.6 was applied on the earnings streams which refer to 1964. The private and social rates of return to three years of secondary education were found to be very close (13 per cent and 12.5 per cent, respectively), but the private rate of return to three years of higher education (14 per cent) was substantially above the social rate of return (6.5 per cent).

The second rate of return study for Great Britain was by Blaug *et al.* (1967) and reported again in Blaug (1967). The study was based on a sample of about 2,800 male employees in five large firms. Private and social rates of return were calculated for various educational qualifications above school-leaving age. The private rate of return to a pass or ordinary university degree was equal to 8.5 per cent, whereas the social rate was 6 per cent.

The third such study for Great Britain is by Richardson (1969). Three sources of earnings were utilized. First, Ministry of Technology data on the earnings of graduate and non-graduate engineers were compared with the earnings of 15-year-old school leavers as collected by the Higher Education Research Unit Industrial Manpower Project.[14] The private rates to non-graduate and graduate engineers were found equal to 26.4 and 15.3 per cent respectively. The corresponding social rates were 18 per cent and 9.2 per cent. The third source of data was the Cornmarket tabulations of earnings of qualified manpower in 1965 and 1968. Rates of return were again calculated using the earnings of the 15-year-old school leavers as the comparative group. These rates were very modest and will be presented in the next chapter where we will deal with profitability estimates by subject.

Another study, by Maglen and Layard (1970) which is more fully reported again in Layard *et al.* (1971), utilized the age—earnings profiles of employees in the electrical engineering industry in 1966; and a variety of profitability estimates was produced corresponding to different combinations of assumptions. Concentrating on the private returns to a first degree, a master's degree and a doctorate, all relative to the secondary "A" level, the results were 12 per cent, 10.5 per cent and 12.9 per cent, respectively. The corresponding social rates were 8.1 per cent, 5.7 per cent and 7.4 per cent. The above estimates incorporate an *a* coefficient of 0.66, include a growth adjustment of 2 per cent per year and are unadjusted for drop-outs.

Benefit—cost ratios for courses in technical colleges in 1964—5

---

[14] For a report on this project see Layard *et al.* (1971).

have been calculated by Selby Smith (1970). His sample was of 17,500 men who were almost exclusively employed by large private companies. The foregone earnings of the control group were based on earnings in agriculture, increased by reference to the average weekly earnings of manual workers in manufacturing. The earnings differentials were standardized for mortality, unemployment, and geographical region. Alpha coefficients of 0.5, 0.65 and 0.8 were used and various growth factors were adopted.

The most recent profitability evidence of investment in education in Great Britain has been provided by Morris and Ziderman (1971) using a 1968 earnings sample of almost 2,500 people with post-secondary qualifications. Social rates of return were estimated for both full-time formal education up to the doctorate level and also for qualifications based on part-time education. Alternate rates using an α adjustment of 0.66 were also calculated. The important results were that, whereas a first degree earned an unadjusted return of 10.8 per cent and a doctorate earned 1.6 per cent, the highest part-time qualification resulted in a return of over 20 per cent.

Ziderman (1971) has elaborated further on the above sample and produced what he considers to be a "best guess" of rates of return to various educational levels in Great Britain. These rates are ability-adjusted, include a 2 per cent adjustment for growth and the social ones exclude research costs. Regarding full-time courses the returns to "A" level over no qualification are 9 (8.5)[15] per cent, first degree over "A" 11.5 (20) per cent, Master's over first degree 3.5 (15) per cent and Doctorate over first degree 5 (16) per cent. Part-time courses gave the highest returns. These were 9.0 (10.5) per cent for Ordinary National Certificate (ONC) over no qualification and 21.5 (25) for HNC over ONC.

The author, using a 10 per cent alternative discount rate for comparison, concludes that social investment in education at "A" level and ONC level in Great Britain has been of the right order of magnitude. On the other hand, there seems to be social under-investment in high-level technicians (HNC). On the question of the low returns to university education, the author wonders whether the externalities associated with this educational level are enough to raise the returns to the order of magnitude of alternative investments.

Norway

The study of the returns to education in Norway is by Aarrestad

---

[15] Numbers in parentheses refer to the private rates.

(1969). Earnings data covered 100 per cent of government employees, teachers, bank and insurance employees, plus 55—80 per cent of members of professional organizations such as engineers and agriculturalists. Aarrestad computed several rates of return for senior secondary and university education on the basis of the different sectors and occupations into which graduates enter. In the case of senior secondary over primary, we have calculated the overall rate of return as a simple average of the individual rates for different sectors. The private rate of return was equal to 7.4 per cent and the social to 7.2 per cent. In the case of university education, for which the cost of different courses is given, we have computed a cost-weighted average of the individual returns in the different occupations. The private rate of return to university education (over secondary) was 7.7 per cent, and the social rate was 7.5 per cent.

Sweden

The study of the returns to education in Sweden is from Magnusson (1970). His calculations were based on information from three main sources; persons employed in private firms, persons employed by the state, and a sample of about 5,000 individuals. The estimation of the rates of return was based on earnings data, except that for secondary education which was based on income data as reported to the inland revenue authorities. The only adjustments made to the data were the familiar ones for taxes and costs borne by the state in distinguishing between the private and social rates of return. The estimated rates vary little according to the source used. The private rate of return to solicitors and social scientists is 9.5 per cent. Civil engineers have a higher private rate of return, 10 per cent, and a lower social one of 7.5 per cent (average of the returns from two different sources). Physicians show the highest private and social rates of return (14 per cent and 13 per cent, respectively).

In terms of overall averages, the private and social returns across subjects were 10.3 per cent and 9.2 per cent respectively. The social return to the holders of the general certificate of secondary education was equal to 10.5 per cent.

It is interesting to note that Magnusson was very reluctant to adjust these rates of return upwards to take productivity growth into account. The reason for this was that he performed a sensitivity test which indicated that it was doubtful whether a correction for changes in productivity should be made: a rate of return calculation from 1956 cross-sectional data was compared with a calculation

48

using time-series data for the first thirteen years (1956—68) and the 1956 cross-sectional data thereafter. The comparison showed that the use of cross-sectional data over-estimates rather than under-estimates the time-series rate of return. This results contradicts the hypothesis usually underlying a rate of return correction for changes in productivity.

Denmark

The rate of return study for Denmark is by Hansen (1966). The study is limited to various branches of higher education and to only three lower-skill professions. Earnings data were taken from collective agreements to estimate "normal" hourly earnings. These earnings included other forms of employee compensation such as an employer's pension payments. There were no adjustments other than wastage, which was reported separately, and the control group consisted of persons who left school at the age of 16. Therefore, the rates of return refer to three years of higher secondary education plus the time spent in the university for the completion of a particular subject.

Rates of return were only computed for higher education and certain apprenticeship schemes. Lawyers show a private rate of return of 11 per cent and a social return of 10 per cent. Civil engineers appear to enjoy the highest returns (13 per cent private and 8 per cent social) and medical doctors the lowest (8 per cent private and 5 per cent social). Incidentally, the rate of return to the apprenticeship scheme for brick-layers has a much higher rate of return (23 per cent private)!

The Netherlands

We have been able to find only one study of the returns to education in The Netherlands. De Wolff and Ruiter (1968) used data from the Central Bureau of Statistics on the earnings of employees in industry and government service in their study. Rates of return were computed without any adjustments and also with adjustments for mortality, labour-force participation rates and the cost of educating women. Earnings differentials were corrected for ability differences as follows, according to a study by Husén (1968) in Sweden:[16]

---

[16] It is interesting to note that the implied α coefficients of this study run in the opposite direction to the ones of Carnoy for Mexico and Kenya.

	Years of schooling		
	under 10	*11—14*	*over 14*
Percentage of earnings differential attributed to schooling	100	75	65

An overall average estimate of the private return to higher education in The Netherlands is 10.4 per cent. The corresponding social rate is 5.5 per cent. The return to secondary education is 8.5 per cent and 5.2 per cent, respectively. The above rates are averages for technical and social-science graduates at university and are unadjusted for mortality and labour-force participation rates.

Belgium

We have computed rates of return to investment in education in Belgium according to age—earnings profiles found in Desaeyere (1969). Earnings data were based on several surveys among professional workers only, the most detailed being for economists who were 10 per cent of the whole sample.

Weighting the returns to applied science, pure science, law and economics by total study costs gave an overall social rate of return of 9.3 per cent. The private rate of return was calculated for applied science only and the estimate of 17 per cent was based on earnings differentials before tax.

Germany

The returns to education in Germany were studied by Schmidt and Baumgarten (1967). Earnings data were based on the 1964 micro-census survey which sampled 200,000 people. The base group consisted of 15-year-old school leavers.

The profitability estimates are only private ones and refer to different branches of higher education. The unadjusted returns to male university graduates were found to be 4.6 per cent and the returns to female graduates 6 per cent. Higher returns were recorded for female graduates from vocational colleges (7.9 per cent).

Greece

There have been two studies of the returns to education in Greece. The first one is by Leibenstein (1967) and the second by Psacharopoulos (1968) and reported again in Psacharopoulos (1970). Although both studies used the same basic sources of data, the purpose of the second study was to test for discrepancies between actual returns and shadow returns to investment in education. Leibenstein used data from three sources: the household survey of 1957—8; salary schedules in the public sector (where the occupations involved have clear-cut educational requirements); and a sample survey of about 1,500 employees for 1964 and about 1,100 employees for 1960 in commerce and industry in the Athens area.

Income foregone was adjusted downwards by 15 per cent to take the possibility of summer employment into account and by a further 5 per cent to allow for the risk of unemployment. The rates for 1964 were 8 per cent for males in higher education and 3 and 5 per cent for males and females respectively in secondary education (all rates unadjusted for growth).

Psacharopoulos estimated internal rates of return to investment in education in Greece on the basis of the marginal social product of labour instead of the observed earnings. A comparison of the shadow with the actual rates of return suggested that privately advantageous decisions with respect to investment in human capital can be very inefficient when assessed in social terms. This study consisted of a test of the assumption, usually made in rate of return calculations, that observed earnings differentials reflect true productivity differentials. The social product of labour of a particular skill was obtained as a solution to the dual of a linear programming model for the economy as a whole. This social product of labour was then introduced on the benefits side for the rate of return calculation. The analysis was carried out at the skill level, as used in the Mediterranean Regional Project of the OECD (1965) and showed that the shadow rates of return for the higher skills are negative.

The result of this exercise suggested that in countries where a discrepancy may exist between actual earnings and the true value of labour productivity, the evaluation of investment in education should be based on a social rather than on a private measure of benefits derived from education. In the case of Greece, investment priorities with respect to investment in skills estimated on the basis of observed earnings would have suggested a change of the educational output in the wrong direction.

Asia

If we include Hawaii in the set of Asian countries, our evidence for this continent amounts to ten case studies.[17] The others are Turkey, Israel, India, Malaysia, Singapore, The Philippines, Japan, South Korea and Thailand.

Turkey

The only study on the returns to education in Turkey is that by Krueger (1971). Her earnings data were based on two surveys made in 1968: one by the Turkish Association of Metal Manufacturers which covered more than 100 firms in four urban areas; and the second by the American military mission in Turkey which was carried out in order to ensure that the remuneration of Americans was competitive with that in Turkish establishments. It covered 42 industrial companies employing 8,300 white-collar and 12,000 blue-collar workers.

The social rate of return to higher education was found to be equal to 8.5 per cent, while the corresponding private rate was equal to 26 per cent. The private rates for secondary general and secondary technical were approximately of the same order of magnitude as the latter figure (24 and 22 per cent respectively).

Israel

The study of the returns to education in Israel is from Klinov-Malul (1966) who estimated present values for different educational levels. The study was based on a family-savings survey of 3,000 urban families in 1957—8. Since the earnings refer to household heads, the profitability estimates are virtually for males only. We have estimated rates of return to investment in three educational levels in Israel on the basis of the data on earnings and costs reported in this study. The social rates of return were found to be 16.5 per cent for primary, 6.9 per cent for secondary and 6.6 per cent for university. The corresponding private rates were 27 per cent, 6.9 per cent and 8 per cent respectively.

---

[17] There is also a comparative study of the returns to Jordanian industrial and general secondary schools by Al Bukhari (1968) but this was of too limited a scope to be included in the international comparison set.

Several studies exist which calculate the profitability of investment in education in India.[18] The first one is by Harberger (1965) who used a sample survey covering the earnings of about 5,800 male workers in Hyderabad in 1956. As these earnings data were not classified by age he had to use certain assumptions about the distribution of the average earnings over the working lifetime. The social rates based on the assumption that the direct costs of education are equal to 50 per cent of the foregone earnings, were 10 per cent for secondary education and 16.3 per cent for higher education. Harberger then compared these returns with those earned on physical capital investments. In another study (Nalla Gounden, 1967) data were derived from an urban income survey of about 5,000 males in 1960—1 by the National Council of Applied Research and from the monthly pay of about 4,000 engineers, as reported by the Council of Scientific and Industrial Research. In estimating the rates of return, an α coefficient of 0.5 was assumed. The social rate of return for primary education was equal to 16.8 per cent; middle yielded an 11.8 per cent rate; matriculation 10.2 per cent; a bachelor's degree 7 per cent, and an engineering degree 9.8 per cent. Selowsky (1967) recalculated the rates of return for India based on Nalla Gounden's data, but without using the assumption of $\alpha = 0.5$.

Nalla Gounden also refers to a study of the returns to education in India by Kothari (1967). The earnings data for this study refer to Bombay only and the social rates of return were 20 per cent for high school over middle school, and 13 per cent for college over high school. This study also produced a social rate for arts and science graduates of 13 per cent and a rate for engineering equal to 25 per cent.

Finally, Blaug *et al.* (1969) estimated rates of return to investment in education in India, in their attempt to diagnose the origins of graduate unemployment in this country. The earnings data for this study were the same as the ones used by Nalla Gounden plus a sample of 20,000 employees in various factories. Adjustments were made for unemployment, wastage, income growth, taxes and other factors influencing earnings (α coefficient).[19] The private rates of

---

[18] In addition to the studies reported here the reader may be interested in some further evidence on earnings differentials between various occupational groups in Bombay (Kothari, 1970).

[19] For a detailed comparison of the assumptions used in the studies by Harberger, Nalla Gounden and Blaug *et al.*, see Woodhall (1969).

return adjusted for wastage, unemployment, other factors ($\alpha = 0.65$) and growth (2 per cent per year) were found to be 18.7 per cent for primary, 10.4 per cent for a first degree (over matriculation) and 15.5 per cent for an engineering degree. The corresponding social rates were 15.2 per cent, 8.9 per cent and 12.5 per cent, respectively. The methodological interest of this study lies in the fact that graduate unemployment is explained by the authors not in terms of "structural imbalances" but by the persistence of an advantageous private rate of return over time.

Malaysia

O. D. Hoerr, of the Harvard Development Advisory Service, has calculated the returns to education in Malaysia (Hoerr, 1970). Using a socio-economic sample of 30,000 households in 1967—8 he estimated social private rates of return for six levels of education. Adjustments to the earnings data included an α coefficient of 0.60, labour-force participation rates and unemployment. The social returns were 8.2 per cent primary, 12.8 to 15.6 per cent secondary and 5.8 per cent university, and the corresponding private returns were 12.9 per cent, 15.6 to 21.1 per cent and 11.4 per cent.[20]

Singapore

Clark and Fong's (1970) main data source in estimating the returns to education in Singapore was the Sample Household survey of 1966. This survey provided earnings data for full-time employees by sex and education. Gross incremental lifetime income streams were adjusted for unemployment and labour-force participation. Private rates of return also contain a tax adjustment. Clark and Fong have computed both present values and rates of return separately for men and women. The rates for men and women are not very different, except for the primary level (men 9.4 per cent, women 3.8 per cent). The overall social rates of return are 6.6 per cent for the primary level, 17.6 per cent for the secondary and 14.6 per cent for the higher. The private rate for the secondary level is 20 per cent and for the higher level 25.4 per cent.

---

[20] The analyses in the rest of this book use only the preliminary results from Hoerr's study since the final results were not in our hands at an early enough date.

The Philippines

The returns to education in The Philippines were studied by Williamson and Devoretz (1967) and again reported in Devoretz (1969). The study was based on a sample household survey in Imus, Cavite. The earnings data refer to the head of the household and were adjusted for survival. No taxes were deducted in calculating the private rates of return. Profitability estimates were made for primary, intermediate, high school, vocational and college education. Social rates of return were computed only for public educational institutions. Primary education yielded a 7 per cent social rate of return, high school yielded 21 per cent and college education 11 per cent. Private rate of return were estimated both for private and public institutions but the rates were not very different from the social rates above. Vocational education gave an 11 per cent social and private rate of return.

Japan

Bowman (1970) used sample surveys of earnings in firms employing ten persons or more in order to estimate rates of return to investment in education in Japan for 1959, 1961 and 1966; and the civil service and service industries were excluded from the sample. The rates were unadjusted for ability, growth or other factors. Bowman has produced a variety of profitability estimates, e.g., based on gross direct costs, low costs, high costs, with or without bonus adjustment, in private and national institutions. Concentrating on the private rates for upper secondary, these were found to be 8 per cent in 1954, 7 per cent in 1961 and 5 per cent in 1966 (based on direct costs and without bonus adjustment). Four years of university without "ronin" gave 19 per cent, 10 per cent and 13 per cent in the respective years.[21] Junior college earned returns of 18 per cent, 11 per cent and 9 per cent in the respective years. On the social side, the average rate of return for private and national institutions in 1961 and without bonus adjustment was 5 per cent for upper secondary, 6 per cent for four years of university without "ronin" and 9.5 per cent for junior college. Commenting on these rates Bowman noted that the most striking aspect of them was the declining pattern over time, obviously due to the increasing proportion of labour with post-secondary education.

---

[21] "Ronin" refers to those who have to re-sit the university entrance qualifying examinations in order to be admitted to the university.

In another study, Danielsen and Okachi (1971) have used 1966 cross-sectional data from the *Statistical Yearbook of Japan* to estimate average and marginal rates of return. Their rates are private and refer to males only. The secondary cycle (twelve over 4.5 years of schooling) yielded a rate equal to 10 per cent, whereas the higher education cycle (sixteen over twelve years of schooling) yielded a rate equal to 10.5 per cent.

South Korea

There is a USAID study on the return to education in South Korea by Kim Kwang Suk (1968). The earnings data were based on a sample survey in the mining and manufacturing industries which covered 13 per cent of total employment. The social rates of return were found to be 12 per cent for middle school, 9 per cent for high school and 5 per cent for university.

Thailand

In a recent report Blaug (1971) has estimated rates of return to investment in education in Thailand. A special sample survey was conducted for this purpose covering 5,000 males and females in the greater Bangkok area in 1970. Multiple regression analysis was used to estimate earnings functions. Earnings were standardized (apart from the familiar age, sex and years of schooling variables) for parents' education, ethnic origin, father's occupation, urban or rural, private or public school, vocational or academic school, hours of work, sector of employment, size of the firm and occupation. According to Blaug, this degree of standardization corresponds approximately to an α coefficient of 0.55. The adjusted private rate of return to lower primary was 24 per cent and the social rate 22 per cent. Upper primary gave a 16 per cent private and a 14 per cent social rate. Both lower and higher secondary yielded 11 per cent private and 10 per cent social rates. Finally, university education gave an 11 per cent private and a 7 per cent social rate. It is also interesting to note that vocational secondary schooling yielded negative private and social rates of return.

Hawaii

Psacharopoulos (1969b) has estimated rates of return to investment in education in Hawaii based on the reports of the 1960 Census of the Population and starting salary offers to University of Hawaii graduates. The private rate of return for elementary schooling had, of course, an infinite value. High school yielded a private rate of 5.1 per cent and college 11 per cent. The social rates of return for the three levels were 24.1 per cent, 4.4 per cent and 9.2 per cent, respectively. In 1965 the private return to a master's degree was 6.7 per cent and to a doctorate 12 per cent.

Africa

Five African countries are represented in our collection of case studies. These are Nigeria, Ghana, Kenya, Uganda and Northern Rhodesia.

Nigeria

There are two studies of the returns to education in Nigeria. The first by Bowles (1967b) refers to Northern Nigeria and the second by Hinchliffe (1969) to the Western Region.

Bowles used earnings data from a sample survey of employment in private firms in 1964 to estimate benefit—cost ratios for different educational levels. His analysis showed that the most profitable level was primary education.

Hinchliffe estimated rates of return for the Western Region by using government pay scales for secondary modern, secondary grammar, sixth form and university graduates. For the earnings of primary school graduates he used weighted earnings in wage farming, transport and the construction industry. Adjustments were made for the effects of unemployment and wastage.

The unadjusted social rates of return were 23 per cent for primary education, 12.8 per cent for secondary grammar and 17 per cent for university over sixth form. Hinchliffe has also estimated private rates of return to investment in education and these were 30 per cent, 14 per cent and 34 per cent for the three respective levels.[22]

---

[22] In estimating the private rates of returns Hinchliffe adopted the proportions of total costs borne by the individual as found in Calcott (1968). It should also be mentioned that the earnings used are before tax and therefore the returns are overestimated.

Ghana

The rate of return study for Ghana is also due to Hinchliffe (1971) and is based on government pay scales for secondary grammar, sixth form and university graduates. Middle-school leavers' earnings were obtained as a weighted average of earnings in wage farming, construction and the mining industry. Primary school leavers' earnings were obtained on the basis of average earnings of wage farming. Adjustments were made for the effects of unemployment and wastage.

The unadjusted social rates which refer to 1967 were 18 per cent for primary, 13 per cent for secondary grammar and 16.5 per cent for university. Hinchliffe later estimated private rates of return for the above three levels and these were 24.5 per cent, 17 per cent and 37 per cent, respectively. The private rates were calculated before adjustments for taxation and are therefore on the high side.

Kenya

There are two studies on the returns to education in Kenya both of which are of methodological interest. The first by Rogers (1972) includes a sensitivity test on the cost side of a rate of return calculation, with the aim of observing how different financing schemes would influence the private returns on post-primary education. For this purpose he used earnings data from government pay scales for civil servants and teachers. The benefit side included salary plus housing subsidy and was net of taxes. The basis of all comparisons was 4th form (seven years of primary school plus four years of secondary). Four alternative financing schemes were examined:

(a) (Existing system): direct costs of schooling plus a subsidy are met by the government.

(b) (Pay-as-you-go): total costs are paid by the student as schooling is received.

(c) (Fixed-amount payments): total costs are paid by fixed-amount annual payments for life or until the costs are repaid.

(d) (Percentage-of-earnings payments): total costs are paid by charging a fixed percentage of earnings each year of the working life.

The returns to secondary 6th form under any scheme were found to be negative. Two years of teacher college yielded the highest return (11.1 per cent) under scheme (a) and the lowest under scheme (b) (6.9 per cent). University yielded 21.4 per cent under the existing scheme and 9.5 per cent under the pay-as-you-go system. In general, the existing scheme proved to be the most advantageous for students and the pay-as-you-go the least. Schemes (c) and (d) ranked in between.

The second study of Kenya, by Thias and Carnoy (1969), attempted two things. First, to isolate the benefits of additional schooling from other socio-economic factors and ability; and second, to project the rates of return into the future. The data were based on a special survey of about 4,800 observations. Regression analysis was used to relate the earnings differentials to educational variables (schooling and examination scores), socio-economic variables (age, tribe, parents' literacy and father's occupation) and specific job-related variables (size and nature of the firm employing the wage earner, their job level and whether they had received on-the-job training). Adjustments were also made for unemployment, mortality and taxation. Private rates were not corrected for life expectancy.

The various adjustments in this study suggested values of the α coefficient ranging from around 0.30 for primary, 0.60 for secondary and 0.80 for university. That is, the lower the levels of schooling compared, less of the income differential is due to education and more is due to other factors like socio-economic background. The private rates of return roughly corresponding to the three educational cycles, are 32.7 per cent for primary, 30.0 per cent for secondary and 27.4 per cent for university. In contrast, the social rates were substantially lower: 21.7 per cent, 19.2 per cent and 8.8 per cent for the respective levels.

Uganda

There are two studies on the returns to education in Uganda. The first one is by Bennett (1967) and the second by Smyth and Bennett (1967). Bennett's results are in the form of benefit—cost ratios, the highest one being for upper secondary schooling and lowest for university. In the other study, Smyth and Bennett used earnings data for graduates of university, higher-secondary and lower-secondary education based on government salary scales. In order to take private-employment opportunities into account, the initial government scales were increased by the following percentages: university graduates 15 per cent, higher secondary graduates 10 per cent and lower secondary graduates 5 per cent. Data on the earnings of primary school graduates and of those who did not complete primary school were obtained from the Ugandan Central Planning Bureau. For the construction of age—earnings profiles, initial earnings were assumed to grow at the following annual rates: university graduates 4 per cent, higher-secondary graduates 4 per cent, lower-secondary graduates 5 per cent, primary school graduates 4 per cent and those with no education 0 per cent. The age—earnings profiles were assumed to continue to infinity.

The social rates of return that resulted from this study were 66 per cent for primary schooling, 22 per cent for lower secondary, 78 per cent for upper secondary and 12 per cent for university.

Northern Rhodesia

The study for Northern Rhodesia was made by Baldwin (1966) and was based on income data by level of education from the 1960[23] African demographic survey of urban areas. Baldwin calculated present values for different discount rates. Since these present values range from positive to negative numbers we have derived the approximate rates of return to each level by plotting them against the discount rates. The social rates of return, which refer only to primary education, range from 4.0 per cent for the third year of primary to 22.5 per cent for the completion of the sixth year of primary education.

Australasia

The only evidence of the returns to education in Australasia that we were able to find refers to New Zealand.

New Zealand

The returns to education in New Zealand were studied by Ogilvy (1968).[24] The basis of the study was starting salaries in various state and quasi-state enterprises, together with the assumption that they increase at 11 per cent per year over the working life of the individual.

An α coefficient of 0.5 was used throughout and rates of return were given separately for males and females. The average social rate to secondary schooling was 19.4 per cent and the private rate was 20 per cent. A university degree yielded a 13.2 per cent social rate and a 14.7 per cent private one.

---

[23] Hence the use of the former name of the country which is now known as Zambia.
[24] For a revised version see also Ogilvy (1970).

Chapter 4. Searching for Rate of Return Patterns

In the previous chapter we have presented all the evidence we were able to discover in 32 countries. In this chapter we will organize this evidence in order to be able to make some international comparisons and see if any obvious patterns emerge.[1] For the countries in which there was only one rate of return study no selection could of course be made, but in other cases we have selected the one which, because of its coverage, methodology and the like, was more comparable with the rest.

The first classification we have attempted is by educational level. Three standard educational levels are distinguished (primary, secondary and higher) and every effort has been made to see that figures are comparable across countries. Other rate of return classifications are by sex, type of graduate programme, type of institution, type of secondary school and subject of higher education.

Organizing the profitability evidence

Our first task in this chapter is to reduce the rate of return evidence presented above into a manageable form. This is done in Table 4.1 where we present social and private rates of return for primary, secondary and higher education. Where several profitability studies are available for a given country we have used the one in which the estimates are apparently most comparable with those in other countries. For example, the rates for the United States were taken from Hines *et al.* (1970) since this is the most recent profitability study for this country and it contains both social and private estimates for all educational levels. Appendix C describes in detail how we arrived at all the country figures in Table 4.1. In the view of the different data, methodologies, assumptions and coverage of the case studies we

---

[1] For the first rate of return comparison ever attempted using evidence from four case studies, see Carnoy (1967b). For another comparative rate of return study using evidence from fourteen countries, see Hansen (1970).

TABLE 4.1

SOCIAL AND PRIVATE RATES OF RETURN BY EDUCATIONAL LEVEL AND COUNTRY (per cent)

Country (1)	Year (2)	Social			Private		
		Primary (3)	Secondary (4)	Higher (5)	Primary (6)	Secondary (7)	Higher (8)
United States	1959	17.8	14.0	9.7	155.1	19.5	13.6
Canada	1961	..	11.7	14.0	..	16.3	19.7
Puerto Rico	1959	17.1	21.7	16.5	> 100.0	23.4	27.9
Mexico	1963	25.0	17.0	23.0	32.0	23.0	29.0
Venezuela	1957	82.0	17.0	23.0	..	18.0	27.0
Colombia	1966	40.0	24.0	8.0	> 50.0	32.0	15.5
Chile	1959	24.0	16.9	12.2	..	..	..
Brazil	1962	10.7	17.2	14.5	11.3	21.4	38.1
Great Britain	1966	..	3.6	8.2	..	6.2	12.0
Norway	1966	..	7.2	7.5	..	7.4	7.7
Sweden	1967	..	10.5	9.2	..	..	10.3
Denmark	1964	..	..	7.8	..	..	10.0
The Netherlands	1965	..	5.2	5.5	..	8.5	10.4
Belgium	1967	..	..	9.3	..	..	17.0
Germany	1964	..	..	..	..	..	4.6
Greece	1964	..	3.0	8.0	..	5.0	14.0
Turkey	1968	..	..	8.5	..	24.0	26.0
Israel	1958	16.5	6.9	6.6	27.0	6.9	8.0
India	1960	20.2	16.8	12.7	24.7	19.2	14.3
Malaysia	1967	9.3	12.3	10.7	..	..	..
Singapore	1966	6.6	17.6	14.6	..	20.0	25.4
The Philippines	1966	7.0	21.0	11.0	7.5	28.0	12.5
Japan	1961	..	5.0	6.0	..	6.0	9.0
S. Korea	1967	12.0	9.0	5.0	..	..	..
Thailand	1970	30.5	13.0	11.0	56.0	14.5	14.0
Hawaii	1959	24.1	4.4	9.2	> 100.0	5.1	11.0
Nigeria	1966	23.0	12.8	17.0	30.0	14.0	34.0
Ghana	1967	18.0	13.0	16.5	24.5	17.0	37.0
Kenya	1968	21.7	19.2	8.8	32.7	30.0	27.4
Uganda	1965	66.0	28.6	12.0	..	..	..
N. Rhodesia	1960	12.4	..	..	..	..	..
New Zealand	1966	..	19.4	13.2	..	20.0	14.7

Source: Appendix C
Note: For explanation of symbol notations see Appendix I.

62

have attempted to include as far as possible only unadjusted rates in this table. Of course this is not possible for countries where there is no choice of studies.[2]

Table 4.1 contains more rate of return estimates than found in the original studies. These extra estimates were made by us, when original earnings profiles and cost data could be found in the case studies. For example, if a case study gave only net present values and not rates of return, the original data were used to estimate rates of return (as for Israel). Or, whenever only a social rate of return was given, the original data were used to estimate a private rate, or vice versa (as in Colombia and Canada). It will be noticed that some cells in Table 4.1 are empty, in particular those for private rates and for the lower educational levels. The reason for this is that most of the authors of the case studies were interested in the social rates of return in view of their implications for educational policy. Moreover, calculations of rates of return for primary schooling are of limited policy interest and are difficult to estimate in countries with a long tradition of compulsory education. In the absence of census data, sample surveys are normally used for earnings data and, since they do not normally include enough individuals with less than primary schooling, a profitability calculation for primary schooling is not possible.

Every effort has been made to see that the figures in Table 4.1 are comparable across countries for each given educational level. However, severe comparability limitations still exist. These limitations are the result of the heterogeneity of the various educational levels, different points in time to which the profitability measures refer and the various adjustments to which these estimates have been subjected. Let us discuss some of these points in detail.

Admittedly, the standard tripartite formal schooling classification varies widely from country to country. For example, the secondary educational level in Great Britain consists in full of seven years of schooling while the same level in the United States includes only four years. Note, however, that a classification according to the number of years of schooling would not necessarily be better. It may be that employers in different countries place a value on the completion of a given level as evidence that the employee possesses the required qualifications. If this hypothesis is true, rate of return comparisons should be done for completed educational levels.

---

[2] e.g., the estimates for New Zealand incorporate an α coefficient adjustment equal to 0.50.

Another disturbing aspect in the comparisons is that the rates do not all refer to the same year. How valid is it to compare the returns in the United States in 1959 with similar returns in Thailand for 1970? Unfortunately, most countries have profitability estimates for one single year and the only country for which time-series evidence on the rates of returns exists is the United States. Rates of return are available for this country for 1939, 1949 and 1959, based on Population Censuses, as well as for more recent years based on special surveys. This time-series evidence suggests that the rates of return have not changed markedly within a quarter of a century.[3] Generalizing the time-series experience of the United States, we could hypothesize that the profitability measures in Table 4.1 are representative of the actual situation in each country for a time period around the year appearing in column (2).

Ideally, all the social returns should have been computed by using before-tax earnings and all private returns by using after-tax earnings. However, the private rates which we have calculated for Venezuela, Colombia, Greece, Nigeria and Ghana have been computed using before-tax earnings. Of course, this leads to an overestimation of the private rate of return but not as much as one might think *a priori*. A more serious objection is that in some cases the costs in calculating the private rate have been taken to be equal only to the foregone earnings (as in the cases of Greece and Colombia).[4]

The returns by educational level across countries

The values of the rates of return in Table 4.1 fluctuate over a wide range and in particular it will be noticed that the private rates for primary education vary more than any other category across countries. The reason for this is that in most cases primary education is provided free and foregone earnings of primary school pupils are virtually zero. Therefore, an infinite private rate of return to this educational level should not be surprising.[5]

---

[3] See Psacharopoulos (forthcoming b).

[4] See Appendix A for the sensitivity of a rate of return estimate to alternative assumptions on costs.

[5] Although mathematically precise, the reader might question the meaning of a private rate of return to primary education in the United States equal to 155 per cent. It is for this reason that in Table 4.2 we have also provided the average private returns to primary schooling excluding countries where the rates are higher than 50 per cent.

Table 4.2 summarizes the rate of return evidence by providing the average rate and standard deviation for each educational level. According to this table the average social returns to investment in education are 25.1 per cent for primary, 13.5 per cent for secondary and 11.3 per cent for the higher level. The private returns are 23.7 per cent, 16.3 per cent and 17.5 per cent for the respective educational levels. It should be noted that the decline is much sharper between the first and second level than between the second and third one. Standard deviations are roughly about half the size of the average rate of return estimates. What this means is that for two-thirds of the students the rates of return are in the range of 50 to 150 per cent of the figure reported in Table 4.2. For example, the most probable social rate of return to higher education for a typical student would be in the range of 6.6 to 16.0 per cent.[6] This range should be borne in mind in any discussion of "rational educational calculus".

TABLE 4.2

AVERAGE RATES OF RETURN BY EDUCATIONAL LEVEL

Educational level	Rate of return (percentage)	Standard deviation	Number of observations
Social			
Primary	25.1	19.1	19
	(19.4)	(8.3)	(17)
Secondary	13.5	6.8	26
Higher	11.3	4.7	28
Private			
Primary	23.7	9.4	8
Secondary	16.3	8.4	21
Higher	17.5	9.7	25

Source: Based on Table 4.1.
Note: The social rate of return figures for primary education exclude Venezuela and Uganda and the private figures for primary education exclude the United States, Puerto Rico, Colombia, Thailand and Hawaii.

The first comparative rate of return study tentatively indicated that the returns to education were declining as the level of schooling rose (Carnoy, 1967b). Today we can confirm this finding after having studied a larger set of data. In order to test the order of the

---

[6] That is 11.3 ± 4.7.

social rates by level of education, we selected the eighteen countries for which we have evidence for all three levels and ranked them as in Table 4.3. The first cell in this table, for example, indicates that in fourteen countries out of the eighteen the rate of return to primary education ranks first, whereas the last cell indicates that in ten countries in our sample the rate of return to higher education is lower in absolute magnitude than the rates for the other two levels. A chi-square test based on this table revealed that the rate of return pattern we are concerned with is statistically significant at the 0.005 level.[7]

TABLE 4.3

RANKING WITHIN COUNTRIES OF THE SOCIAL RATES OF RETURN BY EDUCATIONAL LEVEL

Educational level	Social rate of return rank		
	1st	2nd	3rd
Primary	14	1	3
Secondary	4	9	5
Higher	—	8	10

Source: Based on Table 4.1.
Note: Refers to the eighteen countries for which rates of return are available for all three educational levels.

Private versus social returns

As mentioned in Chapter 2 a divergence between a social and private rate of return can arise because of the following two reasons. First, only a part of the direct cost of schooling is usually borne by the individual, the rest being borne by the state; and second, the after-tax earnings differential combined with after-tax foregone earnings will affect the rate of return in an ambiguous way.[8] In practice, the cost

---

[7] In our case $\chi^2 = 28.0$. The χ^2 statistic at the 0.005 level of significance and 4 degrees of freedom has a value of 14.9.

[8] Of course, there is a host of other reasons for a divergence between true private and social rates such as wages not corresponding to the marginal social product of labour, or higher-educated labour having external effects. Here, however, we deal only with the most common computational reasons for the divergence.

correction is much stronger than the tax one so that the private rate is higher than the social rate.[9]

The divergence between the private and social returns in Table 4.1 can be seen from two points of view. First, as evidence of the net public subsidy education receives in different countries; and second, to what extent this subsidy could be reduced without destroying the private incentive. Consider as an example the case of Mexico where both the private and social returns to higher education are on the high side, 29 per cent and 23 per cent respectively. Obviously, public subsidies to higher education could be reduced in this country as this level of education would still remain a privately advantageous investment opportunity. However, this would not be the case in other countries such as Colombia, where a reduction of the subsidy towards higher education might reduce the private returns to a level at which the incentive to invest would disappear.

Table 4.4 summarizes the differences between private and social rates in two groups of countries in our sample, developed and less

TABLE 4.4

DIFFERENCES BETWEEN PRIVATE AND SOCIAL RATES OF RETURN IN DEVELOPED AND DEVELOPING COUNTRIES (per cent)

| | Educational level | | | | | |
| | Secondary | | | Higher | | |
	Private	Social	Difference	Private	Social	Difference
Developed	11.9	9.5	2.4	11.9	9.4	2.5
countries	(7)	(8)		(11)	(10)	
Developing	18.5	15.2	3.3	22.0	12.4	9.6
countries	(14)	(18)		(14)	(8)	
All countries	16.3	13.5	2.8	17.5	11.3	6.2

Source: Table 4.1 and 5.2.
Notes: (1) Number of observations are in parentheses. (2) The dividing line between developed and developing countries is GNP per capita US $1,000.

---

[9] A tax adjustment is far less important than one might think *a priori*. In Hines *et al.* the unadjusted rate of return to college education over high school was found to be 13.6 per cent. Adjustment for secular income growth raised the rate to 16.2 per cent. A correction for differential ability lowered the rate to 13.2 per cent, but a further correction for taxes had no effect on the rate. See Hines, *et al.*, (1970), p. 334.

developed.[10] The comparison is not made for primary education because of the above-mentioned problem of the very high or sometimes infinite values of the private returns to this educational level.

There are a few interesting points to observe in this Table 4.4. First, it appears that higher education receives more public subsidy than secondary education. This is evidenced in the last row of the table where the discrepancy between the average private and social rates of return in secondary education for all countries is 2.8 percentage points whereas the corresponding discrepancy for higher education is 6.2 percentage points. Second, the less developed the country the higher the discrepancy between private and social rates at both levels under comparison. This is surprising as one would expect *a priori* that the more developed the country the more heavily subsidized would be its educational system.[11]

Males versus females

One might think that investment in the education of men would yield higher returns than corresponding investments for women on the grounds that women have a lower labour-force participation rate than men and, further, are discriminated against in the labour market. A glance at Table 4.5 shows that this is not universally true. Out of twentyone cases for which we have evidence for both males and females, fourteen cases show higher returns for men, while the remaining seven cases show higher returns for women. In fact such results are not surprising since it is not the absolute earnings of men and women that are under comparison in a rate of return calculation but the absolute earnings of more and less educated *women*. Of course, this kind of calculation could lead to a higher or lower rate of return for women relative to that earned by men. However, it is still the case that on the average men make more than women from the resources they invest in similar levels of education. As Table 4.6 shows, the largest differences in the returns to the two sexes occur at primary level. This could easily be explained in terms of the lower

[10] The dividing line between developed and less developed countries is GNP per capita $ US 1,000.
[11] This discrepancy is particularly pronounced in the case of Kenya, Brazil and Mexico.

labour-force participation and higher discrimination against this particular sex-educational group.[12]

TABLE 4.5

RATES OF RETURN BY EDUCATIONAL LEVEL AND SEX IN CERTAIN COUNTRIES (per cent)

| Country | Educational level | | | | | |
| | Primary | | Secondary | | Higher | |
	Males	Females	Males	Females	Males	Females
United States	17.8	5.6	14.0	13.0	9.7	4.2
Puerto Rico	17.1	17.2	21.7	20.9	16.5	6.3
Colombia	15.3	..	26.5	13.5	2.9	3.6
Germany	..	..	..	..	4.6	6.0
Greece	..	..	3.0	5.0	..	..
Kenya	21.7	7.1	23.6	19.5	..	..
Malaysia	9.4	9.3	12.3	11.4	10.7	9.8
New Zealand	..	..	19.4	25.3	13.4	13.5
Brazil	17.9	38.6	..	..	..	..
Singapore	9.4	3.8	18.2	17.0	15.4	13.7

Sources: United States: Hines *et al.* (1970), pp. 326, 328; Puerto Rico: Carnoy (1970), Table 4; Colombia: Schultz (1968), p. 36; Germany: Schmidt and Baumgarten (1967), p. 174; Greece: Leibenstein (1967), p. 13; Kenya: Thias and Carnoy (1969), p. 112; Malaysia: Hoerr's (1970) preliminary results; New Zealand: Ogilvy (1968), p. 100; Brazil: Lerner (1970), Table 12, column 1; Singapore: Clark and Fong (1970), p. 90.
Notes: (1) All rates are social except for Germany and Brazil. (2) Puerto Rico rates refer to urban males and females only. (3) Kenya rates are for junior secondary only.

TABLE 4.6

AVERAGE RATES OF RETURN BY EDUCATIONAL LEVEL AND SEX

Educational level	Males	Females	Difference
Primary	16.3	9.8	6.5
Secondary	17.2	15.5	1.7
Higher	9.6	7.2	2.4

Source: Table 4.4. without Brazil and Singapore

---

[12] For a detailed analysis of the returns to education by sex, see Woodhall (forthcoming).

Secondary general or secondary technical?

An issue which has been widely debated, particularly with regard to developing countries, is the degree to which a country should split the provision of secondary education between "general" and "technical" schooling. In four of the studies we have surveyed, evidence was found on the returns to these two types of education. The results are conflicting. As Table 4.7 shows the returns to secondary technical education in Colombia are substantially higher than the corresponding returns to general education (e.g., 35.4 per cent versus 26.5 per cent). But this is not the case for the Philippines where the social returns to technical secondary (11 per cent) are only one-half the returns to general secondary (21 per cent). And, clearly, this is also the picture in Thailand where the returns to secondary technical education are negative. However, the scarcity of case studies on this subject deters us from drawing any overall conclusion regarding the economic choice between secondary general and secondary technical education.

TABLE 4.7

RATES OF RETURN TO SECONDARY GENERAL AND SECONDARY TECHNICAL EDUCATION IN CERTAIN COUNTRIES (per cent)

| Country | Secondary education | | Type of rate of return | |
	General	Technical		
Colombia	26.5	35.4	males	social
	34.3	52.5	males	private
	13.5	39.8	females	social
	16.0	54.7	females	private
The Philippines	21.0	11.0	social	
	28.0	11.5	private	
Thailand	9.0	−6.0	social	
	10.0	−2.0	private	
Turkey	24.0	22.0	private	

Source: Colombia: Schultz (1968), pp. 28, 36; The Philippines: Devoretz (1969), p. 110; Thailand: Blaug (1971), preliminary results; Turkey: Krueger (1971), p. 39.

Is graduate study worthwhile?

Another interesting classification of rates of return is for higher degrees of university education. From the evidence presented earlier for other levels of education we would expect post graduate returns to be the lowest. Table 4.8 shows that this is only half the truth. The private return to a Bachelor's degree in the United States is 13.6 per cent, that for a Master's degree 7.5 per cent and 9.1 per cent for the Ph.D. For Great Britain Layard *et al.* (1971) estimate the return to a Master's degree as negative, but the private return for a Ph.D. is higher than that for the Bachelor's degree. The same U-shaped pattern appears in Hawaii. If the picture implied by the case studies in Table 4.8 is correct, then employees seem to place a particular value, compared with the immediately preceding qualifications, on both the Bachelor or the Ph.D. degrees, but not on the Master's degree.

TABLE 4.8

RATES OF RETURN TO POSTGRADUATE EDUCATION IN CERTAIN COUNTRIES

Country	Degree					
	Bachelor's		Master's		Doctorate	
	Social	Private	Social	Private	Social	Private
United States	9.7	13.6	..	7.5	..	9.1
	..	..	..	—1.0	..	2.2 to 3.0
Great Britain	8.2	12.0	negative	negative	5.0	16.0
	10.8	..	1.2	..	1.6	..
Hawaii	9.2	11.0	4.8	6.3	8.3	10.0
New Zealand	13.2	14.7	8.8	9.9	..	..

Source: United States: Ashenfelter and Mooney (1969), p. 253, and Hunt (1963), p. 352; Great Britain: Layard *et al.* (1971), pp. 138, 140, and Morris and Ziderman (1971), p. xxvii; Hawaii: Psacharopoulos (1969b), p. 36; New Zealand: Ogilvy (1968), p. 100.
Note: Rates for the Bachelor's degree from Table 4.1.

The returns to different subjects of higher education

Table 4.9 attempts a comparison between the returns to different fields of higher education. The evidence is again rather scanty and no

71

clear-cut pattern emerges. What is of interest are the contrasting returns to engineering in Great Britain (1.4 per cent) and in India (16.6 per cent). This is a nice example of the sensitivity of the rate of return measure to conditions in the labour market.[13]

TABLE 4.9

SOCIAL RATES OF RETURN TO HIGHER EDUCATION BY SUBJECT IN CERTAIN COUNTRIES

Subject	Great Britain	Norway	Sweden	Den- mark	Bel- gium	India	Brazil
Economics	3.9	8.9	..	9.0	9.5	..	16.1
Business administration	..	16.6	9.0	..	..	..	..
Accountancy	7.5	..	..	..	..	..	..
Law	..	10.6	9.5	10.0	6.0	..	17.4
Medicine	..	3.1	13.0	5.0	11.5	..	11.9
Dentistry	..	8.8	..	..	..	..	8.4
Engineering	1.4	8.4	7.5	8.0	..	16.6	17.3
Agronomy	..	2.2	..	..	..	..	5.2
Architecture	..	..	..	9.0	..	..	..
Pure science	..	..	..	..	9.0	..	..
Applied science	1.4	..	..	..	7.0	..	..
Secondary school teacher training	..	6.0	..	9.0	..	..	..
Primary school teacher training	..	..	..	7.0	..	..	..
Overall higher education	8.2	7.5	9.2	7.8	9.3	12.7	15.0

Source: Great Britain: Richardson (1969), p. 113; Norway: Aarrestad (1969), p. 107; Sweden: Magnusson (1970), p. 5.13; Denmark: Hansen (1966), p. 253; Belgium: Desaeyere (1969), p. 266; India: Blaug *et al.* (1969), p. 218; Brazil: Rogers III (1969), table 15; Overall higher education rate: Table 4.1, except Brazil from Rogers III (1969).

In this chapter we have chiefly been concerned with sorting out the rate of return evidence which we have collected for the 32 countries. These results will be used for further analysis in the following chapters in conjunction with other economic variables. Here we were concerned with searching out the existence of patterns

---

[13] But see Layard *et al.* (1971) for a much higher estimate of the returns in engineering education in Britain.

among the rates themselves. At a very general level we have shown that social returns are on average lower the higher the educational level and that private returns to primary schooling are above the returns to secondary and higher education. We have also been able to show that the divergences between social and private rates of return are greater at each educational level in developing countries than in developed countries. All the available evidence has been presented for sub-division of the returns by male—female; general and technical schooling; graduate programmes and subject breakdowns, but the small samples involved have led to the emergence of no overriding trends. In the next chapter we will move on from rate of return patterns to comparisons between the returns to investment in human and physical capital.

Chapter 5. The Allocative Efficiency of Investment in Education

We now turn to consider in this chapter the first question asked in the introduction, namely whether investment in men yields higher returns than investment in machines. The comparison between the returns to alternative investments comes under the heading of "allocative efficiency" in economics. For, if the returns to investment-opportunity A are higher than the returns to investment-opportunity B, then income-growth possibilities exist in devoting more resources to A and less to B. In other words, resources are not efficiently allocated unless the returns to all activities are the same and equal to the market rate of interest.

In a perfectly competitive economy one should expect the private rates of return to investment in each level of education to be equal. That is $r_H = r_i$, for all i where i = primary, secondary and higher education. Further, the average rate of return to investment in education (r_H) should be equal to the private rate of return on physical (or material) capital (r_M), so that the following equation should hold

$$r_H = r_M = r_i \tag{5.1}$$

Equation (5.1) represents the first order condition for the privately efficient allocation of funds between the various investment activities in an economy, whether these activities are in physical or human form. However, the real world is far from perfect. Discrepancies will exist, not only between the returns to each educational level, but also between the returns to education in general and the alternative rate of return on other investments. A situation like equation (5.1) can be interpreted as a case of efficient allocation, while a situation like the one in equation (5.2) can be interpreted as inefficient:

$$r_{primary} \neq r_{secondary} \neq r_{university} \neq r_{material} \tag{5.2}$$

When we consider the social rates of return there is no expectation that an equality of the type (5.1) will exist, even in a perfectly competitive economy, because of the existence of externalities. Public subsidies, and the nonmaximizing behaviour of the state are also reasons why one would not expect an equality of the social rates of return to all levels of education. For example, when higher education is subsidized the total cost is irrelevant to the individual and he may invest to the point where, although the private rate on education is equal to the private rate on alternative investments, the social rate is lower than the alternative. The evidence in Table 4.1 suggests that this example is not far from the truth in many Western European countries.

We shall deal with the relationship between the returns to physical and human capital later in this chapter. Looking for the moment only within the educational sector, the discrepancies of the type in equation (5.2) in Table 4.1 do not suggest that resources have been efficiently allocated within the educational sector in most countries. In many cases, rates of return within countries differ by more than 100 per cent between different educational levels. The average discrepancies between social rates of return across countries are approximately 12 percentage points between the primary and secondary level and 2 percentage points between secondary and higher (see Table 4.2). However, these average discrepancies conceal a tremendous variation between individual countries.

Disaggregating the sample of countries by the level of economic development, we observe that the greater inefficiencies occur within the less-developed-country group (see Table 4.4). Actually, for the developed-country group as a whole, the difference between the return to higher and secondary education is virtually zero.

Remembering that the rates of return to investment in education are calculated on the basis of cross-sectional data, it may be better to interpret discrepancies of the type in equation (5.2) as dynamic disequilibrium situations at any given point in time. The fact that in a particular country the returns at the margin to primary education are higher than the returns to secondary education means that, at present, supply and demand conditions are such that the expansion of primary eduction is desirable.[1] It also means that the country could have enjoyed more income if, during the recent past, more resources had been devoted to primary education relative to secondary education. We do not mean to enter into a discussion here on how the present imbalance between the supply and demand of

---

[1] Assuming that the rate of return on primary education is higher than a criterion rate of return.

primary and secondary school graduates could have been foreseen in the recent past. Suffice it to mention that the higher the discrepancies of the type in equation (5.2), the higher the income possibilities foregone in a given country. And, according to our evidence, the educational level which is most off-balance relative to the other levels is primary education in less-developed countries.

The private demand for education

The rate of return may be considered not only as a summary statistic of costs and benefits associated with education but also, from an individual's point of view, as a decision variable for the amount of schooling to receive. Hanoch (1965) has developed a theoretical model of investment in schooling according to which the utility of an individual is maximized at a given amount of schooling.[2] Since additional amounts of schooling provide a transformation between present costs and future income, we can use the internal rate of return to define a schedule of the marginal efficiency of investment for various amounts of schooling. Similarly, one can obtain a marginal cost curve of financing each additional year of schooling. Following economic theory, the marginal productivity curve is expected to be downward sloping and the marginal cost curve upward sloping. Thus, a person would maximize his utility by investing in that amount of schooling (S^*) for which the internal rate of return is equal to the marginal cost of financing (Figure 5.1).

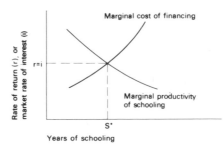

Figure 5.1. An optimum schooling investment decision.

---

[2] See Becker (1967) for the classic piece on the subject. In fact the maximand could be made more concrete in this case by talking about lifetime earnings.

Considering only one individual and a perfect capital market, i is unique. If the marginal cost and marginal productivity curves are well behaved, each individual will maximize his utility by investing at a point such as S^*. When considering a group of individuals and an imperfect capital market, however, we can observe a series of individual optima according to the market conditions facing each individual in the group (Figure 5.2).

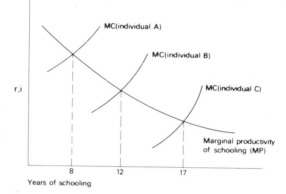

Figure 5.2. A demand schedule for schooling.

For example, individual A does not have good access to the capital market and his marginal cost curve lies above the cost curves of individuals B and C who, for some reason, have managed to obtain cheaper funds for their education. As a result, A will invest in eight years of schooling, while B and C will invest in twelve and seventeen years respectively. It is in this sense that schedule AB can be interpreted as a demand curve for schooling.[3]

To the extent that differences in the supply conditions are greater than differences on the demand side, a set of rates of return for a group of individuals will help us identify the marginal productivity curve for schooling, as a declining function of the amount of schooling received within a given country.

How does the evidence conform to this expected pattern? The answer is: not very well. Out of the thirteen countries for which we have full sets of *private* rates, in only five do the rates decline the

---

[3] This demand curve for schooling should not be confused with the conventional concept of a demand curve for education which is a *positive* function of the rate of return (see Blaug, 1966). Schedule AB in Figure 5.2 represents an *equilibrium* ex post demand curve for schooling.

higher the educational level. And out of a further eight countries where we have sets of rates for secondary and higher education, in only one case are the returns to secondary higher than those to university education (New Zealand).

The reason for this result, when we test the expected pattern of Figure 5.2, is that in the above analysis we have assumed that a single marginal productivity curve (MP) applies to all individuals. A more realistic case would be one in which the marginal productivity curve is systematically related to the marginal cost of financing. That is, individuals who can raise funds more easily for their education also experience a marginal productivity curve higher than those who do not have this ability. This case is illustrated in Figure 5.3.

A combination of these two cases, the first leading to a negatively sloped demand curve and the second to a positively sloped one, could lead to an explanation of the erratic within-country private rate of return pattern in our sample.

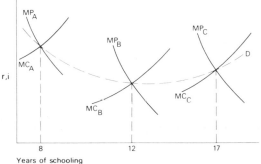

Figure 5.3. A demand schedule for schooling when the marginal productivity and cost of financing are positively correlated.

Investment in men or investment in machines?

It will be remembered that one of the main interests of the economics of education in the sixties was the comparison of the returns to physical and human capital.[4] This interest still holds today in view of its obvious policy implications for the priority direction of investment.

Practically every author of a rate of return calculation to educa-

---

[4] See Harberger (1965) from whom the title of this section is borrowed.

tion has attempted a comparison of his results with alternative rates to other forms of investment. The conclusions of these case-study comparisons fall into three categories. First, studies that have yielded extremely high profitability estimates for investment in education by any standard (e.g., Mexico, Venezuela). Second, studies that show returns of the order of magnitude of the yield on alternative investments (e.g., Canada, Kenya). And finally, studies with rates of return lower than those earned elsewhere (e.g., The Netherlands, Germany).

The authors of the first set of studies do not have much difficulty in sustaining the argument that investment in education is superior to other forms of investment. Even authors of the last type of studies have supported the superiority of investment in education, if by nothing else than bringing in the external and non-monetary effects of education.

Now that we have collected all the existing rate of return evidence in this volume, can we say something more intelligent about this kind of comparison?

There is some disagreement among economists as to what is the correct criterion rate for this type of comparison. Should one use the yield on equities or the returns to manufacturing capital? Should one use the rate of return in risky or relatively safe enterprises? The usual practice is to compare the private rate of return with the real borrowing rate in the economy, and the social rate of return to the before-tax yield on private corporate capital.

It should be remembered, however, that both measures are very imperfect. For example, since there is no collateral in the case of educational loans, a student might not be able to borrow money at all, even if he is willing to pay a very high rate of interest. The student himself is the carrier of the investment which forms an inseparable part of him and which cannot therefore be repossessed like a morgaged house. Markets for student loans have emerged very recently in only a few countries and it is likely to be a long time before it is possible to finance education as one would finance the purchase of a house.[5] Turning to the social rate of return, the before-tax returns to physical capital as normally calculated may be a very poor index of the marginal productivity of capital in the economy as a whole. The reason for this being that the relevant studies are usually based on data taken from the manufacturing sector only and thus are not representative of the economy as a

---

[5] See Woodhall (1971) on educational financing arrangements in a number of countries.

80

whole. The social alternative rate presents the additional complication of the trade-off between the social opportunity cost of capital and the social time-preference rate, since part of educational expenditure is diverted from investment funds and part from consumption funds. For example, in the profitability study for India, Blaug *et al.* (1969, p. 24—25) attached weights to the estimates of the social opportunity cost of capital and the social time-preference rate, each equal to 0.5.

Moreover, for the purist, a comparison of rates of return to investment in education with the yield on private corporate capital is not valid, since most of the returns on corporate capital represent a "book yield" which is derived by dividing the average net book income of the company by the average net book value of its assets. A rate of return to investment in education, on the other hand, represents a "true yield" in the sense that it is derived by using discounted cash flows. As Solomon and Laya (1966) have shown, the book yield seriously overestimates the true yield.

Finally, Pesek and Saving (1967), have argued that one would always expect the returns to human capital to be above the returns to physical capital because of the inferiority of the one kind of capital (non-separability of human capital) relative to the other.

But, despite the difficulties, let us now look at the returns on alternative investments in some countries. Table 5.1 presents estimates of the returns to thirteen countries of our sample. The reader should be as careful in interpreting this set of estimates on the returns to physical capital as he should be careful in interpreting the ones presented above for human capital. The following will give an idea of the diversity of sources, methodology and therefore limitations in comparability of the returns to physical capital. The rates for Canada and Japan are from the work of Minhas (1963) and were estimated on the basis of the following formula applied to manufacturing industries:

$$\frac{\text{net operating profits before tax}}{\text{value of capital stock in use}}$$

One the other hand, Maddison's (1963) rates for The Netherlands and Belgium are the average returns on equities in the 1955—61 period. Denison (1967) computed the returns to physical capital in Great Britain and Germany according to the following formula:

$$\frac{\text{earnings of non-residential structures and equipment}}{\text{net capital stock}}$$

81

The figure on the returns to physical capital in Kenya is the average of the returns to seven World Bank projects in this country plus returns to capital in 31 major companies in 1966—7.

TABLE 5.1

RATES OF RETURN TO INVESTMENT IN PHYSICAL CAPITAL IN CERTAIN COUNTRIES (per cent)

Country	Year	Rate of return
United States	1959	9.7
Canada	1957	12.9
Mexico	1962	14.0
Venezuela	1958	16.7
Chile	1940–61	15.0
Great Britain	1955–59	8.6
Netherlands	1955–61	16.8
Belgium	1955–61	4.4
Germany	1955–59	10.4
India	1960	12.5
Japan	1957	20.4
Ghana	1962	8.0
Kenya	1966–67	18.8

Sources: United States: Jorgenson and Griliches (1967), p. 268; Canada and Japan: Minhas (1963), p. 87; Mexico and Venezuela: Carnoy (1967b), p. 369; Chile: Harberger and Selowsky (1966), p. 22; Great Britain and Germany: Denison (1967), p. 142; The Netherlands and Belgium: Maddison (1963); India: Blaug et al. (1969), p. 25; Ghana: Killich (1966); Kenya: Thias and Carnoy (1969), p. 123.
Note: rates of return are before tax except in the case of the United States, where the rate is after profit taxes, and probably also in the case of Mexico.

There are two questions we could ask in relation to the comparison of profitability rates between physical and human capital. First, are individual educational investments advantageous from the private point of view? Second, do societies allocate the correct amount of resources to the educational sector?

In order to answer the first question we need a set of private rates of return to alternative investments. If the private rate of return to a given level of education is higher than the private rate of return to alternative investments we can say that individuals investing in the former have made a good choice. The profitability estimates to alternative forms of capital in Table 5.1 are social and not private. But we can bias ourselves against investment in human capital and

82

compare social alternative rates with private educational rates from Table 4.1.[6] Out of the twelve countries for which this comparison was possible, we found that in only four the returns to physical capital were higher than the private returns to human capital. This was the case for secondary education in Great Britain, higher education in Germany and both secondary and higher education in The Netherlands and Japan. In all other cases, the private return to any educational level for which such a comparison was possible was higher than the returns to alternative forms of investment.

Turning to the second question we observe that one cannot easily claim the superiority of educational investment over investment in machines from the social point of view. Out of the twelve countries examined, seven show higher returns to physical capital for at least one level of education. This is the case for secondary education in Canada, higher education in Chile, India and Kenya and both secondary and higher education in Great Britain, The Netherlands and Japan. However, *in no case* was the return to primary education lower than the return to alternative forms of investment.

In the above we have compared rates of return to physical capital with rates of return to particular educational levels. It would be of interest, however, to compare the return to physical capital with the returns to investment in education as a whole, so enabling us to assess a country's performance in allocating funds between education and other sectors of the economy.

For this purpose we need to construct a single rate of return estimate to investment in education in each country. The overall (or total) social rate of return (r_H) is estimated as a weighted average of the rates of return at each educational level.[7] The weights used were the total costs of education at each level in a given year. The following formula was applied:

$$r_H = \frac{\sum\limits_{i} r_i \, C_i}{\sum\limits_{i} C_i}$$

---

[6] The private yield on physical capital must be a few percentage points below the figures presented in Table 5.1. Moreover, the private-social relationship of rates of return to physical capital must be less erratic than the one presented above for educational capital.

[7] The adjectives "total", "average", or "overall" have been used in the literature to describe the type of rate computed in this section. In order to avoid confusion with a properly computed average rate of return to a number of schooling years, we will call it an "overall" rate. See also Chapter 2.

where r_i is the rate of return to investment in educational level i; C_i is the total annual costs of education at level i, and i runs over; p = primary s = secondary h = higher.

The cost weights were obtained by multiplying the number of students enrolled at each given level by the annual direct cost of that level of education plus the foregone earnings. Namely, the weights C_i were derived according to the following formula:

$$C_i = E_i \, (C'_i + W_{i-1}), \quad i = p, s, h$$

where E_i is student enrolment at educational level i; C'_i is the direct annual cost of schooling at level i, and W_{i-1} is the earnings of graduates from the previous schooling level.

The detailed data and calculation procedure for determining the overall rates of return are given in Appendix D.

Table 5.2 presents the overall social rates of return in the countries of our sample. Ideally, we should have confined this calculation only to countries for which we had data for a full set of rates of return for *all* three educational levels. As already mentioned, our sample is deficient in evidence on the return to primary schooling in most developed countries. Therefore, the rates of return presented in Table 5.2 should be regarded as lower bounds of the true social returns, since we have already established that the returns to primary are higher than those to any other level and therefore the omission of them under-estimates the overall social rate of return. Bearing in mind this qualification and comparing Tables 5.1 and 5.2 we see that, in just over half of the thirteen countries examined, the social returns to investment in education are higher than the returns to physical capital. But if we break the sample into six developed and seven developing countries, the following interesting pattern emerges in Table 5.3 regarding the returns to the two forms of capital.[8]

The first information Table 5.3 gives is that the returns to both forms of capital are higher in developing countries. This was expected in view of the differences in relative scarcities of capital in either form in developed and developing countries. The second observation is that human capital is a superior investment in developing countries but not in developed countries, as indicated by the reversal of the inequality signs in Table 5.3. This may be ex-

---

[8] "Developed" countries are in this case the United States, Canada, Great Britain, Germany, The Netherlands and Belgium. "Developing" countries are Mexico, Venezuela, Chile, India, Japan, Ghana and Kenya.

84

TABLE 5.2

OVERALL SOCIAL RATE OF RETURN AND PER CAPITA INCOME BY COUNTRY

Country	Rate of return	Per capita income ($ US)
United States	13.6	2,361
Canada	12.4	1,774
Puerto Rico	19.6	761
Mexico	21.9	374
Venezuela	42.0	776
Colombia	25.9	320
Chile	19.3	365
Brazil	13.7	261
Great Britain	4.6	1,660
Norway	7.2	1,831
Sweden	10.3	2,500
Denmark	7.8	1,651
Netherlands	5.3	1,490
Belgium	9.3	1,777
Germany	4.6	1,420
Greece	3.9	478
Israel	9.6	704
India	17.2	73
Malaysia	10.6	280
The Philippines	12.7	250
Japan	5.1	464
South Korea	9.4	146
Thailand	25.2	150
Hawaii	12.5	2,495
Nigeria	18.5	75
Ghana	15.1	233
Kenya	18.9	111
Uganda	39.0	84
N. Rhodesia	12.4	144
New Zealand	17.6	1,931

Source: Appendix D and United Nations, *Yearbook of National Accounts Statistics.* (1968).
Note: Rates for Denmark, Belgium and Germany refer to higher education only.
Rate for N. Rhodesia refers to primary level only. Rate for Germany is private.

plained by the differential rates and levels of expansion of educational systems in the two groups of countries, a point which will be investigated further in this book. Suffice it to say here that the level of development of a country can give an indication of the desired allocation of investment between human and physical capital.

TABLE 5.3

THE RETURNS TO ALTERNATIVE FORMS OF CAPITAL BY LEVEL OF
ECONOMIC DEVELOPMENT

Level of development	Physical capital		Human capital
Per capita income under $1,000 (7 countries)	15.1	<	19.9
Per capita income over $1,000 (6 countries)	10.5	>	8.3

Source: Tables 5.1 and 5.2.

In this chapter we began by presenting the conditions of equilibrium in the investment market and, more particularly, within the educational sector. The large variation in rates of return, particularly in the less-developed countries, was seen to indicate large inefficiencies in the past allocation of resources and relative under-investment in primary education. This discussion led on to the examination of a theoretical model which postulated falling private rates of return to higher educational levels. Finally, the relative profitability of investment in human and physical capital was analyzed for countries where data existed on the returns to physical capital. To aid this comparison, cost-weighted "overall" social rates of return were calculated. The general conclusions were first, that the returns to both physical and human capital are higher in developing countries than in developed countries; and second that, whereas in developing countries returns are greatest to human capital, in the developed countries the greatest returns are to physical capital investment.

Chapter 6. Human Versus Physical Capital
Accumulation in Economic Development

In the preceding chapter the analysis gave an indication that there is a relationship between the rates of return to investment in education and the level of economic development. In the following two chapters we will look first at the relationship between the levels of per capita income, educational development and the returns to education, and then at the contribution of education to the rate of growth of income.

In the first section of this chapter, we present a simple theoretical model of the expected relationship between the rate of return to investment in education, per capita income and human capital accumulation. Then we turn to our data to see how they conform to the theory. Next, we construct a new index of educational development based on costs. This is compared with an index of physical capital per member of the labour force and the two indices are brought together in an effort to explain differential levels of development by means of differential capital endowments. Then an aggregate cross-sectional production function is fitted to the data in two alternative specifications. First, by including human capital in value terms (i.e., using the cost-based educational development index); and second, by disaggregating labour into three distinct categories and including them in the production function in physical terms. The last section of this chapter deals with a generalized human-physical capital accumulation model which, unfortunately, we were unable to test with the existing data.

Rates of return and the level of economic development

Let us first examine the expected relationship between the returns to education presented above in Chapter 4 and the level of economic development of a country. For this purpose we will present a theory of the expected rate of return—economic development pattern and then see to what extent our data fit into this pattern. For the sake of exposition let us make the heroic assumption that a cross-country aggregate production function of the following general form exists:

$$Y = f(K_H, L, Z) \tag{6.1}$$

where Y is an index of output, L is an index of labour, K_H is an index of human capital, and Z is a vector of indices representing all inputs entering the production function except human capital and labour. In order to have a total labour productivity measure on the left-hand side, we further assume linear homogeneity and write (6.1) as

$$\frac{Y}{L} = f\left(\frac{K_H}{L}, Z'\right) \tag{6.2}$$

where $\frac{Y}{L}$ is output per member of the labour force, $\frac{K_H}{L}$ is human capital per member of the labour force, and Z' is the corresponding transformation of Z.

In this case the marginal product of human capital (MP_H) is defined as the first derivative of (6.2) with respect to $\frac{K_H}{L}$, i.e.

$$MP_H = \frac{\partial \left(\frac{Y}{L}\right)}{\partial \left(\frac{K_H}{L}\right)}$$

It is natural to expect that the marginal product of human capital will be a diminishing function of the stock of human capital per member of the labour force. The reason for this negative relationship must be traced back to our original production function (6.1) and the assumption that all other factors (Z) affecting output will remain constant. As the human capital-labour ratio increases, output per person employed increases at a decreasing rate, causing the marginal product of human capital to fall.

How can we bring this elementary analysis into our international comparison of the returns to education? For this purpose we must first re-define our variables and name them after their more popular proxies. For example, we can loosely talk about per capita income instead of output per person employed. Admittedly, differences in labour-force participation rates between countries undermine a perfect relationship between output per person employed and per

88

capita income.[1] Next, we can use the rate of return to investment in education (r_H) instead of the marginal product of human capital (MP_H). This is again a very crude approximation since the rate of return refers to the marginal efficiency of investment which is different from the marginal product of capital.[2] The third of our variables, the human capital—labour ratio, presents the greatest measurement problems. Ideally, one should use a cost-based measure, such as total outlays invested in improving the quality of the labour force, and the construction of an index of this kind will be the subject of a later section in this chapter. In the meantime, one could think in terms of the average number of years of schooling of the labour force or a more sophisticated (and severely criticized) index like the one developed by Harbison and Myers (1964) as proxy measures.

In view of these proxies, what relationships should one expect between the rate of return to investment in education, the per capita income and the level of educational development? In Figure 6.1,

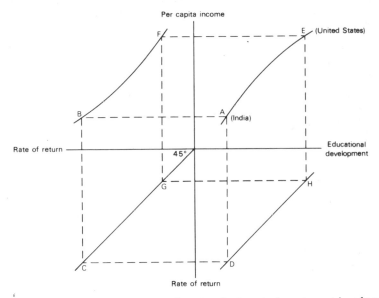

Figure 6.1. The relationship between the rate of return to investment in education, per capita income and level of educational development.

---

[1] For a comparison of the labour-force participation rates in the countries of the sample see Table H.1.

[2] On this matter see Ramsey (1970).

quadrants 1, 2 and 4 present the partial relationships we discussed above. Quadrant 3 is an auxiliary one for connecting the graphs. What Figure 6.1 says is that poor countries like India, with low levels of per capita income and a low index of educational development have a high rate of return to investment in education (ABCD pattern in Figure 6.1). Rich countries like the United States, with high per capita income and a high index of educational development, have a low rate of return to investment in education (EFGH pattern in Figure 6.1).

This analysis has been based on the assumption that all other factors (what we earlier called Z) remain constant. To the extent that various countries differ in Z, one would expect the production function to shift and possibly lead to the rejection of the theory on the basis of empirical observation. To illustrate this point, let us consider one important element of the vector of factors Z which has been assumed to remain constant, namely physical capital. For this we turn to Figure 6.2.

This shows that, because of a higher stock of physical capital in the United States relative to that in India, the true production

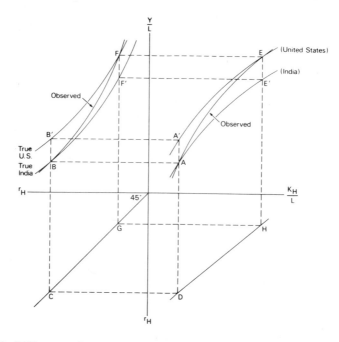

Figure 6.2. Differences between the observed and true rate of return per capita income relationship because of the *ceteris paribus* assumption.

90

functions are EA′ and E′A, respectively. In other words, human capital is more productive in the United States because it cooperates with more of the "other" factors of production. Standardization for differences in Z leads to different true relationships between the rate of return and per capita income in quadrant 2.[3] As can be seen in Figure 6.2 the observed relationship rotates and becomes steeper relative to its true position. To put it another way, failure to standardize for differences in factors other than educational capital tends to make the rate of return more insensitive to changes in per capita income. Or, a narrower range of rates of return could be observed to be consistent with a wider range of per capita incomes. This sensitivity point should be borne in mind when examining the following empirical relationship between the level of development and the returns to educational investment.

Let us now turn and see how our data fit the above theory. In Table 6.1 we have split the 32 countries in our sample into groups of five and classified them in increasing order of average per capita income within each group. The ranking of the average rate of return

TABLE 6.1

AVERAGE RATES OF RETURN BY EDUCATIONAL LEVEL AND PER CAPITA INCOME

Per capita income level ($ US)	Social			Private		
	Primary	Secondary	Higher	Primary	Secondary	Higher
(1)	(2)	(3)	(4)	(5)	(6)	(7)
100	28.7 (5)	19.4 (4)	12.6 (4)	29.1 (3)	21.1 (3)	25.2 (3)
200	15.6 (5)	14.6 (5)	11.6 (5)	24.8 (4)	20.2 (4)	25.4 (4)
350	24.6 (4)	17.5 (4)	13.5 (4)	32.0 (1)	27.5 (2)	22.2 (2)
650	38.5 (3)	10.7 (5)	12.0 (5)	27.0 (1)	11.9 (5)	17.2 (5)
1,600	..	6.8 (3)	9.0 (5)	..	10.3 (3)	12.3 (6)
2,200	21.0 (2)	11.1 (5)	9.8 (5)	155.1 (1)	13.0 (4)	11.5 (5)

Source: based on Tables 4.1 and 5.2.
Note: numbers in parentheses refer to the number of observations. For explanation of symbol notations see Appendix I.

---

[3] It has been assumed for geometric simplicity that the production function shifted in a "parallel" way and therefore does not affect the DH relationship in quadrant 4.

within each group follows, more or less, the above theoretical expectation. For example, the social rate of return to secondary education in the $100 per capita income countries is 19.4 per cent while the corresponding figure for the $2,200 per capita income countries is 11.1 per cent. However, there is tremendous variation within each column, particularly at the intermediate per capita income levels.

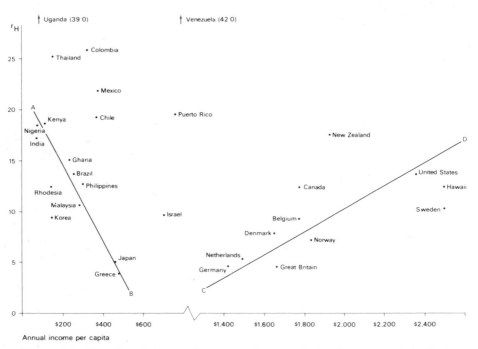

Figure 6.3. Overall social rate of return to investment in education and the level of economic development.

In Figure 6.3 we have plotted the overall social rate of return to investment in education (r_H) against per capita income; in other words we have attempted to see how the theoretical relationship in quadrant 2 of Figure 6.1 looks in practice.[4] A first glance at Figure 6.3 indicates that there is an overall inverse relationship between the level of per capita income and the rate of return to investment in education. This negative relationship is very weak and

---

[4] For the computation of this rate, see Chapter 5, above.

was found not to be statistically significant.[5] However, it will be immediately apparent that there is a discontinuity in the range of per capita incomes in the countries of our sample. This discontinuity occurs between Venezuela (per capita income $ US 776) and Germany (per capita income $ US 1,420). Drawing a dividing line at this point of discontinuity, we have nineteen countries below the $1,000 income mark and eleven countries above it. The average overall social rates of return for the two groups of countries are shown in Table 6.2.

TABLE 6.2

OVERALL SOCIAL RATE OF RETURN BY LEVEL OF DEVELOPMENT

Country group	Overall social rate of return to investment in education (per cent)
Per capita income below $1,000 (19 countries)	17.9 (15.2)
Per capita income above $1,000 (11 countries)	9.6

Source: Tables 4.1 and 5.2.
Note: rate of return in parenthesis excludes Uganda and Venezuela.

Therefore, although we have failed to find a statistically significant relationship between the rate of return and per capita income, we can say that when the returns are divided into only two income groups they are generally higher in the less-developed countries than in the developed ones.

A more careful look at Figure 6.3, however, shows that within each of the two income groups distinguished the rates of return behave differently. First, for countries with per capita income below $ US 1,000, a rather distinct negative relationship between per capita

---

[5] Moreover, a simple linear model was fitted to the above data attempting to explain the rates of return by alternative indices of educational and economic development. The test consisted of pooling together all rate of return observations and adding dummy variables for the educational level the individual rates referred to. The explanatory variables were the percentage of agriculture in the GDP, the Harbison and Myers index of educational development and the percentage of professional and technical workers in the labour force. The result of the test was that the educational level dummy was significant in all cases, simply confirming the χ^2 test presented in Chapter 4. On the other hand, although all development indices had the expected sign none was statistically significant. No index performed better than per capita income. For the detailed results of this test see Appendix G.

income and rate of return can be observed. This is particularly true for eleven countries in this income group through which the free-hand line (AB) has been drawn. Second, for countries with per capita income above $ US 1,000 we observe a *positive* relationship between per capita income and the rate of return as suggested by the free-hand line CD in Figure 6.3. If time-series behaviour in one country can be equated with the cross-sectional behaviour shown above, then we can say this graph suggests that the rates of return decrease as the level of per capita income increases, until some particular stage of economic development is reached and from that point the profitability of education increases alongside increases in per capita income. The particular stage of development seems to be somewhere between $ US 800 and 1,400 per capita income, a region which we were unable to investigate further because none of the countries in the sample belonged to this income group.

The first half of this pattern, namely the declining returns to education by increasing level of economic development, is consistent with our theoretical expectations, namely diminishing marginal returns to investment in human capital. Our immediate speculation for explaining the second part of the pattern is that human capital is a complement to the high level of technology employed in advanced countries.[6]

Another interesting point can be made in this respect by comparing the international cross-sectional rate of return pattern with the corresponding time series pattern in the United States. Rates of return are available in the United States for the three years previous to the Censuses of 1940, 1950 and 1960. The private returns to higher education in these years were 12.5, 10 and 13.6 per cent respectively. The social returns were 9 in 1940 and 1950 and 9.7 per cent in 1960.[7] The contrast we observe is that while in the cross-country comparison there is a definite declining pattern, this was not the case in the United States. The explanation of this phenomenon must lie in the fact that, in the 30-year span represented by these rates, the United States has not experienced the development range represen-

---

[6] For a discussion on the matter see Welch (1970). To put it in Welch's terms, the failure of the rate of return to higher education to decline is due to "changes" that have taken place and which "have resulted in growth in demand for the investment good, education, sufficient to absorb the increased supply with constant or rising returns", p. 36. For a test of the complementary hypothesis between physical and human capital, see Chapter 9.

[7] The rates of return for 1939 and 1949 are from Becker (1964) and the returns for 1959 from Hines *et al.* (1970).

ted by the countries in the international cross-section. Alternatively, one could suggest that once a country is developed the interaction of increased demand and supply of graduates in such that a kind of "liquidity trap" develops and the returns to education do not drop below a given value. Of course this is a tentative hypothesis awaiting further time series evidence within a given country for testing.

Rates of return and relative enrolments

Another way to look at the rates of return is to relate them to enrolments at different educational levels; the argument here being that there might be a closer link between the level of educational development, as represented by enrolments, and rates of return to investment in education, than between rates of return and the general level of economic development, as analyzed in the previous section.

The underlying expectation is that the faster enrolments grow at one educational level relative to another the lower the rate of return will be to investment at the higher level. Of course, this raises serious questions about the dynamics of adjustment of the school system and the labour market for graduates of different types, as well as econometric identification problems, i.e. which causes what. Moreover, the relative *stocks* of people in the labour force with different educational qualifications might be a better variable than school enrolments. We will analyze the relative quantities of educated labour in Chapter 9, below, but at this point we will concentrate on relative enrolments at different levels and relate these to the corresponding rates of return.

Relative enrolments are used since the rate of return itself is a relative concept referring to the relative wages of graduates of a given educational level and the wages of graduates of the preceding level. For example, assuming that investment in higher education takes form in one year, that the direct costs are borne by the state and that the benefits last for ever, the private rate of return to higher education (r_h) could be expressed as

$$r_h = \frac{W_h - W_s}{W_s} = \frac{W_h}{W_s} - 1$$

where W_h and W_s are the average earnings of college and high school graduates, respectively.

Table H.3 in the appendix presents absolute and relative enrolment data for the countries of the sample, and these are related to the social and private rates of return in Table 6.3. Relative enrolments for the secondary to primary level range from a low 0.02 in the case of Northern Rhodesia to a high of 0.98 in the case of Sweden. The higher to secondary ratio varies over a narrower range, from 0.02 in the case of Uganda to 0.43 in the case of The Phillippines. Once again, in interpreting these figures the reader should have in mind the different definitions, lengths of study in terms of years and institutional arrangements in each country. Considering the relationship between the returns to higher education and the higher to secondary enrolment ratio, we see that the declining pattern is more or less repeated in Table 6.3. That is, in countries where the ratio of students enrolled in higher relative to those enrolled in secondary education is below 10 per cent, the average social rate of return to higher education is 11.6 per cent. The higher relative enrolment group of countries (10—20 per cent) experience a similar rate of return to higher education (11.7 per cent). But countries where relative enrolments exceed 20 per cent clearly have a lower social rate of return to higher education (9.2 per cent). The declining rate of return pattern with higher to secondary enrolment ratios is most pronounced in the last column of Table 6.3 referring to the private

TABLE 6.3

RATES OF RETURN AND RELATIVE ENROLMENTS BY EDUCATIONAL LEVEL

Enrolment in higher relative to secondary level	Social		Private	
	Average rate of return to higher education over secondary			
up to 0.10	11.6	(8)	22.5	(7)
0.10 – 0.20	11.7	(16)	16.4	(14)
over 0.20	9.2	(4)	12.8	(4)
Enrolment in secondary relative to primary level	Average rate of return to secondary education over primary			
up to 0.20	16.6	(11)	19.2	(9)
0.20 – 0.40	14.8	(9)	19.4	(7)
over 0.40	5.7	(6)	6.6	(5)

Source: Table 4.1 and Appendix Table H.3.
Note: the numbers in parenthesis are the number of observations.

rates. Turning to the second part of Table 6.3 we see that the same declining pattern holds for both types of rate of return when the ratio of secondary to primary school enrolments is split into three groups, below 20 per cent, between 20 and 40 per cent and over 40 per cent. By way of summary, disaggregating our sample of countries into three groups, we find that there is a clear negative relationship between rates of return to both secondary and higher education and enrolment ratios.

A cost-based measure of educational development

After analyzing the relationships between rates of return, the level of per capita income and relative enrolments, we now turn to the construction of a cost-based measure of educational development. It should be made clear that what we are concerned with here is a measure of the educational level, or stock, of the labour force rather than with the structure and present development of the educational system.

A measure of the human capital stock can be obtained in three ways: first, by the number of years of schooling, second by discounting future earnings, and third by cumulating the schooling costs of persons with different educational qualifications in the labour force. The first measure, although handy from the point of view of data excludes any cost-weighting considerations; one year of schooling at the primary level is clearly not the same as one year of schooling in higher education. The second measure's deficiencies refer to the thorny choice of a discount rate to be used and moreover to the questionable reliability of earnings data. Since cost data are a little better than earnings data we have decided to use a cost-based human capital measure.

In fact there exist two indices of educational development readily at hand; first the Harbison—Myers index and secondly the proportion of professional, technical and related workers in the labour force.[8] Both these indices are inadequate as measures of the educational content of the labour force. The former has been extensively criticized chiefly for the arbitrary weights attached to enrolments in different schooling levels, and in any case it refers to flows rather than stocks, while the latter measure is greatly hindered by vagaries

---

[8] See Harbison and Myers (1964) and Appendix E.

of job classification and performance when measured across countries.[9]

In contrast, we decided to construct our own measure and this is defined as the stock of educational capital per member of the labour force. The great advantage of constructing a capital or cost-based measure is that the weighting of graduates from different educational levels is no longer arbitrary but is based on the actual amount of resources used. The stock of educational capital per member of the labour force was constructed through the following steps:

(a) Obtain an educational profile of the labour force around 1960, by years or level of schooling.

(b) Obtain the total social cost per year of schooling for each educational level.

(c) Calculate the cumulated stock of human capital by totalling the educational inputs devoted to each member of the labour force.

(d) Divide this total stock (K_H) by the labour force (L) so deriving an estimate of educational capital per member of the labour force ($\frac{K_H}{L}$).

The basic sources of data were the OECD's (1969) *Statistics of the Occupational and Educational Structure of the Labour Force in 53 Countries* for the educational distribution profiles and the rate of return studies themselves for the cost data. Unfortunately it was not possible to use all the countries from our rate of return sample since the types of information necessary for the calculations needed to be rather detailed. In particular it was impossible to incorporate countries of continental Europe largely because of a lack of detail below pre-senior secondary level in the educational breakdown of the labour force. Also countries such as Japan, for which we have rates of return, had to be excluded for lack of cost data. Despite these restrictions it was possible to calculate estimates of educational capital per member of the labour force for fourteen countries covering a wide spectrum of development. (For the sources of data and details of calculation, see Appendix E.)

The chief merit of this measure of educational capital is that it incorporates in real terms all the resource inputs which have been used in the creation of this stock, and thus reflects real magnitudes far better than an index based solely on years of schooling. It is apparent, however, that the measure does have certain drawbacks.

---

[9] For an incisive critique of the Harbison and Myers index, see Blaug (1970), pp. 68–70.

The chief practical reservation is that, by using constant prices, we are assuming that the costs of each year of education have remained the same through time, whereas it is probable that over the years the real cost of educational output has increased. But this, however, takes us into the controversial and unresolved areas of questions of the changing quality of education and the true measurement of productivity, and here we are assuming that inputs per unit of output have remained constant.

The theoretical objection to using the stock of educational capital per member of the labour force as a measure of the variations in educational development between countries is perhaps more important. In all branches of the economics of education the real cost of education is measured, correctly, by the direct costs and foregone earnings, and likewise these are the costs used in this analysis. However, if these stock measures are to be used to "explain" variations in per capita incomes, or to rank countries according to the level of educational development, there is a degree of circularity. Foregone earnings in a rich country will be large and so, consequently, will be the stock of educational capital, while in poor countries this component will be small and hence the stock term will also be small. This will also be the case to some extent for direct costs since a large part of these is teachers' salaries which again reflect income levels.

The educational capital stock measure is presented in column (4) of Table 6.4. A glance at the estimates of educational capital per member of the labour force in this table shows that the variations are very wide, the ratio between India and the United States being 1 : 186. By comparing columns (2) and (4), we see that these variations are far wider than differences in levels of per capita income, so to some extent reducing the criticism of circularity. To show further that we are aware of the income problem, Appendix E is concerned with the construction of indices which attempt to mitigate the criticism. Unfortunately this can only be done by constructing index numbers and we are concerned here with absolute values.

Physical capital per member of the labour force

In a human—non-human capital discussion we need to have a measure of the physical capital stock. The corresponding index to that presented in the previous section is a measure of the amount of

TABLE 6.4

PER CAPITA INCOME, PHYSICAL AND EDUCATIONAL CAPITAL PER
MEMBER OF THE LABOUR FORCE IN CERTAIN COUNTRIES (IN U.S. $)

Country	Per capita income $\dfrac{Y}{P}$	Physical capital $\dfrac{K_M}{L}$	Educational capital $\dfrac{K_H}{L}$	Educational capital as a percentage of physical capital
(1)	(2)	(3)	(4)	(5)
United States	2,361	28,045	12,296	44
New Zealand	1,931	17,270	5,745	33
Great Britain	1,660	12,320	3,630	29
Average	1,984	19,212	7,224	38
Israel	704	13,922	2,210	16
Greece	478	4,003	423	11
Mexico	374	4,040	410	10
Chile	365	4,423	877	20
The Philippines	250	3,446	290	,8
Ghana	233	1,236	181	15
S. Korea	146	1,008	403	40
Kenya	111	920	157	17
Average	333	4,125	619	15
Nigeria	75	697	88	13
Uganda	84	539	88	16
India	73	1,197	66	6
Average	77	811	81	10
Overall average	632	6,648	1,919	.
Coefficient of variation	1.21	1.24	1.78	.

Sources: Col. (2) from Table 5.2; col. (3) and (4) from Appendix E; col. (5) =
(Col. (4) : Col. (3) × 100.0).

physical capital per member of the labour force. This index was
constructed in the following steps. First, estimate an incremental
capital—output ratio in a given country and then multiply it by gross
national product. The value of the incremental capital—output ratio
(ICOR) was estimated according to the following formula:

$$ICOR = \frac{\frac{1}{2}(INV_{61} + INV_{62}) + INV_{63} + INV_{64} + \frac{1}{2}(INV_{65} + INV_{66})}{\frac{1}{3}(GNP_{65} + GNP_{66} + GNP_{67} - GNP_{61} - GNP_{62} - GNP_{63})}$$

Verbally, the value of *ICOR* was found for each country by dividing the average level of gross investment over a six-year period by the average annual increase in gross national product.[10] The capital stock was measured by multiplying the *ICOR* by the level of GNP in 1963.

There was in fact a problem in choosing the year to measure GNP and hence the physical capital stock. Since the whole point of the exercise was to compare levels of physical capital with educational capital, the alternatives were: (a) the year corresponding to the educational breakdown of each labour force, or (b) the year to which the unit costs of education refer. Since (a) and (b) are often unequal within countries there is no correct single answer and it was decided therefore to use a "mid-point" year, 1963. The value of the capital stock was then divided by the labour force to derive estimates of physical capital per member of the labour force. These estimates are presented in column (3) of Table 6.4.

Differential factor endowments and the level of economic development

Selowsky (1967) has computed similar measures to the ones presented in Table 6.4, for the United States, Chile, Mexico and India, and compared them with levels of per capita income. He found that the biggest differences in factor—endowment ratios between countries are in the amounts of educational capital per worker and concluded that "the differences in educational capital per member of the labour force explain a big part of per capita income differentials".

Table 6.4 shows that physical capital per worker varies as much as per capita income between the countries of the sample (coefficients of variation 1.24 and 1.21, respectively). However, educational capital varies more (coefficient of variation 1.78) between countries than either per capita income or physical capital. The two extreme countries in the sample are India and the United States, the latter having 32 times the per capita income of the former. In terms of stocks of different kinds of capital the difference is more dramatic. Although the United States has 23 times the amount of physical

---

[10] In this calculation we have followed Robinson (1969).

capital per member of the labour force than India, the corresponding figure for human capital is 186. Moreover, educational capital in the United States is 44 per cent of physical capital, whereas in India the corresponding percentage is 6 per cent.

It is useful to draw an analogy between the cross-sectional stages of development represented by the countries in Table 6.4 and similar time-series evidence in the United States. T. W. Schultz (1971, p. 129) has found that between 1900 and 1957 physical capital in the United States increased four and a half times, whereas the stock of educational capital in the labour force increased eight and a half times.[11] Moreover, he found that the position of the United States in 1900 regarding the educational capital stock as a percentage of physical capital within the country was 22 per cent. It is interesting to note that about two thirds of the countries in our sample had not yet reached this mark by the 1960s.

In another study along these lines, Krueger (1968) attempted to explain per capita income differences between the United States and a number of less-developed countries. Based on an aggregate constant returns to scale production function, she derived inequality statements regarding the part of income differences attributable to three human factors: differences in the number of years of schooling, age distribution and urban-rural distribution of the population. For example, in the case of Mexico, she states that "even if Mexico had had the United States endowment per head of land, capital and other resources, Mexican per capita income would have been less than 45.6 per cent that of the United States". In other words, "Mexico could not hope to increase her per capita income above 45.6 per cent of the United States unless her stock of human resources were improved. Further, even if data were available on capital, land, etc., smaller Mexican endowments of these factors would turn out to be far less important than the human capital stock differential." Krueger concluded that "differences in human resources between the United States and the less-developed countries account for more of the difference in per capita income than all other factors combined".

The type of data which we have collected in this study allows us actually to fit an aggregate production function of the type implicit

---

[11] It should be noted that Professor Schultz's figures refer to the total stock of capital of each kind and not to the stock of capital per member of the labour force as our figures in Table 6.4.

in Krueger's and others' work.[12] In fact we can attempt two specifications of such an aggregate production function. First, one in which we distinguish physical and human capital; and second, one in which we distinguish several kinds of educated labour.

Meta-production functions with non-homogeneous capital and labour inputs

The first kind of function we have attempted to fit is

$$Y = f(K_H, K_M, L) \tag{6.3}$$

where Y is gross domestic product; K_H is the stock of human capital embodied in the labour force; K_M is the stock of physical capital, and L is the size of the labour force.

The problems of such an aggregate production function are too well known to be repeated here (see Nelson, 1968). The basic issue centres around the assumption of lumping into a common production function countries differing in their micro-production functions because of differences in technological standards. Morever, a relationship of the type (6.3), above, might not be a real "production function" in the textbook sense. The reason being that a production function implies a maximizing behaviour and, of course, there is no guarantee that the observations generated by the collection of country cases represent an efficient production frontier. Therefore, purists might prefer to call fitted empirical relationships of the type (6.3), above, simply "regressions" instead of production functions.

In spite of these difficulties Hayami and Ruttan (1970a, b) have defended the use of such functions by specifying that they may relate to the secular period, that is, beyond the long run. In this case criticisms based on the non-availability of the fund of technical knowledge disappear altogether and "production relationships can be described by a meta-production function which describes all potentially discoverable technical alternatives".

The functional form used was a Cobb—Douglas one, since more complicated functions of the CES type do not necessarily yield better results than the traditional form (see Layard *et al.* 1971,

---

[12] It should be noted that a time-series aggregate production function is also implicit in Denison's (1967) work, although this production function is never fitted directly because of problems of data availability. On this matter see also Blaug (1970), pp. 89- 100.

103

chapter 11). Moreover, the function was fitted by means of two-stage least squares in order to purge the K_M variable of its correlation with the equation error term.[13] Utilizing capital stock and labour-force data from Appendix E the regression gave the following result[14] in log linear form:

$$\log Y = 2.085 + 0.472* \log K_H + 0.263 \log K_M + 0.193* \log L \quad (6.4)$$
$$(0.281) \qquad\qquad (0.311) \qquad\qquad (0.126)$$

with an R^2 of 0.961. The coefficients of human capital and raw labour are statistically significant at the 90 per cent probability level, whereas the coefficient of the physical capital variable is not significant.

Looking first at the sum of the elasticities of output with respect to the three inputs we see that they come to 0.928. Therefore, we can conclude that the constant—returns-to-scale assumption used earlier in this chapter is not completely implausible. More interesting, however, is that the crude labour share (19 per cent) is far below the actual share of labour derived from actual wages data in the sample (70 per cent).[15] This would be expected in view of the fact that wages include the return not only to crude labour but also to the human capital component embodied in the person employed. But the highlights of the above estimate are the different sizes and degrees of statistical significance of the coefficients referring to the two forms of capital. The elasticity of output with respect to the human capital input is 0.472 and statistically significant, while that to the physical capital input is 0.263 and moreover is statistically insignificant. What equation (6.4) says, in words, is that differential income levels are better explained by means of differences in human capital endowments than by more traditional inputs such as physical capital and the number of persons employed.

The marginal product of human capital derived from this equation is equal to 34.0 per cent while the corresponding figure for physical

---

[13] In effect what we have here is a system of two equations with two endogenous variables (Y and K_M). Therefore, we first construct an instrument of K_M as a function of the exogenous variables and then use the estimated value of K_M in the final equation. On two-stage least squares, see Goldberger (1964), Chapter 7.

[14] Countries providing observations for this test were the United States, New Zealand, Great Britain, Israel, Greece, Mexico, Chile, The Philippines, Ghana, South Korea, Kenya, Nigeria and Uganda.

[15] See Table 7.4, below.

capital is 8.0 per cent. On the other hand, crude labour shows an average annual shadow wage of $870. These shadow estimates are not far from the average actual values found in the sample.

In the above analysis we related output mainly to inputs in value terms, namely physical capital and human capital. We now attempt another formulation of the cross-country production function in which income is expressed as a function of physical capital and three distinct labour inputs. The production function is of the type

$$Y = f(L_{op}, L_s, L_h, K_M) \tag{6.5}$$

where Y is a measure of total GDP in a given country; L is the number of persons in the labour force with the subscripted educational qualification (op = primary or less, s = secondary and h = higher), and K_M is an index of the capital stock. Since we do not have data on the proportion of people in the labour force with no schooling for most of the developed countries in the sample, we aggregated the less than primary and primary educational levels into one single category L_{op}.

Although this is a sensible specification of a production function, empirical fitting of it has been very rare because of the difficulty in collecting data on disaggregated labour inputs. The only case that we know of which has attempted to fit empirically a production function of this form was the LSE Industrial Manpower Project using data from firms in the electrical engineering industry in Great Britain.[16] The results of this exercise were very high R^2s and very low t-ratios of the estimated coefficients. Our data in Appendices E and F permitted us to run the above function in a Cobb-Douglas form for seventeen of the countries of our sample.[17] The two-stage least squares estimates of this equation gave the following result:

$$\log Y = 0.357 + 0.140 \log L_{op} + 0.365** \log L_s + 0.031 \log L_h$$
$$\quad\quad\quad\quad (0.112) \quad\quad\quad (0.206) \quad\quad\quad\quad (0.096)$$
$$+ 0.503** \log K_M \tag{6.6}$$
$$(0.181)$$

with an R^2 of 0.955. The coefficients for physical capital and labour with secondary qualifications are statistically significant at the 95 per cent probability level. On the other hand, the coefficients for labour

---

[16] See Layard *et al.* (1971), Chapter 11.
[17] Countries in the sample included the United States, Canada, Mexico, Colombia, Chile, Great Britain, Norway, The Netherlands, Greece, Israel, The Philippines, Japan, South Korea, Nigeria, Ghana, Kenya and Uganda.

with lower and higher educational qualifications are not statistically significant.

The first point to observe in this result is that the sum of the coefficients is virtually equal to one (1.038), thus giving further strength to the constant—returns-to-scale assumption. The second point is that the overall shadow share of labour (53.6 per cent) is now nearer the actual share of labour than in the previous formulation of the function. The reason clearly is that labour as defined in equation (6.6) now contains the human capital component.

Looking at the individual elasticities of output with respect to the three categories of labour distinguished, we see that they rank as follows: secondary, primary or less, and higher. However, one should bear in mind the high standard error of the exponent of the most educated category of labour. Table 6.5 compares the actual and

TABLE 6.5

ACTUAL VERSUS SHADOW SHARES OF LABOUR BY EDUCATIONAL LEVEL (per cent)

Educational level	Actual	Shadow
Primary or less	35	14
Secondary	26	37
Higher	11	3

Source: Equation (6.6) and Table 7.4.
Note: The shadow figure for secondary education is based on a statistically significant regression coefficient at the 95 per cent level of probability.

shadow shares of labour by educational category. (The actual shares of labour are from Chapter 7 where their calculation is fully explained). In this table we see that the primary or less and higher levels receive more than they actually contribute to production, whereas the opposite is true for the secondary level. Viewed in another way, the shadow wages and the average actual wages of labour are presented in Table 6.6. The marginal productivity of physical capital according to equation (6.6) is 13 per cent. The marginal products of labour are $826, $4,563 and $1,038 for the primary or less, secondary and higher educational levels, respectively.

It should be remembered that the only shadow price in Tables 6.5 and 6.6 which is based on a statistically significant regression coefficient is that for secondary school graduates. Therefore, we cannot conclude from this test that secondary school graduates contribute

106

TABLE 6.6

ACTUAL VERSUS SHADOW WAGE RATES BY EDUCATIONAL LEVEL
(in US $)

Educational level	Actual	Shadow
Primary or less	1,178	826
Secondary	2,625	4,563
Higher	4,025	1,038

Source: Equation (6.6) and Table F.2.
Note: See note to Table 6.5.

more to production than higher education graduates. However, this last finding resembles a previous result by Psacharopoulos (1970) for Greece, where the shadow rate of return to university graduates had a negative value.

On the relationship between human capital, physical capital and the rate of return

Up to this point we have dealt with bits and pieces of what might be a generalized model of physical and human capital accumulation (see Johnson, 1964). Assuming that all countries start life with given resource endowments and transform these into different forms of capital, the question is how the division between investments in human and physical capital takes place. To answer this question the rate of return concept can be introduced.

We can hypothesize that in any given country there is a long-run equilibrium ratio of the stock of human to physical capital and that the country approaches this ratio through investment. The form of capital which will receive priority will depend upon the rates of return on physical and human capital and the market rate of interest. When human capital cheapens (or shows a higher rate of return) relative to physical capital, more will be invested in human capital relative to physical capital.

Figure 6.4 illustrates the adjustment process towards a desired stock of higher education graduates, L_h^*. The long-run equilibrium rate of return r^*_h to investment in higher education graduates is consistent with preferences in the given country. But at the 1970 cross-section there is a divergence (AB) between the returns to higher education graduates and the opportunity cost of capital. This

107

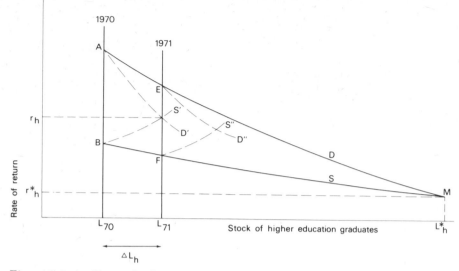

Figure 6.4. An illustrative human capital accumulation model.

divergence will give rise to investment of ΔL_h graduates as an adjustment towards the desired equilibrium stock $L_h{}^*$. So long as the short-run marginal rate of return (as defined by the intersection of the short run supply S' and demand D' schedules for 1970) is above the long-run one (r^*_h) investment will take place.[18] A testable proposition derived from this analysis is that the larger the difference in the returns between human capital and physical capital, the greater the speed of adjustment towards M, or the greater the size of ΔL_h.

For test purposes one could rely on the short-run supply and demand functions. That is

$$\text{Demand} \quad r_h = f(\frac{L_h}{L}, \frac{Y}{P}) \qquad\qquad (6.7)$$

---

[18] Readers must have recognized the analogy of this scheme to the classical capital accumulation model. The long-run demand curve is the marginal efficiency of capital (MEC) whereas the long-run supply curve is the marginal rate of time preference (MRTP). The latter has been drawn with a mild negative slope to indicate that as capital accumulation takes place, people are less willing to sacrifice today's consumption for tomorrow. The short-run supply and investment schedules apply only to the cross-sectional year. Therefore D' lies below D because of diminishing returns in adding to the existing stock (holding all other variables constant). Also, S' lies above S as people must have an incentive to save above what is considered normal in the long run.

108

Supply $\quad \Delta L_h = f(\dfrac{r_h}{r_M}, \dfrac{Y}{P})$ $\qquad\qquad\qquad$ (6.8)

In other words, the proportion of higher education graduates in the labour force ($\dfrac{L_h}{L}$) determines the rate of return to investment in university education while increases in the stock of graduates are a function of the relative return to human and physical capital ($\dfrac{r_h}{r_M}$). Per capita income has been included in both equations as a shift variable. The expected signs of the partial derivatives are

$$\frac{\partial r_h}{\partial \left(\dfrac{L_h}{L}\right)} < 0 \quad \text{and} \quad \frac{\partial \Delta L_h}{\partial \left(\dfrac{r_h}{r_M}\right)} > 0$$

Equation (6.7) and (6.8) form a system of two equations with two unknowns (ΔL_h and r_h). The proportions of higher education graduates in the labour force ($\dfrac{L_h}{L}$), the return to physical capital (r_M), and the level of per capita income ($\dfrac{Y}{P}$) can be assumed exogenous in the short run. To put it another way, the proportion of graduates in the labour force determines relative wages, which in turn determine the rate of return to investment in higher education. Then, a comparison of the return to the two forms of capital determines the size of the future investment. Symbolically, the sequence is

$$\frac{L_h}{L} \to \frac{W_h}{W_s} \to \overset{C_h}{\searrow} r_h \underset{\underset{\dfrac{Y}{P}}{\uparrow}}{\to} \overset{r_M}{\searrow} \Delta L_h$$

where C_h is the direct cost of higher education.

Ideally, one should test this model with time-series data within a country. The second best method is to test whether countries with higher discrepancies between the return to human capital and physical capital show a greater propensity to accumulate human capital than others. Our data proved deficient in testing this model since we lack data on the change in the stock of the labour force with different qualifications. The change in enrolments was tried as a substitute but no clear pattern emerged.[19] Moreover, the ratio

---

[19] This was done on the assumption that there is a positive correlation between changes in enrolments and changes in the stock of qualified persons in the labour force.

$\dfrac{r_H}{r_M}$ has shown no clear pattern when viewed across countries.

Is it true, then, that "...because of the existing institutional and social framework and because of imperfections in the capital market we cannot expect human capital to respond to economic pressures and incentives in the same manner as material capital"? (Friedman, 1962, p. 245). The answer is no, for, as we shall see in Chapter 9 below where the model is tried in an alternative specification, the accumulation of human capital was clearly found to be associated with economic rewards.

Chapter 7. The Contribution of Education to Economic Growth

In this chapter we look into the contribution of education to economic growth in a number of countries and numerical estimates are presented derived on the basis of three alternative procedures. First, Schultz-type calculations are made in which the contribution of education to growth takes a rental form (rate of return times educational investment). These estimates are compared with a variety of time-series calculations based on the methods developed by Denison. Finally, cross-sectional Denison-type calculations are attempted in which the per capita income difference between groups or pairs of countries is accounted for by differences in the use of educated labour.

Alternative ways of growth accounting

Since educational expenditures came to be considered as a form of capital, the question arose of how much this capital contributes to national income and to its growth. The natural analytical framework for answering these questions is a "growth accounting equation".[1] This equation links the rate of growth of the economy as a whole to the rate of growth of different inputs. Let us consider first the basic derivation of this equation and then proceed to the three computational variants.

Assume that output (Y) in a given country is produced by a series of inputs as below

$$Y = f(K, L, D) \tag{7.1}$$

---

[1] See Solow (1957), Selowsky (1969) and Griliches (1970). For an overview of the many issues related to education in the process of economic growth see Bowman (1971).

111

where K is a capital index: L is a total labour index, and D is a land index.

As we are interested in increases of output over time, let us differentiate (7.1) with respect to time,

$$\frac{dY}{dt} = \frac{dK}{dt} f_K + \frac{dL}{dt} f_L + \frac{dD}{dt} f_D \qquad (7.2)$$

where f_K is the marginal product of capital; f_L is the marginal product of labour, and f_D is the marginal product of land.

To simplify our formulas let us assume that the importance of land increments over time on the growth of output is insignificant. In this case we can set $\frac{dD}{dt} = 0$. Next, let us divide every term in (7.2) by Y and get

$$\frac{1}{Y} \frac{dY}{dt} = \frac{dK}{dt} \frac{f_K}{Y} + \frac{dL}{dt} \frac{f_L}{Y} \qquad (7.3)$$

The left-hand side in (7.3) represents the rate of growth of output, call it g_y. If we multiply and divide the last term of (7.3) by L and use the following definitions: $\frac{dK}{dt} = I =$ the investment rate; $\frac{1}{L} \frac{dL}{dt} = g_L =$ the rate of growth of the labour input; $\frac{f_L L}{Y} = s_L =$ the share of labour in total output, and $\frac{I}{Y} = k =$ the investment—output ratio, we can rewrite (7.3) as

$$g_y = \frac{I f_K}{Y} + g_L s_L \qquad (7.4)$$

or

$$g_y = k f_K + g_L s_L \qquad (7.5)$$

Equation (7.5) relates directly the rate of growth of output (g_y), to the investment—output ratio (k), the marginal product of capital (f_K), the rate of growth of the labour input (g_L) and the share of labour in total income (s_L).

Investment in education can enter this accounting scheme in alternative ways. First, by distinguishing two kinds of capital — human capital and physical capital — or by distinguishing several non-homogeneous labour inputs based on educational levels. If we differentiate capital (K) in (7.4) into physical (K_M) and human (K_H) we can rewrite equation (7.4) as

$$g_y = \frac{I_M}{Y} r_M + \frac{I_H}{Y} r_H + g_L s_L \qquad (7.6)$$

112

but where L should be interpreted now as raw labour. According to this formula the contribution of education to growth is equal to the educational investment—output ratio $\frac{I_H}{Y}$, (i.e. the proportion of national income devoted to education in a given year), times the social rate of return (r_H) on this kind of capital. Note also that one can further disaggregate the contribution of the education term $\frac{I_H}{Y} r_H$ into the contribution of particular educational levels, e.g.,

$$\frac{I_H}{Y} r_H = \frac{I_p}{Y} r_p + \frac{I_s}{Y} r_s + \frac{I_h}{Y} r_h \qquad (7.7)$$

where the subscripts p, s and h refer to primary, secondary and higher education, respectively. We will denote this method of measuring the contribution of education to growth as "Schultz-type" growth accounting (See Schultz, 1961).

The second variant of growth accounting is known as "Denison-type". For this purpose we will have to distinguish at the outset the different kinds of educated labour entering the production function. For example, if L_h, L_s and L_{op} represent labour with higher, secondary and primary or less educational qualifications, we can rewrite equation (7.1) (ignoring the land input) as

$$Y = f(L_{op}, L_s, L_h, K),$$

which implies

$$g_Y = k f_K + \sum_i g_i s_i$$

where i runs over the three educational levels. In this case, the contribution of education to growth would be

$$g_{op} s_{op} + g_s s_s + g_h s_h$$

In other words, in a Denison-type calculation we multiply the rate of growth of a given educational input by the income share of persons in the labour force with the same educational qualification,[2] whereas in the Schultz-type calculation the contribution of education to growth is derived from measures of factor rentals.

The two methods can be shown to be logically equivalent under certain assumptions. For instance consider the case of, say, higher education,

---

[2] See Denison (1967).

Schultz   Denison

$$\Delta K_h \times r_h \quad \simeq \quad \Delta L_h \times (W_h - W_s)$$

where ΔK_h is a discrete increment in the higher educational capital stock over a period of time in monetary terms and ΔL_h is the corresponding measure in physical (number of persons) terms. Remembering that the investment part of the Schultz measure consists of direct costs of higher education C_h and foregone earnings W_s, and that the rate of return r_h can be approximated by the following formula

$$r_h = \frac{W_h - W_s}{C_h + W_s}$$

we can say that in the case of horizontal and infinite age—earnings profiles the two types of calculations will give identical results.[3]

Finally, the third variant consists of using a growth accounting equation in a cross-sectional sense, where observations are now countries instead of years within countries. We will denote this as "cross-sectional Denison-type" growth accounting and elaborate it further in the last section of this chapter.

Schultz-type growth accounting

The main ingredients of a Schultz-type calculation are social costs per student year by educational level and social rates of return for the corresponding levels. Social costs include, of course, foregone earnings. Therefore, the total educational investment in any given year is

$$I_H = \sum_i E_i (C_i + W_{i-1})$$

where E_i is enrolments in educational level i; C_i is direct cost per student/year at level i, and W_{i-1} is the foregone earnings of

---

[3] See Chapter 2, above, and Appendix A. For a thorough comparison of the Schultz and Denison approaches see Bowman (1964). For Schultz and Denison—type calculations using the same sources of data, see Psacharopoulos (forthcoming a), where the contribution of education as a percentage of the rate of growth of the Hawaiian economy was found equal to 12 per cent according to the Schultz method and 16 per cent according to the Denison method. It is pointed out that the degree of inequality is due to the roughness of data.

114

students in educational level i (which is equal to the earnings of graduates of level $i-1$ and of the same age).

As already mentioned, by estimating the value of the expression

$$\frac{I_H}{Y} r_H \tag{7.8}$$

(where Y is gross domestic product and r_H the social rate of return to investment in education), one can calculate the contribution of education to growth in any given country. Before we proceed with the empirical estimation we should mention some qualifications of this simple accounting scheme.

In the first place, the ratio $\frac{I_H}{Y}$ will give an exaggerated picture of the resources a country devotes to education since I_H includes foregone earnings, whereas Y, as conventionally measured in the national accounts, does not. Therefore formula (7.8) as it stands will overstate the contribution of education to growth.

Another reason why formula (7.8) will do this is that not 100 per cent of the students become members of the labour force. The construction of the I_H variable is based on enrolments, whereas what we are interested in for *ex post* growth accounting purposes is how much of the educational investment has been actually embodied in the labour force. However, it appears reasonable to adjust formula (7.8) for this by multiplying by the labour force participation rate (π). In this case, the contribution of education to growth will be

$$\pi \cdot \frac{I_H}{Y} \cdot r_H \tag{7.9}$$

Another qualification refers to the fact that the contribution of education to growth, as in the formula above, is gross of deaths, retirements and maintenance of the labour force at a given educational level. But in order to avoid too many adjustments, we have estimated the contribution of education to growth according to formula (7.9).

In Appendix Table H.1 we have constructed the educational investment—output ratios for countries for which we have a full set of data on foregone earnings and costs. As can be seen in this Table, investment varies from a high of 22 per cent of GDP in South Korea to a low of 3.3 per cent in Venezuela. Developed countries such as the United States, Norway, Great Britain, New Zealand and The Netherlands seem to devote a more or less similar share of their resources to education (7 to 12 per cent) whereas less-developed countries vary considerably in the magnitude of this share. After

TABLE 7.1

THE CONTRIBUTION OF EDUCATION TO ECONOMIC
GROWTH ACCORDING TO ALTERNATIVE ACCOUNTING
SCHEMES, BY COUNTRY (per cent)

Country	Accounting scheme	
	Schultz	Denison
(1)	(2)	(3)
United States	17.9	15.0
Canada	..	25.0
Great Britain	8.4	12.0
Norway	6.3	7.0
The Netherlands	4.0	5.0
Belgium	..	14.0
Denmark	..	4.0
Germany	..	2.0
Italy	..	7.0
France	..	6.0
Greece	..	3.0
Israel	4.7	..
New Zealand	18.3	..
Hawaii	12.0	16.1
Mexico	13.2	0.8
Venezuela	14.8	2.4
Colombia	24.5	4.1
Chile	11.4	4.5
Argentina	..	16.5
Brazil	..	3.3
Equador	..	4.9
Honduras	..	6.5
Peru	..	2.5
Malaysia	14.7	..
The Philippines	10.8	10.5
S. Korea	15.9	..
Nigeria	16.0	..
Ghana	23.2	..
Kenya	12.4	..

Sources: Col. (2) based on Table 5.2, and Appendices D and H.
Hawaii from Psacharopoulos (forthcoming a).
Col. (3) U.S. and European countries other than
Greece from Denison (1967). Greece from
Bowles (1967a), Table 5.1. Latin American
countries from Correa (1970), p. 27. The
Philippines from Williamson and Devoretz
(1967), p. 13. Canada from Bertram (1966),
p. 46.

Note: For explanation of symbol notations see Appendix I.

averaging, however, there is little difference between the shares devoted in the developed-country group (9.4 per cent) and the developing-country group (9 per cent). The figures represent the percentage of the average rate of growth in the 1960—5 period which is explained by educational investment.[4]

The United States, Hawaii and New Zealand are the only developed countries which appear with a contribution of education to growth above 10 per cent. Great Britain, Norway and The Netherlands show much lower contributions ranging from 4 per cent to 8 per cent of their rate of growth. On the other hand, less-developed countries appear with substantially higher contributions than those found in developed countries (cf. in particular Colombia 25 per cent, and Ghana 23 per cent).

Splitting the sample into three groups according to the level of per capita income we observe that the contribution of education to growth is generally higher in the less-developed countries. (Table 7.2).

TABLE 7.2

THE CONTRIBUTION OF EDUCATION TO ECONOMIC GROWTH BY LEVEL OF PER CAPITA INCOME

Per capita income ($ US)	Contribution of education to growth (per cent)
180	15.5
500	13.7
2,000	11.2

Source: Tables 5.2 and 7.1, column (2).

As is shown in the above table, the contribution of education ranges on the average between 11 and 15 per cent of the observed rate of growth. The declining rate of return pattern discussed in Chapter 4, above, is repeated here, although the difference in the contributions between countries at different development stages is much less pronounced. This is so because the relatively low rates of return are swamped by the relatively high shares of educational investment thereby producing only small differences in the contribu-

---

[4] In other words, $\pi \frac{I_H}{Y} r_H/g_y$

tion of education to the rate of economic growth in rich and poor countries.

Table 7.1, column 3, also presents estimates of the contribution of education to growth in some of the countries of our sample as well as in other countries, based on the Denison methodology. These estimates come from a variety of sources. Bearing in mind differences in methodology and data used, the Schultz-type estimates are rather close to the Denison-type estimates for the United States, Great Britain, Norway, The Netherlands and Hawaii. However, the Denison estimates from Correa (1970) referring to Latin American countries are in sharp contrast to ours, partly because he uses more limited educational and income data sources. On the other hand, Selowsky's (1967) estimate for Mexico using a Denison-type procedure is almost identical to ours (13 per cent), while his corresponding calculation for Chile is 21 per cent which is well above the estimates produced here and by Correa.

As already mentioned, it is possible to disaggregate the total contribution of education to growth by educational level. This was done for thirteen countries only, for which we have a full set of rate of return estimates. Table 7.3 shows the percentage distribution of the explained rate of growth by educational level. Once again, it is primary education which in most countries makes the greatest contribution to economic growth. On the average, primary education contributes 46 per cent of the total educational contribution to the rate of growth, secondary 40 per cent and higher 14 per cent.

Regarding this last set of estimates and the apparent superiority of investment in primary, secondary and, lastly, higher education, it should be noted that these contributions are based on rates of return using unadjusted earnings differentials. This is of crucial importance because if, as Thias and Carnoy (1969) seem to have established in Kenya, the α coefficient is lower the lower the educational level, it might be that secondary education has actually been a greater source of growth than primary education.

Cross-sectional Denison-type growth accounting

All Denison-type estimations presented in the previous section have been based on time-series data. The average rate of growth of the economy as a whole over a number of years was related to the rate of growth of educational and other inputs over time. However, it is quite possible to attempt a Denison-type calculation where the

118

TABLE 7.3

THE CONTRIBUTION OF EDUCATION TO ECONOMIC GROWTH BY EDUCATIONAL LEVEL AND COUNTRY

Country	Percentage contribution by educational level			Total contribution = 100 per cent
	Primary	Secondary	Higher	
United States	43	31	26	17.9
Mexico	59	29	12	13.2
Venezuela	69	22	9	14.8
Colombia	54	39	7	24.5
Chile	56	34	10	11.4
Israel	46	36	18	4.7
India	35	53	12	34.4
Malaysia	43	49	8	14.7
The Philippines	18	50	32	10.8
South Korea	38	56	6	15.9
Nigeria	63	25	12	16.0
Ghana	37	49	14	23.2
Kenya	38	50	12	12.4
Average	46	40	14	16.4

Source: based on Table 4.1, and Appendices D and H.

unit of observation is countries instead of years. That is, one can observe the difference in income between two given countries and attempt to attribute this difference to the various amounts of inputs used in the two countries. Of course, the essential assumption in this case is that both countries will operate on the same production function, otherwise the averaging involved is meaningless. As noted in Chapter 6, above, Hayami and Ruttan (1970a) have rationalized this kind of aggregation in terms of a secular or meta-production function. We attempt here to use implicitly in a Denison-type calculation the production function fitted explicitly in Chapter 6, above. For the application of the meta-production function we need data on the distribution of the labour force by educational qualification in different countries, as well as data on income shares of the different categories of labour. Then, the percentage difference in per capita income between any two countries can be partly explained in terms of differences in the proportions of educated labour in the labour force. Namely,

$$\Delta \left(\frac{Y}{P}\right)\bigg/ \frac{Y}{P} = \sum_i s_i \, \Delta \left(\frac{L_i}{L}\right)\bigg/ \frac{L_i}{L} + \binom{\text{differences in non-}}{\text{educational inputs}} \qquad (7.10)$$

where $\Delta(\frac{Y}{P})$ is the per capita income difference between the two countries (or group of countries) under comparison: $\Delta(\frac{L_i}{L})$ is the difference in the proportion of persons with educational qualifications i in the labour force, and s_i is the average share of labour with educational qualification i in the two countries.[5] Tables F.1 and F.2 in the Appendix contain data on the distribution of the labour force by educational level and on average wages, respectively. Income shares of labour constructed on the basis of these data are presented below in Table 7.4 for five advanced and four less-developed countries.

TABLE 7.4

INCOME SHARES OF LABOUR BY EDUCATIONAL LEVELS AND COUNTRY

Country	Less than primary	Primary	Secondary	Higher	Total labour share	Per capita income ($ US)
(1)	(2)	(3)	(4)	(5)	(6)	(7)
United States	..	0.19	0.35	0.25	0.78	2,361
Canada	..	0.24	0.44	0.14	0.82	1,774
Great Britain	..	0.38	0.35	0.17	0.90	1,660
The Netherlands	..	0.42	0.33	0.18	0.93	1,490
Norway	..	0.40	0.26	0.05	0.71	1,831
Average	..	0.33	0.35	0.16	0.83	1,823
Israel	0.03	0.29	0.23	0.12	0.67	704
Chile	0.03	0.16	0.15	0.03	0.37	365
The Philippines	0.07	0.50	0.18	0.11	0.86	250
Ghana	0.29	0.13	0.02	0.03	0.47	233
Average	0.11	0.27	0.15	0.07	0.61	388
Overall average share	0.35		0.26	0.11	0.72	°

Source: Tables F.1, F.2 and 5.2.

---

[5] The reader will detect two implicit assumptions in this accounting scheme. First, the underlying production function is first-degree homogeneous and, second, per capita income is used as a proxy for income per member of the labour force in the left-hand side.

Before proceeding with the cross-sectional Denison-type growth accounting, let us pause here and consider the data on income shares. The first point to note is that these shares are on the high side, as judged from the total labour share they produce (column 6 of Table 7.4). This can be explained in view of the fact that we are not using average national wage figures but wages and salaries of particular groups—mostly in the urban sector of the economy. This is particularly true in the case of Great Britain, The Netherlands and The Philippines, the latter having an implausibly high total share of labour. The second point to observe is that in the developed countries the top income share goes to secondary school graduates, whereas in the less-developed countries this position is held by primary school graduates.

Another use of the income-share data is in assessing the elasticity of output with respect to labour inputs of different educational qualifications. This is based on the well known competitive assumption, according to which the wage rates are equal to the value marginal product of labour. In this case the income shares in Table 7.4 can be considered as an approximation of the exponents of a production function of the following type:[6]

$$Y = A L_o^{s_o} L_p^{s_p} L_s^{s_s} L_h^{s_h} K^{s_k}$$

According to the competitive model the shares of labour can be interpreted as the elasticities of output with respect to different labour inputs. For example, the results indicate that if labour with secondary qualifications in the United States increased by 10 per cent, then output would increase by 3.5 per cent. In fact, it is this property of the income shares that is exploited in the following growth-accounting scheme.

The growth accounting will proceed in three steps; first between the two groups of five developed and four less-developed countries; second, between two countries within the upper-income group, and third between two countries in the lower-income group. In other words we compute the average of the growth parameters for each country group and then apply equation (7.10) to account for income differences between groups.

According to the last column of Table 7.4 the average per capita income in the rich-countries groups is US $1,823 and in the lower-income group is US $388. The difference in per capita income in the

---

6 For an actual fitting of this function, see Chapter 6, above.

two groups of countries as a percentage of the income in the rich countries is 79 per cent. This is the percentage we will try to account for by differences in the proportions of educated people employed in the two groups of countries. According to Table F.1 the average proportion of primary-or-less educated persons in the labour force is 0.51 in the developed countries and 0.78 in the less-developed ones. The corresponding proportions for secondary educated persons in the labour force are 0.39 and 0.17, and for higher educated persons 0.11 and 0.05 respectively. The difference in the proportions of educated labour in the two groups of countries as percentages of the proportions in the rich-country group are: minus 53 per cent with primary or lower qualifications, plus 56 per cent with secondary qualifications and plus 55 per cent with higher education qualifications. To these percentages we have applied the all countries average income shares of primary-or-less (0.35), secondary (0.26) and higher (0.11) from Table 7.4. The result of this exercise is that out of the 79 per cent difference in per capita income *minus* 19 percentage points are accounted for by developed countries having less "primary-or-less" labour than poor countries in their labour force, but plus 15 percentage points for having more secondary educated labour and plus 6 percentage points for having more labour with higher educational qualifications. The net result is that educational inputs explain 2 percentage points of the 79 per cent difference in per capita income between developed and less-developed countries. Or, if the income difference is set at 100, educational inputs explain 3 per cent of the income difference.

Table 7.5 presents this comparison (column 2) as well as separate comparisons within each country group. The first set of figures in each of columns (2), (3) and (4) represent percentage-point differences and the second set represent percentage differences. There are less dramatic income differences between the countries at this level of comparison. When the sample is disaggregated into the two sets of countries, the labour inputs seem to explain more (10 per cent) of the income difference within each income group than when we considered all the countries together (3 per cent). Of course, the relationships are too crude to make any generalizations.

This chapter has dealt with three different methodologies for calculating the contribution which education has made to increases in the rate of economic growth in a number of countries at varying levels of economic development. The first section spelled out these approaches at the theoretical and methodological level while the later sections presented the results. Schultz-type calculations based essen-

TABLE 7.5

CROSS-SECTIONAL DENISON-TYPE GROWTH ACCOUNTING

Differences in per capita income explained by	Comparison between					
	Two groups of 5 developed and 4 developing countries		Two developed countries: United States vs. Great Britain		Two developing countries: Israel vs. Chile	
(1)	(2)		(3)		(4)	
Less than primary educated labour	·	·	·	·	−3	(−6)
Primary educated labour	·	·	−15	(−50)	−3	(−6)
Primary or less educated labour	−19	(−24)	·	·	·	·
Secondary educated labour	15	(19)	8	(27)	5	(10)
Higher educated labour	6	(8)	10	(33)	6	(12)
Net explanation	2	(3)	3	(10)	5	(10)
Per capita income difference	79	(100)	30	(100)	48	(100)

Source: Tables 7.4 and F.1.
Note: Figures may not add up because of rounding. Figures not in parentheses are percentage points, figures in parentheses are percentages.

tially on rental values were calculated for seventeen countries using data from our rate of return studies and were then compared with results of Denison-type computations taken from various sources. On the whole, the two approaches gave similar results for the developed countries but for the developing countries the Denison-type estimates were much lower than those using the rental-value approach. The last section of this chapter developed an experimental Denison-type approach using countries rather than years as the unit of observation. This led to income differences being partly explained by variations in the proportions of educated labour in the labour force. The empirical estimates were too crude for any generalizations to be made.

123

Chapter 8. Cost and Earnings Structures

The rate of return to investment in education is purely a discount rate or a summary statistic which conveniently relates the costs of a particular level of education to the monetary payoff. In giving emphasis to such a statistic much of the detail is lost. Therefore in this chapter we will disaggregate the rate of return into its components and analyze separately the costs and relative earnings.

Educational costs by component and level of education

One of the most interesting questions concerning investment in education is the proportion of earnings foregone in total cost by level of education. Such knowledge may be illuminating if private behavioural decisions are being investigated or if public finance questions are being asked. Table 8.1 presents, for fourteen countries, the proportion of foregone earnings in total costs for secondary and higher education.

To give more meaning to the columns of figures, the countries have been divided into three groups by level of income and the proportions averaged. Several points may be made about these averages. First it is apparent that the proportions of foregone earnings at both secondary and higher education levels are similar for both the high and middle income groups: at the secondary level 67 and 66 per cent, and at the higher level 53 and 50 per cent. In other words, two-thirds of total investment takes the form of foregone earnings in secondary education and about one half in higher education in these countries. It should be obvious from these figures that to speak of educational costs without considering students' opportunity costs can be very misleading.[1] Turning to the low-income countries of Africa and Asia the proportions of foregone earnings are much lower, averaging 53 per cent at the secondary level and 34 per

---

[1] But for an opposite view see Vaizey (1962), p. 43.

TABLE 8.1

FOREGONE EARNINGS AS PERCENTAGE
OF TOTAL SOCIAL COST PER STUDENT
YEAR BY EDUCATIONAL LEVEL AND
COUNTRY

Country	Secondary	Higher
United States	62.4	63.4
New Zealand	65.0	50.4
Great Britain	72.4	44.3
Average	67	53
Israel	75.3	34.7
Mexico	62.0	64.9
Chile	66.4	48.6
Colombia	61.0	52.7
Average	66	50
Malaysia	38.5	19.5
Ghana	62.6	24.3
S. Korea	69.5	62.0
Kenya	43.6	23.0
Uganda	42.6	34.3
Nigeria	59.4	27.7
India	56.2	47.1
Average	53	34

Source: Table D.3.

cent at the higher educational level. One thing which is obvious within this group is that the African countries, especially at the higher education level, have very similar cost structures involving relatively low proportions of foregone earnings. The reason for this is that universities in African countries, especially those in ex-British and ex-French colonial countries, attempt the same level of quality as residential European universities. This has meant that buildings, equipment and teaching staff have been of the same quality and hence of at least equal cost. Therefore, the actual direct cost per student year varies little between universities in, say, Ghana and Britain, while foregone earnings are much lower in Ghana. Therefore the proportion of direct costs in total costs is much higher in poor than in rich countries.

After looking at the components of total annual costs, we now turn to the relative costs of one year of schooling at the primary, secondary and higher educational levels. In Table 8.2 two types of cost ratios are produced, first direct costs alone and second total costs. The levels of comparison are secondary and primary education, and higher and primary education. Once again, countries are grouped by income levels and the ratios averaged.

Concentrating on the averages, the first point to make is that the cost ratios for both direct and total costs are larger the lower the income level. This is most true of the direct costs for higher/primary education levels. The addition of foregone earnings to direct costs widens the ratios further, implying that the ratios of foregone

TABLE 8.2

RATIOS OF DIRECT AND TOTAL COSTS PER STUDENT YEAR BY EDUCATIONAL LEVEL AND COUNTRY (primary = 1)

Country	Direct costs		Total costs	
	Secondary/ primary	Higher/ primary	Secondary/ primary	Higher/ primary
United States	1.2	3.7	2.9	9.5
New Zealand	2.3	7.1	6.5	14.4
Great Britain	2.9	16.1	10.5	28.9
Average	*2.1*	*9.0*	*6.6*	*17.6*
Israel	2.7	16.8	10.8	25.6
Mexico	5.1	9.0	5.7	11.0
Chile	1.5	7.9	4.4	15.5
Colombia	2.7	17.9	5.7	31.7
Average	*3.0*	*12.9*	*6.6*	*20.9*
Malaysia	1.9	13.0	3.1	16.1
Ghana	6.3	119.6	11.6	109.7
S. Korea	2.4	5.5	8.0	14.4
Kenya	12.3	167.3	21.9	217.0
Uganda	14.3	115.9	25.0	176.0
Nigeria	7.3	100.8	8.4	65.8
India	4.9	17.1	5.6	16.2
Average	*7.1*	*77.0*	*11.9*	*87.9*

Source: Table D.3

127

earnings are greater than the ratios of direct costs. The importance of foregone earnings can be seen most clearly in the middle- and high-income country groups where the ratios are doubled or trebled by their inclusion. The most outstanding result, however, is that, taking direct costs, one year of university in the lower-income sample of countries costs 77 times one year in primary school, and for total costs the cost is 88 times as great. Even in middle-income countries, one year of higher education costs 21 times as much as one primary school year. Figures such as these strikingly point out the need for low-income countries to analyze the potential benefits of higher education before planning expansion.

Division of total educational resources between levels

Finally, in this section we take a look at the way in which total annual educational investment is distributed between the three levels of education. This is done by utilizing the cost data from Table D.3 and enrolments from Table H.3. What patterns of resource distribution should we expect? For enrolments — assuming the length of secondary schooling is no longer than primary schooling — we would expect no reversals in the ordering of schooling levels, primary enrolment > secondary enrolment > higher enrolment. Table H.3 shows that in fact this is the pattern for all countries. When ordering the schooling levels by resource inputs, however, we may expect variations between countries, since the cost of one pupil/year varies by level.

At the early stages of educational development, the resource cost of primary education will be above that of secondary which in turn will be above that for higher education, since enrolments at these levels will show large differences. Later, enrolments at secondary level will increase and, since this level is more expensive per student year, the total cost of secondary education will grow to be above that for primary education. Eventually this will also be the case for higher education vis-à-vis the primary level. With the approaching universality of higher education, this level will take over as the greatest resource-consuming educational level. Table 8.3 presents the actual resource distributions in this respect.

Of the fifteen-country sample in Table 8.3, three countries correspond to the first pattern and nine to the second as described above; the odd countries out being the United States, Great Britain and The Philippines. It is interesting to note that in the United States

TABLE 8.3

DISTRIBUTION OF TOTAL RESOURCES DEVOTED TO
EDUCATION BY LEVEL AND COUNTRY (per cent)

Country	Primary	Secondary	Higher
United States	32	31	37
New Zealand	27	54	19
Great Britain	10	70	20
Israel	29	47	24
Mexico	53	35	12
Chile	46	38	16
Colombia	37	38	25
Malaysia	44	47	9
The Philippines	33	31	36
Ghana	33	57	10
S. Korea	29	59	12
Kenya	30	47	23
Uganda	18	25	7
Nigeria	51	38	11
India	31	56	13

Source: Tables D.3 and H.3.

higher education already takes the major share of educational resources.

The conclusions from this analysis of educational costs are:

(a) Between one-half and two-thirds of the cost of secondary and higher education takes the form of foregone earnings for almost all countries divided into three income groups. The only major exception to this is at the higher education level for poor countries, where foregone earnings represent only one-third of total cost.

(b) Ratios between the annual student cost in primary, secondary and higher education are much wider for poor countries than for others. The cost of one year in university is equivalent to over 80 primary years in this country group.

(c) The majority of countries of our sample devote most resources to secondary education, then primary and least to higher education.

Relative earnings and education

After isolating the cost side of the rate of return calculation and noting the general importance of foregone earnings, attention is now

129

turned to the benefit side of the calculations — the age—education—earnings profiles. This is interesting not only because of the relationship with the rate of return but also because of the importance which education has for earnings distribution. The analysis takes the form of comparing average annual earnings by educational level.[2]

The first practical problem to be solved concerns the equivalent schooling groups which are to be used. Two possibilities exist — years of schooling or level of schooling completed — and there are advantages and disadvantages for both. The advantage of using years of schooling is that absolute equivalence could be arrived at, but unfortunately the data for all our countries are not this comprehensive. As to levels, the advantage is that earnings do not increase smoothly by years of schooling, rather they are often geared to the completion of a particular level. The disadvantage of this procedure is the non-equivalence of levels across countries, for instance, primary school length varies from five to eight years in our sample of countries.

In fact, it was decided to use a mixture of the two methods. At the primary schooling level the most satisfactory procedure for equalizing the level of education is to use eight years of schooling. We have average earnings associated with this level for ten countries. For the rest, earnings relate to seven years of schooling except for Chile, Greece, Korea, and Malaysia where data exist only for six years.

The second division is a little more complicated but generally comes about four years after the first division. For some countries this corresponds to the end of the secondary cycle and immediately before university. For the others, chiefly those educational systems based on British influence, the break is pre-sixth form. In all countries, the division corresponds to eleven or twelve years of schooling except for Norway, Ghana and Malaysia where it is after thirteen years. The final category, higher education, corresponds to university or sixth forms plus university and in most cases is five years in length. The whole schooling cycle for fifteen of the nineteen countries is sixteen years, the exceptions being The Philippines (fifteen years), Norway (eighteen years), Ghana (eighteen years) and India (fifteen

---

[2] The countries chosen for this analysis are: United States, Canada, Great Britain, The Netherlands, France, Norway, Greece, Israel, Mexico, Chile, Colombia, Malaysia, Philippines, Ghana, South Korea, Kenya, Uganda, Nigeria and India. The data for all these countries come from the individual rate of return studies except for France for which Denison's (1967) study is utilized.

years). It should be noted that the years per course explained above are in many cases the minimum number and, particularly in under-developed countries, the actual time taken to complete each course may be much longer (this also applies to higher education in many European countries). The divisions above are not perfect, especially at the secondary level, but there is no gain in re-arranging them further. Generally, the primary, secondary and higher divisions of education correspond to eight, twelve and sixteen years of schooling respectively.

The only earnings-stream calculations which require special explanation are those for people with primary level education. To derive the earnings of the eight years of schooling for Mexico, Colombia, Ghana and Nigeria, countries where primary schooling is five or six years, was a relatively simple matter. For Mexico, Carnoy (1967b) actually provides an age—earnings profile for eight years of schooling as does Selowsky (1968) for Colombia, and Denison (1967) refers to eight years for France. In Ghana, primary school is followed by four years of middle school so here the half way points between the primary and middle school earnings profiles were used. The same procedure was followed in Western Nigeria where the four-year secondary-modern school operates. But for Chile, Greece, Korea and Malaysia, this was not possible and our first division corresponds in all these cases to six years; for Kenya, Uganda, The Netherlands, Norway and The Philippines it is seven years. In the case of Great Britain, no earnings profile is available for primary school leavers, but since the rest of the earnings data used for this country is from the electrical engineering industry, the average wage of primary school leavers has been assumed to equal the average paid to labourers and the semi-skilled in that industry during the same period in which the other data were collected, (Ministry of Labour, 1967).

At this point the whole set of lifetime-earnings streams was brought to hand. From these the average annual earnings were calculated for the three educational levels described above plus, where possible, the average earnings for those with no schooling (see Appendix Table F.2). For greater ease of comparability, the earnings were expressed in ratios. Table 8.4 presents the results with the nineteen countries divided up into high-, middle- and low-income groups.

Observing the individual country earnings ratios in the context of the group averages brings out some very clear patterns. In the high-income group, the six countries display a large similarity in the ratios and in each case the higher to secondary ratio is above the

TABLE 8.4

RATIOS OF AVERAGE ANNUAL EARNINGS OF LABOUR BY EDUCA-
TIONAL LEVEL AND COUNTRY

	Educational levels compared				
Country	Primary over none	Secondary over primary	Higher over secondary	Higher over primary	Higher over none
(1)	(2)	(3)	(4)	(5)	(6)
United States	..	1.48	1.65	2.44	..
Canada	..	1.44	1.83	2.63	..
Great Britain	..	1.45	1.61	2.33	..
The Netherlands	..	1.29	1.74	2.24	..
France	..	1.50	1.73	2.59	..
Norway	..	1.40	1.50	2.13	..
Average	..	*1.43*	*1.68*	*2.39*	..
Greece	..	1.39	1.58	2.20	..
Israel	1.60	1.36	1.51	2.05	3.28
Mexico	3.32	1.40	2.25	3.15	10.46
Chile	1.67	2.22	2.00	4.88	8.15
Colombia	3.00	3.00	1.50	4.50	13.50
Average	*2.40*	*1.87*	*1.81*	*3.36*	*8.85*
Malaysia	3.81	4.28	1.80	7.73	29.49
The Philippines	2.03	1.60	1.41	2.24	4.55
Ghana	2.28	1.87	4.87	9.11	20.77
S. Korea	..	2.14	1.20	2.57	..
Kenya	1.63	2.33	2.35	5.47	8.92
Uganda	2.40	3.27	3.69	12.07	28.97
Nigeria	2.38	2.20	4.36	9.55	22.63
India	2.45	1.42	1.67	2.37	5.81
Average	*2.43*	*2.39*	*2.67*	*6.39*	*17.31*

Source: based on Table F.2 for all countries except France. France from Denison
(1967), p. 376.

secondary to primary one, although by only relatively small margins. Countries in the middle-income group show greater variation — the three South American countries having higher ratios than the high-income countries, while both Israel and Greece have very low ratios. The result for Israel can be explained by the conscious policy of the government and the Histadrut in the 1950s to equalize earnings. Recent evidence suggests that this policy has been breached somewhat and it is likely that the earnings ratios are now widening. One major variation within this group is the ordering of the ratios between levels. Israel and Mexico have the lowest ratios for the secondary to primary comparison and the highest for the primary to no schooling one, while Chile has the reverse pattern and Colombia has equal and relatively large ratios at both levels of comparison. For the group as a whole, we see a decrease in the ratios as we move up the educational hierarchy (2.40, 1.87, and 1.81). On the other hand, if the whole schooling system is split into two parts equal in length (eight years) primary/no schooling, higher/primary, then the ratio increases for the second cycle (3.36 as against 2.40). Looking further at the overall earnings ratio between those with sixteen years of schooling and those with none, here there are very wide variations — the highly educated in Israel earning just over three times the amount earned by the illiterate, while in Colombia the disparity appears to be over thirteen times.

Finally, we turn to the low-income group. At the primary/no schooling level, the earnings ratio is similar to that for the middle-income group of countries but the other comparisons indicate a much wider spread of earnings for the low-income group. For the post-primary schooling cycle, relative earnings increase greatly as can be seen from column (5), a university graduate averaging over six times the earnings of a primary school graduate. The effect of the whole educational cycle is to increase earnings seventeen-fold on average over the illiterate in these countries. The dispersion in earnings for Kenya is lower than for the other African countries probably because the earnings data relate to urban workers only, whereas the data for the other three countries include rural earnings which are generally only about one half to one third the size of urban earnings in developing countries.

The conclusions to be drawn from the empirical investigation of the relationships between earnings and educational level across a wide range of countries are:

(a) High-income countries have narrower earnings ratios than the other income groups at all educational levels. Ratios increase up the educational hierarchy in this group.

(b) Medium- and low-income countries appear on the average to share similar earnings ratios for the primary/no schooling levels but for secondary/primary levels and the higher/secondary levels, the earnings ratios are much greater in the low-income countries.

(c) The higher/primary earnings ratios increase markedly as we move from high- to low-income countries.

(d) The earnings ratios between graduates of higher education and people with no education vary widely between countries but on the whole they are again much larger in the low-income countries.

(e) For all low- and middle-income countries, except Mexico and India, the eight years of secondary and higher education increase earnings relative to the primary level more than the eight years of primary education in relation to no education.

(f) On the evidence of other countries, the low-income countries cannot expect the primary/no schooling ratios to narrow until higher levels of development are reached. On the other hand the evidence indicates that the higher/secondary ratio and the secondary/primary ratio should narrow rapidly, the average ratio at this level for the middle-income countries being much below that for the low-income countries.

The average earnings of graduates of different educational levels vary widely in developing countries. These variations are far greater than those found in the more economically advanced countries and, in the countries of the sample with the lowest per capita incomes, a university graduate can expect to earn over twenty times as much as an individual with no schooling. In the United States a university graduate can expect to earn under three times as much as the primary school leaver while in Ghana the figure is over nine times. On the other hand it may be said that such a degree of inequality is due largely to the recent occurrence of the educational expansion and that the experience of other countries shows that, over time, earnings inequalities based on education will decrease.

A main problem in interpreting the present range of earnings in under-developed countries is that we have little time-series evidence for these countries and therefore it is impossible to know whether

134

(a) differentials by level of education have been narrowing, or (b) whether the present wide range of earnings has been introduced by education, or (c) whether such a range existed previously, based on factors other than education. These interesting questions cannot be developed further here, and attention is turned in the next chapter to a possible explanation of the "vertical" patterns in Table 8.4.[3]

---

[3] For an attempt to relate earnings inequality to educational and economic development see Chiswick (1971). Developing his earlier theoretical work with Becker (Becker and Chiswick, 1966) on the relationships between investment in human capital, rates of return and earnings inequality, Chiswick formulated a model predicting a positive relationship between earnings inequality and the level of economic development. Using data from Lydall (1968) on earnings inequality and schooling inequality, the model was tested. Although many of the results were ambiguous and of low levels of significance, it is possible to say that the above-postulated relationship was not found, rather earnings inequality and economic development were negatively related. Chiswick argues, however, that the negative simple correlation between earnings inequality and the level of economic development is not directly due to the latter but to the greater equality in educational provision in developed economies.

Chapter 9. Testing some Behavioural Models

In this last chapter we report the results of a number of tests using the data collected in this study. These tests fall into two groups: first, we examine whether there is any relationship between relative earnings and relative numbers of people in the labour force with different educational qualifications. Second, we construct a new profitability measure based on the original age—earnings profiles and attempt to explain international migration.

Educated labour and relative wages

In this section the proportions of people in the labour force with different educational levels are related to the wages which correspond to these levels. The hypothesized direction of causation in the short run disequilibrium situation discussed in Chapter 6 was that an increase in the proportion of higher education graduates (L_h) relative to secondary school graduates (L_s) in the labour force will lead to a fall in the relative wages $\frac{W_h}{W_s}$. This case is illustrated in Figure 9.1 where a shift of the supply curve results in identifying two points A and B on the more stable demand curve for educated labour.

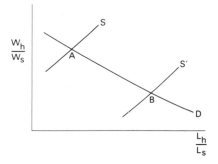

Figure 9.1. The relationship between relative wages and relative quantities of educated labour.

137

Alternatively, if relative wages are considered to be the exogenous variable, a fall in the wages of university graduates relative to the wages of secondary school graduates will lead to the employment of more university graduates relative to secondary school graduates in the economy. The important point for our purposes is not so much the direction of causation as the sign and size of the slope of the curve AB. With these determined, one would have a way of assessing either the effect of an incomes policy on the demand for different kinds of labour, or the effect of a given expansion of the educational system on the distribution of earnings in the economy.

It will be useful to organize our discussion on this point around the concept of the elasticity of substitution between different types of educated labour.[1] This statistic tells us by how much the proportion of one type of labour will change relative to another type, after their relative marginal products have changed (and of course keeping all other variables constant). The elasticity of substitution (σ) between university graduates and secondary school graduates can be defined as

$$\sigma_{hs} = -\frac{\dfrac{\partial\left(\dfrac{L_h}{L_s}\right)}{\dfrac{L_h}{L_s}}}{\dfrac{\partial\left(\dfrac{MP_h}{MP_s}\right)}{\dfrac{MP_h}{MP_s}}} \tag{9.1}$$

Assuming perfect competition, wages can be substituted for marginal products (MP) and σ estimated by fitting the following function

$$\log\left(\frac{W_h}{W_s}\right) = a + b \log\left(\frac{L_h}{L_s}\right)_i \tag{9.2}$$

where i is the country providing the observation. According to definition (9.1) the elasticity of substitution in this case is

---

[1] On this topic see Allen (1938) and McFadden (1963).

138

$$\sigma_{hs} = -\frac{1}{b}$$

The estimation of the elasticity of substitution using equation (9.2) is of course an econometric compromise. Ideally, one should start from a production function such as the one we have attempted to fit in Chapter 6 where labour of different categories appears as separate elements. The problem of estimation via this procedure is that it involves the second derivative of the function.[2] A highly sophisticated attempt which has followed this procedure has failed to produce any convincing results.[3] An alternative is to avoid the first differentiation of the production function and assume that observed market wages are equal to marginal products. In this case the elasticity of substitution can be estimated by fitting the partial relationship described in equation (9.2). This relationship was fitted using our wage and labour force data from Appendix F for 21 countries. The sample was then split into nine advanced and twelve less advanced countries and the same relationship was fitted to each group.[4] When equation (9.2) was fitted using the data from all countries it gave the following results:[5]

$$\log \frac{W_h}{W_s} = 0.034 - 0.420^{**} \log \frac{L_h}{L_s}, \quad R^2 = 0.36, \sigma_{hs} = 2.4 \qquad (9.3)$$
$$(0.129)$$

$$\log \frac{W_s}{W_p} = 0.339 - 0.163^{**} \log \frac{L_s}{L_p}, \quad R^2 = 0.21, \sigma_{sp} = 6.2 \qquad (9.4)$$
$$(0.072)$$

---

[2] The first derivative of the function provides the estimate of the marginal products, e.g.,

$$MP_h = \frac{\partial Y}{\partial L_h}$$

and relative marginal products are further differentiated in order to yield an estimate of σ (equation (9.1), above).

[3] See Layard *et al.* (1971), chapter 11.

[4] Countries in the higher-income group included the United States, Canada, Great Britain, The Netherlands, France, Norway, Greece, Israel and Japan. Countries in the lower-income group included Mexico, Chile, Colombia, The Philippines, Ghana, Nigeria, Kenya, Uganda, India, Turkey, Brazil and South Korea.

[5] Numbers in parentheses are standard errors.

$$\log \frac{W_p}{W_o} = 0.787 - 0.020 \log \frac{L_p}{L_o}, \quad R^2 = 0.02, \sigma_{po} = 50 \qquad (9.5)$$
$$\qquad\qquad\qquad (0.054)$$

where h, s, p, o are higher, secondary, primary and no education, respectively.

The first point to note from these results is that the relative quantities of people employed with different skills explain 36 per cent of wage differentials between university and secondary school graduates and 21 per cent of the wage differentials between secondary and primary school graduates, but for the lower educational categories there is practically no relationship at all between the variables we have examined. Moreover, the elasticity of substitution between the top two educational categories was found equal to 2.4 between primary and secondary school graduates equal to 6.2 and between lower educational categories equal to 50. The first two estimates were based on statistically significant relationships, whereas this was not the case for the last one.

We should mention at this point the results of two similar exercises, Bowles (1969 and 1970) and Dougherty (1971a). Bowles used cross-sectional earnings and employment data from twelve countries, and distinguishing labour with seven years of schooling or less, eight to eleven years and twelve years or more, (i.e., roughly corresponding to our p, s and h categories), found the following elasticities of substitution $\sigma_{ps} = 12.0$ and $\sigma_{sh} = 202.0$. Dougherty used both cross-sectional and time-series earnings and employment data in the United States to estimate elasticities of substitution between different occupations or educational levels. His results have shown that the elasticity of substitution between different types of educated labour is significantly higher than unity but less than infinity. For example, the following statistically significant estimate at the 99 per cent level of probability was found:

$$\sigma_{op} = 10.4$$

Moreover, the elasticities of the lower educational levels are higher than the elasticity of adjacent categories of highly qualified labour.

Our results are more consistent with Dougherty's than Bowles's. They differ from Bowles's in two respects: first, the elasticity of substitution increases the lower the educational levels of the labour categories compared; and second, the most significant relationship is the one involving the top two labour categories. In view of these findings we have concentrated our further investigations only on a

140

comparison of higher and secondary education graduates.

The second experiment consisted of splitting the sample into two groups of nine developed and twelve less-developed countries so as to reflect in part the underlying differences in production functions within the 21 country sample. The results were as follows:

Developed countries;

$$\log \frac{W_h}{W_s} = 0.440 - 0.001 \log \frac{L_h}{L_s}, \quad R^2 = 0.00 \tag{9.6}$$
$$(0.111)$$

Less-developed countries:

$$\log \frac{W_h}{W_s} = 0.127 - 0.419** \log \frac{L_h}{L_s}, \quad R^2 = 0.33, \sigma_{hs} = 2.4 \tag{9.7}$$
$$(0.191)$$

These results indicate that we really are dealing with two separate groups of countries and that the possibilities of substitution between secondary and higher education graduates are much greater in developed than in under-developed countries. Or, in other words, relative labour supplies explain relative earnings better in less-developed countries than in advanced countries.

As noted above, estimation of the elasticity of substitution via equation (9.2) is based on the assumption that countries are similar in every respect other than relative wages and relative quantities of educated labour. The construction of the physical capital variable in Chapter 6 enables us to move some way from such a restrictive assumption and to experiment with a shifter of the function. That is, we have included the physical capital variable in the basic estimating equation, in order to be able to estimate the elasticity of substitution keeping all other variables constant. The following equation was fitted in this respect

$$\log \left(\frac{W_h}{W_s}\right)_i = a + b \log \left(\frac{L_h}{L_s}\right)_i + c \log \left(\frac{K}{L}\right)_i \tag{9.8}$$

where $\frac{K}{L}$ is the physical capital–labour ratio in country i (see Chapter 6, above and Appendix E). The results for the two groups of countries were as follows:

Developed countries:

$$\log \frac{W_h}{W_s} = -0.549 + 0.050 \log \frac{L_h}{L_s} + 0.114* \log \frac{K}{L}, \quad R^2 = 0.37 \tag{9.9}$$
$$(0.099) \qquad (0.060)$$

141

Less-developed countries:

$$\log \frac{W_h}{W_s} = -0.030 - 0.432^* \log \frac{L_h}{L_s} + 0.018 \log \frac{K}{L}, \ R^2 = 0.33, \sigma_{hs} = 2.3$$
$$\phantom{\log \frac{W_h}{W_s} = -0.030 } (0.232) \phantom{\log \frac{L_h}{L_s}} (0.166)$$

$$(9.10)$$

Comparing regressions (9.6) and (9.7) with (9.9) and (9.10) we can see that the inclusion of the capital variable had two effects. First, it "explained" relative wages in the developed countries better than did the relative labour supplies. Most interesting, however, is the positive sign corresponding to the significant capital variable for the developed-countries group. What this implies is that the greater the amount of physical capital per man, the wider the difference between the earnings of higher and secondary education graduates. Seen in another way, physical-capital accumulation shifts the demand schedule for educated labour to the right resulting in a greater wage differential for any given labour ratio (Figure 9.2). In other words, highly educated workers appear to be complementary to physical capital.[6]

This result is also consistent with findings by Dougherty (1971b) who fitted time-series CES-derived wage functions for different kinds of labour. His findings indicate that there exists a positive relationship between the level of skill and the relative upwards shifting of wages. Although Dougherty is very cautious in attributing

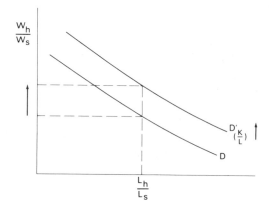

Figure 9.2. Widening of the wage differential due to the increase in the capital intensity of production.

---

[6] For detailed discussions on this subject see Griliches (1969 and 1970) and Welch (1970).

this phenomenon to any particular cause, he hints that this positive correlation might be a consequence of technical progress or the accumulation of capital.

Empirical estimates of the elasticity of substitution between different types of educated labour such as those derived above, are important for at least three reasons: for educational planning, for income growth accounting and for policies of income distribution. The implication of our findings for educational planning is that we are now in a better position to make a choice between the two alternative approaches: i.e., manpower requirements or rate of return analysis. The manpower-requirements approach implicitly assumes that the elasticity of demand for any type of educated labour is zero, and that the elasticity of substitution between one kind of labour and other factors of production is zero. Therefore, educational planning according to this approach should proceed on the basis of fixed-coefficients (Leontief production functions) stipulating the "needs" of the economy for educated labour. At the other end of the scale the rate of return approach, as usually advocated, implicitly assumes that the elasticity of demand for labour of a given kind is infinite, or that the elasticity of substitution between labour and other factors of production is infinite. Therefore, educational planning according to this approach should proceed on the basis of cost-benefit analysis, for the actual numbers of persons employed do not matter. Educational planning around the world has proceeded on the basis of assumptions regarding the elasticity of substitution of educated labour rather than on factual evidence. A major educational planning exercise, the Mediterranean Regional Project, was based on the zero substitution assumption whereas elsewhere the assumption of infinite substitution has been used.[7]

Bowles's (1969 and 1970) and Dougherty's (1971b) evidence were the first steps towards factual evidence on this crucial assumption. Their results showed that although the elasticity of substitution is not infinite it is high enough for us to assume the real world lies closer to the assumptions underlying the rate of return approach. Our results have confirmed this view. However, the lower elasticity between secondary and higher education graduates in the less-developed countries suggests that possibilities of substitution may be

---

[7] See OECD (1962), Blaug (1967) and Bowles (1967b). For an empirical comparison between alternative approaches see Bowles (1969) and Psacharo-poulos (1968).

143

more limited and that a fixed coefficients approach may be justified in this case.

In accounting for the sources of income growth it is often necessary to construct a total labour index over a number of years in the past, either within a country or between countries (see Chapter 7, above). An estimate of the elasticity of substitution will suggest the weighting scheme of different categories of labour. If the elasticity is near infinity, then one can weight different labour inputs by their wages so as to arrive at the total input. Denison (1967) has used such a linear combination to account for rate of growth differences in several countries. On the other hand, Bowles (1969 and 1970) has suggested an extension of Sato's (1967) two-level CES function for taking into account the exact value of σ in constructing a labour index. What our findings suggest is that Denison's method is a very crude approximation and that more attention should be given to Bowles's use of the two-level CES function.

For policies of income distribution we are interested in knowing how earnings differentials will be affected if the proportions of educated labour in the economy change. The *ad hoc* hypothesis would be that a reduction in income inequality would result from a reduction in the inequality in the provision of education (Layard, 1971). What our findings suggest in this respect is that, whereas in developing countries a decrease in the ratio of higher education graduates to secondary graduates will lead to narrower earnings differentials, in developed countries increases in the capital intensity of production work in the opposite direction and may lead to a more unequal earnings distribution.

Relative wages, cross-rates of return and international migration

The kind of data assembled in this study permit us to test hypotheses regarding international migration. Over the last twenty years the world has experienced the so-called "brain drain", namely the flow of highly qualified manpower from developing to more advanced countries and also between the more advanced countries. This flow of professional people has been attributed to the higher living standards in the more advanced country, intellectual unemployment in the country of origin, or simply better research opportunities in the country of destination. (Thomas, 1954 and 1967).

The literature on the economics of the brain drain is rich but mainly concentrates on the welfare aspects, considering such

144

questions as whether the remaining population is better, the same or worse off after emigration of highly qualified manpower.[8] In contrast, in this section we are concerned with the positive aspect of the brain drain and we attempt to measure the significance of economic factors in determining the emigration of high-level manpower.[9]

The key to our analysis is the estimation of the economic returns a university graduate enjoys by completing his degree in the home country and then emigrating in order to work in a foreign country. The decision to graduate and then work abroad is treated as an investment decision with the prospective migrant comparing the costs and benefits involved. The costs consist of private direct outlays for university education, foregone earnings while at university and moving expenses to the country of destination. The benefits consist of the difference between what the emigrant will be earning in the country of destination and what he would be earning as a secondary school graduate if he remained in the country of origin. Therefore, the cost-benefit analysis and the resulting profitability measure refer to the combined activity of graduating in the home country *and* moving immediately after graduation.

Our investigation is limited to the flow of professional workers from different countries into the United States. Although this limitation is suggested on grounds of data availability, this particular direction of movement also represents the salient characteristic of international migration today.

The costs and benefits associated with university graduation and subsequent migration can be summarized into a single statistic which we will call a "cross-rate of return", in the sense that it is a hybrid of costs in the home country and earnings differentials between the country of destination and the country of origin. The cross-rate of return (r_c) was obtained by solving the following equation for r_c:

$$\sum_{t=1}^{n} Q_{10} (W_{1h} - W_{0s})_t (1+r_c)^{-t} = \sum_{t=0}^{-s} (C_{0h} + W_{0s}) (1+r_c)^{-t} + D$$

(9.11)

where Q_{10} is a cost-of-living adjustment factor between the country

---

[8] For the highlights of the controversy on the welfare effects of the brain drain see Grubel and Scott (1966), Thomas (1967), Johnson (1967), Patinkin (1968), Berry and Soligo (1969) and Scott (1970).
[9] For econometric investigations of the determinants of *internal* migration see Sahota (1968) and Greenwood (1969).

of origin (0) and the country of destination (1); W_{1h} is the earnings of higher education graduates in the country of destination; W_{0s} is the earnings of secondary school graduates in the country of origin; C_{0h} is the direct annual cost of attending higher education in the country of origin; D is the moving costs from the country of origin to the country of destination; s is the length of the university cycle in years, and n is the number of working years in the lifetime of a university graduate.

The necessary data for the calculation of the cross-rates of return were obtained from the same sources which provided the domestic rate of return estimates (see Psacharopoulos, 1971). Unfortunately, not all 32 case studies report the detailed age—earnings profiles by educational level. Therefore, we were able to estimate cross-rates of return for only fourteen countries.

The basis of all calculations has been the age—earnings profiles of university graduates in the United States. These were obtained from Hanoch (1967). Hanoch's age—earnings profiles were based on a sample of the 1960 Census of Population and were subsequently adjusted for a host of factors other than education influencing earnings. Accordingly, the estimated cross-rates of return are biased downwards, as the earnings of secondary school graduates in the home country were in each case subtracted from the adjusted US earnings.

The above United States earnings refer to 1959. These earnings were brought to the year to which the country-of-origin data refer by applying a growth factor equal to the annual rise of wages in the United States manufacturing industries. This growth factor was very close to 3 per cent.[10]

Another adjustment to the United States graduate earnings was intended to allow for differences in the cost of living. The nominal earnings differential between a United States university graduate and an Indian secondary school graduate certainly exaggerates the advantage of moving. It is for this purpose that we have applied international cost-of-living adjustments to the United States earnings.[11] In addition, we opted to under-estimate rather than over-estimate the cross-rates of return by assuming that the cost of moving would be equal to twice the one-way air fare from the capital of

---

[10] The data for this adjustment were based on International Labour Office (1963 and 1968).

[11] The United Nations (*Monthly Bulletin of Statistics*, 1968) cost-of-living index was used for this purpose.

TABLE 9.1

DOMESTIC AND CROSS-RATES OF RETURN BY COUN-
TRY OF ORIGIN (per cent)

| Country | Rate of return | |
	Domestic	Cross
(1)	(2)	(3)
Canada	19.7	18.5
Mexico	29.0	45.0
Colombia	15.5	44.0
Chile	12.2	48.0
Great Britain	12.0	36.0
Norway	7.7	18.5
Belgium	17.0	18.0
Germany	4.6	14.0
Israel	8.0	34.0
India	14.3	> 50.0
The Philippines	12.5	> 50.0
Nigeria	34.0	> 50.0
Ghana	37.0	> 50.0
Kenya	27.4	> 50.0

Source: Column (2) from Table 4.1. Column (3) from
Psacharopoulos (1971), p. 234.
Note: All domestic rates of return are private except for
Chile where the rate is social.

the country of origin to Chicago, USA.[12]

The results of our calculations are shown in the last column of
Table 9.1. These figures should be interpreted as *private* cross-rates
of return and therefore be compared with the ones in column 2 of
the same Table.

The first point to observe in Table 9.1 is that the cross-rates of
return are substantially higher than the domestic rates of return. The
cross-rates of return range from over 50 per cent in five less-
developed countries to 14 per cent in the case of Germany. The
cross-rate of return for Canada is very close to the domestic one
because of the similar earnings of graduates in the two countries. The

---

[12] See Table 9.2, column (6).

147

fact that the Canadian cross-rate of return is slightly lower than the domestic rate is the result of our bias towards underestimating rather than overstimating the returns. The second point to observe is that the cross-rates of return are substantially higher than the returns to alternative investments, and this is particularly true for less-developed countries.[13] The third point is that, while in some countries university education might not be profitable when undertaken *per se* (e.g., Germany), university education and subsequent emigration to the United States shows a substantial pecuniary payoff.

Interpreting the cross-rates of return as they stand, one should expect a higher propensity of qualified people to emigrate to the United States from less-developed than from developed countries. This proposition will be tested below. Suffice it to mention at this point the qualification that these rates refer only to the strict pecuniary costs and benefits. Family ties, ignorance of the English language and friction at both ends of the emigration pipeline certainly prevent a clearing mechanism from operating and therefore reduce the effect of the high cross-rates of return.

Another qualification that has to be made at this point is that in a sense these rates represent the polar case in which someone emigrates immediately after graduation and remains in the United States over his lifetime. The cross-rate of return would be much lower than the one indicated in Table 9.1 in the case of someone who decides to emigrate after he has been in the home labour market for a number of years or for someone who decides to return to the home country before the end of his working life. However, the rates we have computed can be interpreted as the expected rates of return for someone who considers the combined graduation—emigration activity.

The determinants of the brain drain

Out of the many "push" and "pull" factors which have been proposed in the literature as affecting the brain drain we will test here the importance of only two: differences in the standard of living as a whole and differences in the lifetime earnings of professional workers in various countries.

---

[13] Using 14 per cent as the alternative criterion rate, only the cross-rate of return estimate for Germany is not well above that mark. See also Table 5.1 above.

148

For this purpose, let us first present the variable to be explained. The Immigration and Naturalization Service of the US Department of Justice publishes annually the number of professional, technical and related workers admitted as immigrants to the United States by country of origin. Column (2) of Table 9.2 shows the average annual number of professional workers who emigrated to the United States in the 1958—69 period.[14] Immigration of professionals has ranged from a few hundred in the case of most countries to well above 1,500 in the case of The Philippines, Germany, Canada and Great Britain. In column (3) of the same table the 1969 immigration figures are singled out. The reason for this is that the United States immigration law has recently been changed, the emphasis of the criterion for admission being shifted from quotas to the skill of the prospective immigrant. It is in this sense that 1969 could be considered a "quota free" year.[15] The difference between the average annual admissions in the earlier period and in 1969 are a sharp decline in the number of immigrants from the developed countries (Canada, Great Britain and Germany) and a corresponding increase from less-developed countries (India and the Philippines in particular). In order to avoid our dependent variable picking up the old quota system, we have decided to work only with the 1969 immigration figures. The implicit assumption is that the 1969 figures will reflect the behaviour of the emigrants rather than the quotas.

Our next task was to standardize the absolute number of emigrants by the size of the country of origin. For this purpose we have chosen the number of students enrolled in higher education in the country of origin. Column (4) of Table 9.2 shows the number of emigrants relative to the size of the university student body in each country. Therefore, although almost the same absolute numbers of professionals emigrated from Brazil and Sweden to the United States in 1969, column (4) of Table 9.2 shows that the Swedes had a much greater propensity to emigrate to the United States than the Brazilians (0.254 and 0.090 per cent, respectively).

One should mention at this point the particular position of Canada. Although Canada appears to have one of the highest emigration rates to the Unites States, this may be due to a statistical

---

[14] For the rate of immigration in particular years see Table H.5 in the appendix.
[15] Numerical limitations to entry, however, do still exist. The difference between the new and the old quota systems is that the previous one specified quotas for each country whereas now the prospective immigrants compete within two hemispheres, the Eastern and the Western.

illusion. The point is that we are dealing with "gross" emigration figures and the figures of Canadians emigrating to the United States may be more "gross" than for any other country. This must be attributed to the geographic proximity of the two countries as well as common language and, to some extent, common culture. Therefore, we have excluded the observation for Canada from the statistical analysis to follow.[16]

Before we test the strength of our hypothesis which relates cross-rates of return to rates of migration, it will be interesting to use more conventional variables. The first set of explanatory variables that one could propose in explaining the brain drain is per capita income and distance.[17] The underlying hypothesis is that emigrants respond to international differences in the standard of living and distance. One would expect the propensity to migrate to be greater the higher the per capita income difference between the country of origin and the United States, and the less the distance between the two countries.

The last two columns of Table 9.2 present the two explanatory variables. United States income has first been adjusted for cost-of-living differences between countries and then divided by the per capita income of the country of origin (column 5). Relative per capita income ranges from 1.1 in the case of Sweden to 26.6 in the case of India. The distance factor was based on a one-way air ticket from the capital of the country of origin to Chicago, USA (column 6).

Multiple regression was used in an attempt to explain the 1969 emigration proportions (column (4) of Table 9.2) by the relative per capita income and distance (columns (5) and (6) of the same Table, respectively). The attempt proved unsuccessful. The statistical analysis showed that the variation of the emigration variable bears absolutely no relation to differences in per capita income and distance. The regression result was:

---

[16] What would be more appropriate, however, would be to consider in the test North America as a whole as the place of destination. Quoting Parai on this point:

"Immigrants arriving in Canada could be considered as having migrated to North America (rather than just Canada), with the subsequent movement across the border being essentially of the nature of interregional migration". Parai (1965), p. 87.

[17] See Watanabe (1969). Language is another variable that could be added as a dummy in the regression. However, the small size of our sample did not justify the use of a third independent variable.

150

TABLE 9.2

PROPORTIONS OF QUALIFIED MANPOWER EMIGRATING TO THE UNITED STATES BY COUNTRY OF ORIGIN AND OTHER FACTORS

Country	Average annual number of emigrants 1958–69	Number of emigrants 1969 M	Number of emigrants 1969 as a percentage of enrolment in higher education M/E_h	Per capita income relative to the U.S. $\frac{Y_1}{Y_0} Q_{10}$	Distance D
(1)	(2)	(3)	(4)	(5)	(6)
Canada	3,646	2,431	1.887	1.34	72
Mexico	559	484	0.315	6.18	107
Venezuela	57	40	0.079	3.84	205
Colombia	562	647	1.729	9.04	189
Brazil	224	157	0.090	12.13	591
Chile	150	116	0.535	4.33	337
Great Britain	3,720	2,513	1.257	1.39	247
Norway	274	134	0.638	1.73	289
Sweden	355	153	0.254	1.14	319
Denmark	214	126	0.848	1.52	289
The Netherlands	396	221	0.344	1.99	269
Belgium	139	73	0.136	1.79	269
Germany	1,737	924	0.442	1.60	289
Greece	340	585	2.225	4.55	401
Israel	205	383	1.434	2.17	457
India	896	2,857	0.243	26.58	631
Japan	241	400	0.038	3.33	485
The Philippines	1,580	7,138	11.032	11.76	545
New Zealand	73	108	0.444	1.36	596

Source: See Psacharopoulos (1971), p. 239.

$$\frac{M}{E_h} = -17.325 + 4.728 \, \frac{Y_1}{Y_0} \, Q_{10} + 0.317 \, D \qquad (9.12)$$
$$\qquad\quad (11.435) \qquad\quad (0.469)$$

with an R^2 of 0.075, where $\frac{M}{E_h}$ is the number of professional, technical and related workers immigrating to the United States (M) as a percentage of student enrolment in higher education in the country of origin (E_h) times 100.0, $\frac{Y_1}{Y_0}$ is the relative per capita income between the United States (Y_1) and the country of origin (Y_0) adjusted for cost of living differences (Q_{10}) and D is the distance between the country of origin and the United States. (Numbers in parentheses are standard errors.)

The probable reason why this experiment was not successful is that, although the response to differences in the standard of living is intuitively plausible, the relative per capita income is not the ideal measure of such differences. Per capita income differences overstate the standard of living differences between qualified people as they reflect the earnings of the unskilled workers as well. To the extent that India has more low paid unskilled workers than the United States, the relative per capita income of the two countries will overstate the Indian university graduates' income position before emigration. Actually, it is very hard to believe that an Indian professional worker will be 26 times better off if he emigrates to the United States.

We turn now to test the strength of the cross-rates of return, estimated above in explaining the brain drain. The underlying hypothesis is that prospective migrants respond to lifetime wage differentials. According to this theory the number of university graduates emigrating to the United States is a function of the cross-rate of return applicable to their country. The higher the rate of return, the higher the propensity of graduates to emigrate. Moreover, domestic enrolment in higher education can be assumed to be a function of the domestic rate of return. The higher the private rate of return within a given country, the higher the propensity of students to enrol in higher education. Under these circumstances it is postulated that the percentage of university graduates who emigrate is positively related to the cross-rate of return and negatively related to the domestic rate of return. For example, assume that the per capita emigration flow of graduates ($\frac{M}{P}$) from any given country is a function of the cross-rate of return (r_c) and that per capita enrolment ($\frac{E_h}{P}$) in the same country is a function of the domestic private rate of return to higher education (r_o). Specifying, for algebraic simplicity, these functions as:

152

$$\frac{M}{P} = a\,r\frac{\alpha}{c} \tag{9.12}$$

$$\frac{E_h}{P} = b\,r\frac{\beta}{o} \tag{9.13}$$

and dividing (9.12) by (9.13) we get

$$\frac{M}{E_h} = \text{const.}\,r_c^{\alpha}\,r_o^{-\beta} \tag{9.14}$$

Equation (9.14) says, in words, that the number of university graduates emigrating to the United States from a given country relative to total enrolment in higher education is positively related to the cross-rate of return and negatively related to the domestic private rate of return to higher education.

We have proceeded to test this theory, namely attempting to explain the same emigration variable (column (4) of Table 9.2) by the domestic and cross-rates of return presented earlier. The statistical test was satisfactory in the sense that about 68 per cent of the variation in the propensities of professionals to emigrate to the Unites States is explained by the variation in the domestic and cross-rates of return. Equation (9.14) was fitted and the regression result was:

$$\log\frac{M}{E_h} = 0.488 + 1.563^{**}\log r_c - 1.072^{**}\log r_o, R^2 = 0.685$$
$$(0.521) \qquad\quad (0.391)$$

The elasticities of the brain drain with respect to the cross and domestic rates of return have the expected signs (positive and negative, respectively) and moreover they are statistically significant.

Although the domestic and cross-rates of return seem to conform to our theory, the test is by no means conclusive. The major limitation is the small number of observations on which it is based. Another limitation is the nature of the dependent variable which represents actual emigration figures. A more correct measure for testing the behaviour of potential migrants would be the number of applicants for United States visas. Furthermore, the measure by which we have standardized the number of emigrants from different countries is not ideal. One should have used the number of higher education graduates rather than enrolment as we did. However, even with these data limitations, it is clear that movements of highly trained manpower are closely linked to lifetime earnings differentials between the country of origin and the country of destination.

Appendix A. The Sensitivity of Rate of Return Estimates to the Shape of the Age-earnings Profile

A common short-cut assumption in some of the rate of return studies we have examined is the adoption of horizontal age—earnings (or cost) profiles. Although this short-cut estimation method has been criticized in principle, no one has shown to what extent the "flat" net-benefits assumption affects the rate of return. In the following, we take an actual net-benefits profile and compute a series of rates of return based on alternative assumptions about the shape of the profile. These sensitivity tests will give us some idea of the magnitude of the bias involved when such assumptions are made.

The net-benefits profile in the following Table refers to university graduates in Canada. The first four years represent the costs of study whereas the rest represent excess earnings (over the earnings of secondary school graduates).

The rate of return estimated on the basis of the above data is equal to 19.7 per cent. We will denote this as the *real* rate of return, because it is based on the actual (real) shape of the net benefits profile.

Shortcut variations for the computation of the rate of return may involve the following:

(a) *Cost side:* Assumption that the annual university costs are equal to the four year average, i.e. $1,852 per year in our case.

(b) *Benefits side:*

(i) Assumption that the annual earnings are equal to the lifetime average earnings. In our case the resulting constant lifetime differential would be $3,425 per year.

(ii) Assumption that the annual earnings are equal to the earnings of the 35—44-year-old. In our case the differential according to this assumption would be $4,040.

Table A.2 presents the rates of return calculated on the basis of various combinations of the above assumptions.

TABLE A.1

AN ACTUAL NET AGE—EARNINGS PROFILE: HIGHER EDUCATION OVER SECONDARY SCHOOL GRADUATES, CANADA 1961 (Canadian dollars)

Age	Net benefits	Average of values in brackets
19	−1,493	
20	−1,526	
21	−2,022	−1,852
22	−2,366	
23	447	
24	694	
25—34	2,117	
35—44	4,040	3,425
45—54	4,323	
55—64	3,798	

Source: Podoluk (1965), p. 61.

TABLE A.2

RATE OF RETURN ESTIMATES ACCORDING TO ALTERNATIVE ASSUMPTIONS (per cent)

Benefits	Costs	
	Real	Average
Real	19.7	19.2
Average	31.0	30.0
As of 35—44	35.0	35.5

Source: Table A.1.

The estimated rates of return in this table range from 19.2 per cent to 35.5 per cent (the real rate being 19.7 per cent).

The first point to observe is that the assumption which averages the cost side does not have a significant effect on the rate of return. The true rate was underestimated by only 0.5 per cent. Had the real rate been lower, say around 10 per cent, such a bias could be considered negligible.

The second point to observe is that the use of average annual earnings grossly overestimates the rate of return. The estimate changes by more than 50 per cent when horizontal age-earnings profiles are assumed. This overestimate is due to the neglect of the two initial positive differentials which are low relative to the others and which play a key role in the discounting. Had we taken into account the real differentials at the ages of 23 and 24 while assuming average earnings thereafter (i.e., from 25 to 64), the rate of return estimate would have come to 24.0 per cent,[1] which is much closer to the real value.

By way of summary, averaging on the cost side of a rate of return calculation is not likely to affect the rate appreciably. Averaging on the benefits side, however, is likely to lead to a gross overestimate.

---

[1] This particular estimate was obtained on the assumption of average costs.

Appendix B. Comparative Information on the Contents of Existing Profitability Studies

This appendix shows (by the mark "x") what data are included in the original profitability studies reviewed in this book.

COUNTRY	United States					Canada		Puerto Rico
Author	Becker (1964)	Hansen (1963)	Hanoch (1967)	Lassiter (1966)	Hines et al (1970)	Wilkinson (1966)	Podoluk (1965)	Carnoy (1970)
Year	1961	1949	1959	1949,1959	1959	1961	1961	1959
Sample size			57,000		107,000		1,280,596	
EARNINGS DATA								
Census	x	x	x	x	x	x	x	x
Sample of total population								
Urban only								
Government pay scales								
Given industry or profession								
By subject								
Shadow wages								
PROFITABILITY TYPE								
Social	x	x			x			x
Private	x	x	x	x	x	x	x	x
Marginal	x	x	x	x	x	x	x	x
Average		x	x		x		x	
Present values						x	x	x
SEX								
Males and females		x			x			
Males separately	x		x	x	x	x	x	x
Females separately					x			x
ADJUSTMENTS								
Regression analysis			x					
α coefficient	x							
Private is after tax	x	x			x	x		
Unemployment	x	x	x		x	x	x	
Wastage		x			x			x
Growth	x	x			x			
Mortality	x	x			x			x

159

COUNTRY	Mexico	Venezuela	Colombia		Chile		Brazil	
Author	Carnoy (1967b)	Shoup (1959)	Schultz (1968)	Selowsky (1968)	Selowsky (1967)	Harberger & Selowsky (1966)	Hewlett (1970)	Castro (1970)
Year	1963	1957	1965	1966	1964	1959	1962	
Sample size	4,000		1,000	10,715				
EARNINGS DATA								
Census								
Sample of total population								
Urban only	x		x	x	x	x	x	x
Government pay scales								
Given industry or profession								
By subject								
Shadow wages				x				x
PROFITABILITY TYPE								
Social	x	x	x	x	x	x	x	x
Private	x		x				x	x
Marginal	x	x	x	x	x	x		x
Average	x		x		x			
Present values	x		x				x	x
SEX								
Males and females			x	x	x	x	x	
Males separately	x	x	x	x				
Females separately	x	x	x					
ADJUSTMENTS								
Regression	x		x					
α coefficient								
Private is after tax	x			x				
Unemployment			x	x				
Wastage				x				
Growth								
Mortality								

COUNTRY	Brazil (contd.)		Great Britain					
Author	Rogers III (1969)	Lerner (1970)	Blaug (1965)	Blaug et al (1967)	Richardson (1969)	Layard et al (1971)	Selby Smith (1970)	Morris and Ziderman (1971)
Year	1960	1960	1964	1965	1965,1968	1966	1965/66	1968
Sample size		4,700	6,500	2,800	19,947	25,884	17,500	2,500
EARNINGS DATA								
Census								
Sample of total polation		x	x					x
Urban only								
Government pay scales								
Given industry or profess.on				x	x	x	x	
By subject					x			
Shadow wages								
PROFITABILITY TYPE								
Social	x		x	x	x	x	x	x
Private	x	x	x	x	x	x		
Marginal	x		x	x	x	x	x	x
Average			x	x	x			x
Present values				x	x		x	x
SEX								
Males and females								
Males separately			x	x	x	x	x	x
Females separately								x
ADJUSTMENTS								
Regression analysis		x	x			x		
α coefficient			x			x		
Private is after tax	x		x	x	x		x	x
Unemployment								
Wastage					x	x	x	x
Growth				x		x		x
Mortality	x						x	x

COUNTRY	Norway	Sweden	Denmark	The Netherlands	Belgium	Germany	Greece	Greece
Author	Aarrestad (1969)	Magnusson (1970)	Hansen (1966)	De Wolff and Ruiter (1968)	Desayere (1969)	Schmidt (1967)	Leibenstein (1967)	Psacharopoulos (1970)
Year	1966	1967	1964	1965	1967	1964	1960,1964	1960
Sample size		5,000				124,000	2,600+	2,600+
EARNINGS DATA								
Census						x		
Sample of total population		x						x
Urban only			x				x	
Government pay scales							x	
Given industry or profession	x	x	x	x	x			
By subject	x	x	x		x			
Shadow wages								x
PROFITABILITY TYPE								
Social	x	x	x	x	x		x	x
Private	x	x	x	x		x	x	
Marginal	x	x	x	x	x	x	x	x
Average							x	
Present values	x	x	x	x	x		x	
SEX								
Males and females	x	x						
Males separately		x	x	x	x	x	x	x
Females separately						x	x	
ADJUSTMENTS								
Regression analysis								
α coefficient				x				
Private is after tax	x	x	x			x	x	x
Unemployment				x	x	x		
Wastage			x	x	x			
Growth				x		x	x	
Mortality	x							

COUNTRY	Turkey	Israel	India			Malaysia	Singapore	The Philippines
Author	Krueger (1971)	Klinov-Malul (1966)	Harberger (1965)	Nalla Gounden (1967)	Blaug et al (1969)	Hoerr (1970)	Clark and Fong (1970)	Williamson & Devoretz (1967)
Year	1968	1957–58	1957	1960	1960	1967	1966	1966
Sample size		3,000	2,895	8,650	28,650	30,000		1,063
EARNINGS DATA								
Census								
Sample of total population	x	x				x	x	
Urban only	x		x	x	x			x
Government pay scales								
Given industry or profession		x	x	x	x			
By subject								
Shadow wages						x		
PROFITABILITY TYPE								
Social	x	x	x	x	x	x	x	x
Private	x	x			x	x	x	x
Marginal	x	x	x	x	x	x	x	x
Average			x	x	x	x		
Present values		x				x	x	x
SEX								
Males and females	x					x		
Males separately		x	x	x	x	x	x	x
Females separately						x	x	
ADJUSTMENTS								
Regression analysis α coefficient				x				
Private is after tax		x			x	x	x	
Unemployment					x	x	x	
Wastage		x			x	x		
Growth		x			x			
Mortality								x

163

	Japan	S. Korea		Thailand	Hawaii	Nigeria		Ghana
COUNTRY	Japan	S. Korea	Thailand	Hawaii	Nigeria		Ghana	
Author	Bowman (1970)	Danielsen and Okachi (1971)	Kim (1968)	Blaug (1971)	Psacharopoulos (1969b)	Bowles (1967)	Hinchliffe (1969)	Hinchliffe (1969)
Year	1961	1966	1967	1970	1959	1965	1966	1967
Sample size				5,000				
EARNINGS DATA								
Census		x			x			
Sample of total population								
Urban only				x				
Government pay scales						x	x	x
Given industry or profession	x		x			x	x	x
By subject								
Shadow wages								
PROFITABILITY TYPE								
Social	x		x	x	x	x	x	x
Private	x	x		x	x			
Marginal	x	x	x		x	x	x	x
Average		x	x	x	x			
Present values						x		
SEX								
Males and females	x		x	x	x	x	x	x
Males separately		x						
Females separately								
ADJUSTMENTS								
Regression analysis				x				
α coefficient						x		
Private is after tax					x			
Unemployment					x			
Wastage				x	x	x	x	x
Growth				x		x	x	x
Mortality				x				

COUNTRY	Kenya		Uganda	N. Rhodesia	Neu Zealend
Author	Rogers (1972)	Thias and Carnoy (1969)	Smyth and Bennett (1967)	Baldwin (1966)	Ogilvy (1968)
Year	1967	1968	1965	1960	1963
Sample size		4,850			
EARNINGS DATA					
Census					
Sample of total population					
Urban only	x	x	x	x	x
Government pay scales					
Given industry or profession					
By subject					
Shadow wages					
PROFITABILITY TYPE					
Social		x	x	x	x
Private	x	x	x	x	x
Marginal	x	x	x	x	x
Average	x	x	x	x	
Present values			x	x	
SEX					
Males and females	x		x	x	x
Males separately		x			
Females separately		x			
ADJUSTMENTS					
Regression analysis		x			
α coefficient	x				x
Private is after tax		x			x
Unemployment		x			
Wastage		x	x		
Growth		x			
Mortality		x			

Appendix C. Sources of Rate of Return Estimates Used in this Study

This appendix gives the sources and methods of computation of the rate of return estimates by educational level appearing in Table 4.1 in the text.

United States

Hines *et al.* (1970), Table 2. Primary refers to 8 over 0, secondary to 12 over 8 years and higher to 16 over 12 years of schooling. Rates are for white males and are unadjusted for factors other than education and age.

Canada

Podoluk (1965), pp. 61—2. Secondary refers to 4—5 years of schooling. Higher refers to a university degree. We have estimated the social rates of return in this country according to the social-to-private relationship of the corresponding rates in the United States.

Puerto Rico

Carnoy (1970), Tables 2b and 4b. Primary refers to the average of the returns up to 5.5 years of schooling. Secondary refers to the average of the returns for 5.5 to 12 years of schooling. Higher refers to 13—16 years of schooling. Rates are for urban males, not corrected for labour force participation or growth.

Mexico

Carnoy (1967b), pp. 366—7. Primary refers to up to 6 years of schooling, secondary to 7—11 years and higher to 12—16 years. Private rates are weighted averages of the two rates within each cycle. The weights were equal to the implicit ones used by Carnoy in a similar calculation for the derivation of the social rates (Carnoy, 1967b, p. 367). Rates are for urban males and are unadjusted.

Venezuela

Shoup (1959), pp. 407—9. Primary refers to 6 years of schooling, secondary to 5 years and university to 4 years. The social rate of return for primary is the lower of the two estimates provided and relates to urban workers only. We have estimated private returns based on the earnings data in Shoup and assuming zero direct costs.

Colombia

Selowsky (1968), p. 54b. Primary refers to the 5th year of primary over illiterates, secondary to the 6th year bachillerato over primary, and higher to the 5th year of university over secondary. Rates are for men and women before any adjustment. We have calculated the private rates of return based on the earnings data in Selowsky (1968), tables XX-A and XXI-A.

Chile

Harberger and Selowsky (1966), p. 29. Secondary education excludes "special".

Brazil

Hewlett (1970), pp. 57—8. Secondary refers to the average rates for the two cycles (ginasio and secundario). Higher is for university over the completion of secundario (16 over 12 years of schooling).

Great Britain

Layard *et al.* (1971), pp. 138, 140. Secondary refers to "A" level over "O" level, and higher to first degree over "A" level. Rates are unadjusted for growth, wastage and ability.

Norway

Aarrestad (1969), tables 6 and 7 for private rates, and tables 13 and 14 for social rates. Secondary refers to the average rate for graduates in insurance, banking and local authority work. Higher refers to the average rate earned in eight occupations in both the public and private sectors.

Sweden

Magnusson (1970), p. 5.13. Social secondary refers to holders of the general certificate. The rates for higher education are averages of the return to legal professionals, social scientists, civil engineers, business administrators, natural scientists and physicians in private and State enterprises.

Denmark

Hansen (1966), p. 253. Rates refer to 3 years of senior secondary plus higher education and are cost weighted averages for economists, lawyers, secondary school teachers, medical doctors, civil engineers, technical college graduates and primary school teachers. Rates are unadjusted for wastage.

The Netherlands

DeWolff and Ruiter (1968), p. 135. Rates are averages for employees in private industry and Government. Higher refers to social and technical science at university level over general secondary school and the secondary rate refers to 5—6 years of general secondary schooling. Rates are adjusted for mortality and labour force participation.

168

Belgium

Desaeyere (1969), tables 13, 24 and 25. We have estimated social rates of return to applied science, pure science, law, economics, medicine and architecture based on the costs and earnings from the above tables. The cost—weighted average is 9.3. The private rate is for applied science only.

Germany

Schmidt and Baumgarten, (1967), p. 174. The rate of return is for male university graduates, unadjusted for growth.

Greece

Leibenstein, (1967), p. 13. Secondary refers to 12 over 6 years of schooling and higher to 15 over 12 years of schooling. Rates of return are for males and are unadjusted for growth. Private rates were derived from costs and earnings data as found in the above source (p. 60).

Turkey

Krueger (1971), p. 39. The rate of return for the secondary level refers to secondary general. The observation for Turkey has not been included in the averaging and standard deviation calculations in chapter 4 as it was not in our hands at an early enough date.

Israel

We have estimated rates of return based on the cost and earnings data in Klinov-Malul (1966), pp. 29, 41, 44, 47, 51, 54, and 100—1.

India

Blaug *et al.* (1969), tables 9.1 and 9.2. Primary is over illiteracy. Secondary is the average of the rates for middle over primary and matriculation over middle. Higher refers to first degree over matriculation. Rates are unadjusted for wastage, unemployment and growth.

Malaysia

The rates in Table 4.1 are preliminary findings from Hoerr's (1970) study, and are taken from a private letter. Primary refers to 6 years of schooling, the secondary rate to 12 over 3 years of schooling and the university rate to 16 over 3 years of schooling.

Singapore

Clark and Fong (1970), p. 90. Rates of return refer to unweighted averages for men and women. The observation for Singapore has not been included in the averaging and standard deviation calculations in chapter 4 as it was not in our hands at an early enough date.

The Philippines

De voretz (1969), p. 110. Primary is the average for primary over illiteracy and intermediate over primary. The private rates are the averages for private and public schools.

Japan

Bowman (1970), table 1. Secondary refers to upper secondary only. Higher refers to 4 years of university without "ronin". Social rates are averages for national and private institutions. All rates are unadjusted for bonus. Private rates are based on the "low direct costs" option.

South Korea

Kim (1968), p. 10. Primary refers to "middle school".

Thailand

Blaug (1971). Primary refers to the average of the rates for lower primary and upper primary. Secondary refers to the average returns for lower secondary and upper secondary.

Hawaii

Psacharopoulos (1969b), pp. 28, 30. Primary is 8 over 0 years of schooling, secondary is 12 over 8 years of schooling and higher is 16+ over 12 years of schooling.

Nigeria

Hinchliffe (1969), pp. 192, 201. All rates are for the Western Region. Primary refers to 6 over 0 years of schooling, secondary refers to the cost weighted average rate for secondary modern and secondary grammar. Higher refers to 3 years of university. Rates are unadjusted for unemployment and wastage. Private rates were estimated using private cost assumptions from Calcott (1968).

Ghana

Hinchliffe (1971), table II. The secondary rate is a cost weighted average rate for middle school and grammar school. Rates are unadjusted for wastage and unemployment. Private rates were estimated on the assumption that book fees are the only private direct costs and using earnings data from Hinchliffe (1969), appendix 1.

Kenya

Thias and Carnoy (1969), p. 112. Secondary is the average rate for lower and higher secondary. Rates are for male Africans and are unadjusted for factors other than education and age.

171

Uganda

Smyth and Bennett (1967), p. 319. The rate for secondary school is the cost-weighted average to lower and upper secondary.

Northern Rhodesia

Baldwin (1966), p. 211. The overall rate of return to primary education is the average of the rates for each individual year of primary education derived by interpolation of the net present values for given discount rates.

New Zealand

Ogilvy (1968), p. 100. Secondary refers to the completion of the "school certificate". Higher refers to a Bachelor's degree. Rates are for males and females.

Appendix D. Unit Social Costs by Educational Level

The purpose of this appendix is to provide relative unit costs by level of schooling. This information provides the basis for the construction of the overall social rate of return weights and the educational capital stock variable. All values are converted into U.S. dollars at the official exchange rate for the year to which they refer. In view of wide exchange-rate fluctuations in some countries, the exchange values used in this study are also presented.

TABLE D.1

SOCIAL UNIT COSTS PER STUDENT YEAR BY EDUCATIONAL LEVEL IN NATIONAL CURRENCIES

| Country | Educational level | | | | | |
| | Primary | | Secondary | | Higher | |
	Direct	Foregone	Direct	Foregone	Direct	Foregone
United States	582	31	670	1,112	2,128	3,692
Puerto Rico	112	..	174	116	1,294	..
Mexico	414	545	2,082	3,412	3,720	6,875
Venezuela	400	..	1,200	5,000	5,000	12,000
Colombia	756	150	2,017	3,150	13,564	15,120
Chile	107	..	159	314	853	807
Brazil (US $)	50	..	145	..	900	..
Great Britain	60	..	173	455	964	766
Norway	..	..	3,000	11,351	6,850	16,899
Denmark	..	..	..	..	18,600	29,300
The Netherlands	..	..	..	3,050[a]	..	7,680[a]
Belgium	..	..	..	..	243,000	111,000
Israel	155	..	412	1,255	2,600	1,379
India	65	69	330	424	1,142	1,017
Malaysia	341	..	649	407	4,420	1,070
The Philippines	..	115[a]	..	614[a]	..	1,794[a]
S. Korea	15,710	..	38,006	86,700	85,894	139,800
Hawaii	272	..	480	..	1,034	..
Nigeria	9	10	65	95	900	345
Ghana	9	4	55.5	93	1,068	342
Kenya	8.2	..	97	75	1,315	393
Uganda	8.8	..	127.8	95	1,035	541
N. Rhodesia	6.0	14.1	..	..	..	..
New Zealand	87.0	..	199	370	620	631

Note: a includes direct costs.

173

Source:
United States: Direct costs and foregone earnings are from Hines *et al.* (1970), p. 339 and are for white males only. Direct cost is the difference between social and private cost, the latter being equal to foregone earnings. The annual costs were derived by dividing total cost by the number of years of schooling in each cycle.

Puerto Rico: Direct costs are from Carnoy (1970), pp. 20—1 and are for urban pupils in 1961—2. Secondary costs are the average annual costs in junior and senior high school. Foregone earnings are from Carnoy (1967b), Table III and for the secondary level they are computed by averaging those for the 5th to the 12th grade. No foregone earnings for university students are available.

Mexico: Direct costs from Carnoy (1967b) table 5. Foregone earnings from the same source, table 4. Annual foregone earnings at primary level are averages of those corresponding to 2 to 6 years, at secondary level 7 to 11 years and university 12 to $17\frac{1}{2}$ years.

Venezuela: Direct costs from Shoup (1959), table XV-2 and foregone earnings from same source table XV-1.

Colombia: Direct costs from Selowsky (1968), pp. 15, 17 and 19. Foregone earnings based on hourly wages for males and females (p. 91) grossed up by number of hours worked per week by educational level (p. 24) and multiplied by 50 to obtain annual foregone earnings.

Chile: Direct costs and foregone earnings from Harberger and Selowsky (1966), table 3.

Brazil: Direct costs from Hewlett (1970), p. 42. Earnings profiles for foregone earnings could possibly be derived from this study (pp. 47, 49).

Great Britain: Direct costs from Layard *et al.* (1971) appendix E, table E3 and p. 342. Foregone earnings from Appendix D. Both types of estimates are for science and engineering students only.

Norway: Direct costs from Aarrestad (1969), table 12. The figure for secondary school corresponds to *Gymnas* or senior secondary school. For higher education, the direct cost figure is the average of the arts and science faculties. Foregone earnings are from table 2 and at the secondary level refer to insurance workers and at the higher educational level to local authority workers.

Denmark: Direct costs and foregone earnings from Hansen (1966), table 1. These are the average figures from seven fields of higher education.

The Netherlands: Total annual costs for general secondary school and university from De Wolff and Ruiter (1968), p. 128. University costs are the average for science and social science courses.

Belgium: Direct costs and foregone earnings are from Desaeyere (1969), table 24. These are the average figures for pure and applied science, law and economics.

Israel: Direct costs were taken from Klinov-Malul (1966), tables 5-4, 5-7, 5-10 and foregone earnings from the same source, tables 3-7, 4-8 and A-14.

India: Direct costs from Blaug *et al.* (1969), table 8-12. Foregone earnings from same source table 7-1. Monthly earnings were grossed up to annual earnings.

South Korea: Direct costs for primary, high school and college are from Kim (1968), table 1 and they include in-school and out-of-school expenses. Foregone earnings from table III of same source.

Hawaii: Direct costs from Psacharopoulos (1969b), pp. 22, 24.

174

Nigeria: Direct costs and foregone earnings from Hinchliffe (1969) p. 192 and appendix, respectively. Secondary refers only to first stage of secondary grammar school.

Ghana: Direct costs and foregone earnings from Hinchliffe (1969), p. 207 and appendix, respectively. Again, secondary refers only to first stage of secondary grammar school.

Kenya: Direct costs from Thias and Carnoy (1969), table 6.2. Foregone earnings from same source, table 6.1. Secondary refers to first stage of secondary grammar school.

Uganda: Direct costs and foregone earnings are from Smyth and Bennett (1967), table III.

N. Rhodesia: Direct costs and earnings foregone are from Baldwin (1966), table 8-11 and refer only to the average from six years of primary school.

New Zealand: At the primary level, costs are for state primary schools as shown in Ogilvy (1968), p. 57. At the state secondary level, total annual cost was £ 569 and it is stated that 65 per cent of total costs are foregone earnings (p. 61). At university level, foregone earnings are shown to be £ 631, and total costs £ 1,250 (pp. 69—70).

Malaysia: Direct costs and foregone earnings from Hoerr (1970), table 2. The figures for secondary education are averages for "lower secondary" Forms III and IV and Higher School Certificate.

The Philippines: The basic cost data is from Devoretz (1969), table 1. His estimates of total cost were divided at the primary level by 6 years, at the secondary level by 4 years and at the higher level by 5 years to derive cost per student year.

175

TABLE D.2

VALUE OF 1 US $ IN NATIONAL CURRENCIES

Country	Year	Value	
Mexico	1963	12.49	pesos
Venezuela	1957	3.35	bolivars
Colombia	1966	13.5	pesos
Chile	1959	1.053	escudos
Brazil	1962	475.0	cruzeiros
Great Britain	1966	0.358	pounds
Norway	1966	7.14	krones
Sweden	1967	5.165	krones
Denmark	1964	6.9	krones
The Netherlands	1965	3.61	guilders
Belgium	1966	49.63	francs
Germany	1964	3.98	marks
Greece	1964	30.0	drachmas
Israel	1957	1.8	IL
India	1960	4.77	rupees
Malaysia	1967	3.07	$ M
The Philippines	1964	3.91	pesos
Japan	1962	358	yen
S. Korea	1967	274	wan
Thailand	1970	20.8	baht
Nigeria	1966	0.357	£ N
Ghana	1966	0.357	£ G
Kenya	1968	0.357	£ K
Uganda	1966	0.357	£ U
Rhodesia	1960	0.357	£ R
New Zealand	1966	0.361	£ NZ

Source: United Nations *Statistical Yearbook* (respective years)

176

SOCIAL UNIT COSTS PER STUDENT YEAR BY EDUCATIONAL LEVEL AND COUNTRY (US $)

Country	Primary			Secondary			Higher		
	Direct	Foregone	Total	Direct	Foregone	Total	Direct	Foregone	Total
United States	582	31	613	670	1,112	1,782	2,128	3,692	5,820
Puerto Rico	112	..	112	174	116	290	1,294	..	..
Mexico	33	44	77	167	273	440	298	550	848
Venezuela	120	..	120	360	1,500	1,860	1,500	3,600	5,100
Colombia	56	11	67	149	233	382	1,004	1,119	2,123
Chile	102	..	102	151	298	449	810	767	1,577
Brazil	50	..	50	145	..	..	900	..	..
Great Britain	167	..	167	483	1,269	1,752	2,690	2,137	4,827
Norway	..	..	..	420	1,589	2,009	959	2,366	3,325
Denmark	..	..	..	..	..	..	2,695	4,246	6,941
The Netherlands	..	..	..	..	..	854	..	..	2,150
Belgium	..	..	..	..	..	..	4,860	2,220	7,080
Israel	86	..	86	229	697	926	1,444	766	2,210
India	14	14	28	69	89	158	240	214	454
Malaysia	111	..	111	212	133	345	1,441	349	1,790
The Philippines	..	..	29	..	..	157	..	..	459
S. Korea	58	..	58	141	321	462	318	517	835
Hawaii	272	..	272	480	..	..	1,034	..	..
Nigeria	25	28	53	182	266	448	2,520	966	3,486
Ghana	25	11	36	157	260	417	2,991	958	3,949
Kenya	22	..	22	271	210	481	3,682	1,100	4,782
Uganda	25	..	25	358	266	624	2,898	1,515	4,413
N. Rhodesia	17	39	56	..	..	..	..	..	..
New Zealand	241	..	241	551	1,025	1,576	1,717	1,748	3,465

Source: Tables D.1 and D.2.

Appendix E. Estimation of Human and Physical Capital per Member of the Labour Force

Tables E.1 and E.2 below, present the construction of the human and physical capital indices used in the analysis in Chapter 6. The human capital index was constructed by multiplying the number of persons in the labour force with a given educational level by the number of years of schooling corresponding to that level, times the annual social cost of schooling at the same level. The physical capital index was constructed in two steps. First, investment was summed over 6 years and divided by the one year lagged increase of output in order to calculate the incremental capital-output ratio (ICOR). Next, the ICOR was multiplied by Gross National Product so as to arrive at an estimate of the stock of physical capital used in the economy.

In Chapter 6 the measure of the stock of educational capital per member of the labour force as an indicator of the level of educational development was criticized on the basis that components of total cost figures used have differences in income levels built in. Thus, variations in the stock of educational capital which undoubtedly exist will be over-inflated by this procedure. In the analysis contained in Chapter 6, we were dealing with absolute numbers and this problem could not be side stepped, but it is possible to construct indices which whilst retaining the essence of the former measure, remove the "income" effect. This can be done first by deflating the stock of educational capital by the level of G.N.P. for 1963 in each country. Column (3) of Table E.3 presents the results of these computations and while there are a few surprises, for example the relatively poor showing of Israel and Ghana and the high placing of Korea, the rankings generally follow the pattern of countries ranked by educational capital per member of the labour force. Even after completely allowing for income differences, differences in educational capital are still very wide.

A second variation on the initial index was made by extracting the individual cost element almost completely. The aim here was to construct an index of educational development by applying a constant set of weights to the stocks of primary secondary and higher educated members of the labour force in each country. But rather than using an arbitrary set of weights as Harbison and Myers did, the three weights reflect the average proportional costs of each level of education in the fourteen countries under analysis. The data was taken from Appendix Table D.3. On average, each secondary school year costs 6.3 times one primary school year and the figure for higher education is 21.3. The weights applied therefore were:

1.0 for each year of primary education.
6.3 for each year of secondary education.
21.3 for each year of higher education.

Applying these weights to the stocks of manpower with the appropriate level of education and dividing by the total labour force produces an educational index which reflects the educational composition of the labour force, assuming that the same amount of resources are diverted to each particular year of education in all countries. Column (4) of Table E.3 presents the results of these computations. It is interesting to note that this index, which is clearly the most "physical" as opposed to "economic" of the three measures bears a close similarity to the Harbison—Myers index to the extent that the rank correlation for the thirteen countries which appear in both indices (The Philippines is missing from the Harbison—Myers index) is 0.85.[1]

Table E.3 presents the results of all three sets of computations made to measure levels of educational development together with the index numbers computed by Harbison and Myers.

---

[1] The Harbison—Myers index used enrolments only at the secondary and tertiary levels with a weighting ratio of 1 : 5.

TABLE E.1

EDUCATIONAL CAPITAL PER MEMBER OF THE LABOUR FORCE, BY COUNTRY

Country	Educational capital (million US $) K_H	Labour force (thousands) L	Educational capital per member of the labour force (US $) $\dfrac{K_H}{L}$
(1)	(2)	(3)	(4)
United States	836,234	68,007	12,296
New Zealand	1,038	1,026	5,745
Great Britain	86,487	23,824	3,630
Israel	1,569	710	2,210
Greece	1,551	3,663	423
Mexico	4,465	10,890	410
Chile	2,094	2,389	877
The Philippines	2,725	9,395	290
Ghana	464	2,560	181
S. Korea	2,831	7,028	403
Kenya	357	2,300	157
Nigeria	1,544	17,500	88
Uganda	243	2,722	88
India	12,458	188,676	66

Source: Col. (2): Labour force distribution from Table F.1.

Costs: all countries except Greece from Table D.3. Greece from Leibenstein (1967), Appendix 1, Table 2.

Col. (3): from Table E.2, Col. (5). Col. (4) = Col. (2) : Col. (3).

180

TABLE E.2

PHYSICAL CAPITAL PER MEMBER OF THE LABOUR FORCE BY COUNTRY

Country	Incremental capital-output ratio	Gross National Product, 1963 (in million US $)	Physical capital (in million US $)	Labour force (in thousands)	Physical capital labour force (in US $)
	ICOR	Y	K_M	L	$\dfrac{K_M}{L}$
(1)	(2)	(3)	(4)	(5)	(6)
United States	3.18	599,705	1,907,301	68,007	28,045
Norway	4.33	6,931	30,008	1,407	21,328
Canada	3.51	38,112	133,853	6,472	20,682
New Zealand	3.99	4,446	17,719	1,026	17,270
Great Britain	3.40	86,227	293,517	23,824	12,320
The Netherlands	2.88	17,210	49,523	4,169	11,879
Israel	3.80	2,598	9,885	710	13,922
Greece	3.12	4,703	14,664	3,663	4,003
Japan	3.38	65,633	221,839	43,687	5,078
Mexico	2.86	15,376	43,999	10,890	4,040
Chile	3.87	2,685	10,403	2,389	4,423
Colombia	4.59	5,354	24,563	4,907	5,006
The Philippines	4.21	7,691	32,376	9,395	3,446
Ghana	1.90	1,667	3,163	2,560	1,236
S. Korea	1.81	3,904	7,084	7,028	1,008
Kenya	2.36	898	2,117	2,300	920
Nigeria	2.96	4,120	12,191	17,500	697
Uganda	2.89	509	1,468	2,722	539
India	5.46	41,325	225,809	188,676	1,197
Brazil	4.48	20,443	91,585	17,117	5,331
Turkey	2.43	7,669	18,636	12,993	1,434

Source: Col. (2), (3): Investment and GNP from United Nations, *Yearbook of National Accounts Statistics* (1969). For the construction of ICOR see Chapter 6.
Col. (4): Column (2) x Column (3).
Col. (5): United States, Norway, Canada, Great Britain, The Netherlands, Israel, Greece, Japan, Chile, The Philippines, Ghana, Korea and India from OECD (1969). Nigeria: Education and World Affairs (1967); Mexico: Selowsky (1967); New Zealand: New Zealand Department of Statistics (1969), Vol. IV; Kenya: Government of Kenya (1965); Uganda and Brazil: *United Nations Demographic Yearbook* (1964). Refers to population 16 years and more; Colombia: International Labour Office (1968); Turkey: Krueger (1971).
Col. (6) = Col. (4) : Col. (5).

181

TABLE E.3

ALTERNATIVE MEASURES OF EDUCATIONAL DEVELOPMENT, BY COUNTRY

Country	Educational capital per member of the labour force (US $)	Educational capital deflated by Gross National Product	Constant cost weighted index	Harbison—Myers composite index
(1)	(2)	(3)	(4)	(5)
United States	12,296	1.39	34.1	261.3
New Zealand	5,745	2.33	24.5	147.3
Great Britain	3,630	1.00	27.2	121.6
Israel	2,210	0.60	26.6	84.9
Greece	423	0.33	11.2	48.5
Mexico	410	0.29	6.5	33.0
Chile	877	0.78	10.7	51.2
The Philippines	290	0.35	11.8	...
Ghana	181	0.28	2.5	23.1
S. Korea	403	0.72	7.7	55.0
Kenya	157	0.40	2.5	4.7
Uganda	88	0.59	1.7	5.4
Nigeria	88	0.34	1.2	4.9
India	66	0.30	1.8	35.2

Source: Col. (2): Table E.1
Col. (3) = Col. (2): GNP from Table E.2.
Col. (4): Based on Table F.1, and the following weights: primary 1.0, secondary 6.3 and higher 21.3, taken from Table D.3.
Col. (5): Harbison and Myers (1964), p. 33.

182

Appendix F. The Distribution of the Labour Force by Educational Level and Relative Wages

Data on the distribution of the labour force by years or levels of schooling are still scanty in many countries. A recent OECD (1969) publication has covered most of the ground in this respect, but the long list of sources in Table F.1 emphasizes the difficulty one still faces to raise such data in some countries. Relative wage data (Table F.2) were derived from the original rate of return studies.

TABLE F.1

DISTRIBUTION OF THE LABOUR FORCE BY EDUCATIONAL LEVEL AND COUNTRY

Country	Number of persons employed (thousands)					Percentage			
	L_o	L_p	L_s	L_h	L	L_o	L_p	L_s	L_h
United States	..	24,214	30,735	13,058	68,007	..	35.6	45.2	19.2
Canada	..	2,621	3,283	568	6,472	..	40.5	50.7	8.9
Mexico	4,143	5,682	777	286	10,890	38.0	52.2	7.1	2.6
Colombia	623	3,174	996	108	4,907	12.7	64.7	20.3	2.2
Chile	445	1,350	538	56	2,389	18.6	56.5	22.5	2.3
Great Britain	..	13,005	8,343	2,476	23,824	..	54.6	35.0	10.4
Norway	..	913	436	57	1,407	..	64.9	31.0	4.1
The Netherlands	..	2,376	1,334	459	4,169	..	57.0	32.0	11.0
Greece	..	3,269	290	105	3,663	..	89.2	7.9	2.9
Israel	63	360	213	74	710	8.9	50.7	30.0	10.4
India	169,663	13,750	4,068	1,147	188,676	90.0	7.3	2.2	0.6
The Philippines	1,588	5,900	1,325	582	9,395	16.9	62.8	14.1	6.3
Japan	..	30,748	10,039	2,900	43,687	..	70.4	23.0	6.6
S. Korea	3,156	2,764	942	166	7,028	44.9	39.3	13.4	2.4
Nigeria	15,750	1,488	228	33	17,500	90.0	8.5	1.3	0.2
Ghana	2,089	423	39	9	2,560	81.6	16.5	1.5	0.3
Kenya	1,766	465	63	6	2,300	76.8	20.2	2.7	0.3
Uganda	1,811	840	68	3	2,722	66.5	30.9	2.5	0.1
Turkey	1,540	4,974	1,145	329	7,988	19.3	62.2	14.3	4.1
Brazil	8,253	8,309	467	88	17,117	48.2	48.5	2.7	0.5

Source: Chile, Greece, Israel, The Philippines, Canada, India, Japan, Korea and Ghana: OECD (1969).

United States:OECD (1969) and Miller (1960).

Mexico: Selowsky (1967), p. 30.

Great Britain: Moreh (1971), tables 1b and II, preliminary results.

Colombia: Total labour force from ILO (1968). Percentage distribution from Selowsky (1968) p. 42a.

Norway: OECD (1969) p. 73. Of the joint categories "Not Completed Secondary Education" and "Completed Secondary General Education" it was assumed that the total was distributed between them in a ratio of 3 : 1.

The Netherlands: Denison (1967) p. 393. Higher education category refers to those with 13 years + of education.

Nigeria: The actual figures are approximations based on 1963 stocks of secondary and higher educated manpower from Nigeria National Manpower Board (1964) p. 23, from the National Development Plan 1971—4 and educational output flows from Education and World Affairs (1967) Table IV-5.

Kenya: Government of Kenya (1965), pp. 5, 10.

Uganda: United Nations Demographic Yearbook (1964), Jolly (1975) and Uganda Manpower Planning Division (1967). Data refer to African population only.

Turkey: Krueger (1971), p. 18.

Brazil: Instituto Brasileiro de Estatistica (1960), vol. I.

Notes: (1) L_O category in Chile and Korea includes labour with "unknown" educational qualifications. (2) In Kenya, the assumption made is that all wage earners have had some primary education at least. (3) Data on Turkey refer to males only.

184

AVERAGE ANNUAL WAGES BY EDUCATIONAL LEVEL AND COUNTRY

Country		Absolute wages (US $)				Relative wages		
	W_o	W_p	W_s	W_h	W_p/W_o	W_s/W_p	W_h/W_s
United States	..	3,769	5,567	9,206	..	1.48	1,65
Canada	..	3,484	5,022	9,209	..	1.44	1.83
Mexico	572	1,898	2,663	5,993	3.32	1.40	2.25
Colombia	372	1,117	3,351	5,027	3.00	3.00	1.50
Chile	342	570	1,265	2,530	1.67	2.22	2.00
Great Britain	..	2,660	3,858	6,224	..	1.45	1.61
Norway	..	3,012	4,217	6,433	..	1.40	1.53
The Netherlands	..	3,044	4,263	6,944	..	1.29	1.74
Greece	..	968	1,344	2,128	..	1.39	1.58
Israel	699	1,120	1,519	2,293	1.60	1.36	1.51
India	151	370	527	882	2.45	1.42	1.67
Malaysia	168	641	2,747	4,955	3.81	4.28	1.80
The Philippines	296	602	966	1,358	2.03	1.60	1.41
Japan	..	..	..	..	..	1.20	1.20
S. Korea	..	507	1,088	1,304	..	2.14	1.20
Hawaii	..	3,690	4,637	7,321	..	1.26	1.58
Nigeria	224	532	1,168	5,088	2.38	2.20	4.36
Ghana	260	594	1,111	5,412	2.28	1.87	4.87
Kenya	507	828	1,929	4,542	1.63	2.33	2.35
Uganda	..	..	..	..	2.40	3.27	3.69
Turkey	..	669	1,959	5,518	..	2.92	2.82
Brazil	..	620	945	3,344	..	1.52	3.54

Source: United States: U.S. Bureau of the Census (1962), p. 119.

Canada: Podoluk (1965), p. 69.

Mexico: Carnoy (1967b), p. 362. Monthly earnings multiplied by 12.

Colombia: Selowsky (1968), pp. 91—2. Annual earnings were derived by grossing up hourly earnings by hours worked per week and multiplying by 50 weeks.

Chile: Harberger and Selowsky (1966), p. 26.

Great Britain: Layard et al. (1971) Appendix D, and Ministry of Labour (1967). Primary graduates earnings were assumed to be equal to the average of unskilled and semi-skilled workers' earnings in the engineering industry.

Norway: Aarrestad (1969), pp. 33—4. Primary level refers to insurance workers, secondary level to local authority workers and higher to secondary school teachers.

The Netherlands: De Wolff and Ruiter (1968), p. 128. The earnings for the "higher" category are an average of those for semi-higher and higher education.

Greece: Leibenstein (1967), p. 60. Earnings refer to males only.

Israel: Klinov-Malul (1966), pp. 100—1.

India: Blaug et al. (1969). p. 171. Monthly earnings multiplied by 12. The earnings refer to middle school, matriculates, the arts and science graduates.

Malaysia: Hoerr (1970), p. 21. Secondary refers to school certificate.

The Philippines: Williamson and Devoretz (1967), p. 24.

Japan: Relative wages were obtained by an approximation of the private rate of return formula

$$r_i = \frac{1}{\lambda} \left(\frac{W_i}{W_j} - 1\right)$$

where λ is the length of the ith schooling cycle in years and r_i is the known (Bowman, 1970) private rate of return to the same schooling level.

S. Korea: Kim (1968), p. 7.

Hawaii: Psacharopoulos (1969b), p. 26.

Nigeria and Ghana: Hinchliffe (1969), Appendix.

Kenya: Thias and Carnoy (1969), pp. 82, 92. Monthly earnings multiplied by 12.

Uganda: Earnings ratios based on gross figures for discounted lifetime earnings, Smyth and Bennett (1967), pp. 315—7.

Turkey: Krueger (1971), p. 35.

Brazil: Hewlett (1970).

Appendix G. Rate of Return Patterns and Alternative Measures of Development

In this appendix we attempt to find whether there are any statistical relationships between the level of economic or educational development of a country and the rates of return to investment in education. Although the two kinds of development (economic and educational) are highly correlated, two alternative proxies are used for each of them.

Economic development is here measured first by the level of per capita income and secondly by the percentage contribution of agriculture to Gross Domestic Product. The values of these variables for the 27 countries on which the following test is based, appear in Table G.1. The reason why we have used two alternative measures in our investigation is that neither measure is perfect. Per capita income has been widely criticized as an index of development due to the inadequacy of the official exchange rates to reflect differences in the cost of living between countries. The percentage contribution of agriculture to GDP has the advantage that one does not have to deal with monetary units. The logic of this measure is that the more developed the country, the lower will be the contribution of agriculture to GDP.* Therefore, on theoretical grounds, one would expect a positive relationship between the percentage contribution of agriculture to GDP and the rate of return to investment in education.

The level of educational development is measured first by what is known as the "Harbison and Myers index", and alternatively by the percentage of professional, technical and related workers in a country's labour force. The Harbison and Myers "composite index of human resource development" is based on the educational enrolment rates by level of education in each country.

---

* For an example of the use of this index in examining development patterns, see Chenery and Taylor (1968).

Although this index is readily available it has two major limitations for our purposes.[1] First, it is constructed on the basis of enrolment ratios in secondary and higher education, and thus refers to potential manpower stocks rather than existing ones. Secondly, the index numbers all refer to the same year, whereas our rates range over eleven years. For these reasons we have also used the number of professional workers in the labour force, which has the additional advantage of being more "price-free" than any other measure. The values of these two measures appear in Table G.1.

For the purpose of examining the statistical significance of the relationships involved, the following function was fitted

$$r_{ij} = a + bD_{ij} + cI_j$$

where r_{ij} is the rate of return to investment in educational level i in country j; D_{ij} is a dummy variable indicating the educational level to which the rate of return refers, and I_j is the index used as a proxy for the level of development of a country j. The regression results appear in Table G.2.

The results of these tests are very similar for whichever index of economic or educational development is used. In all cases, the explained variation of the rate of return is about one-fifth of the total variance. The development variable has in all cases the expected sign — that is, the higher the level of development, the lower the rate of return to investment in education — although in no case is the coefficient statistically significant.

The regression coefficient of the educational level to which the rate of return refers, on the other hand, is negative and strongly significant in all cases. That is, the higher the level of education within a given country, the lower the rate of return. This last finding simply confirms our previous results of the χ^2 test presented in Chapter 4, above.

---

[1] For a sharp criticism of this index, see Blaug (1970), chapter 3.

TABLE G.1

ECONOMIC AND EDUCATIONAL DEVELOPMENT INDICATORS, BY COUNTRY

Country	Percentage of agriculture in GDP	Harbison and Myers index	Percentage of professional workers in the labour force
(1)	(2)	(3)	(4)
United States	4.0	261.3	10.8
Canada	6.1	101.6	10.6
Puerto Rico	12.4	. .	7.8
Venezuela	7.2	47.7	. .
Colombia	30.5	22.6	3.9
Chile	12.6	51.2	4.9
Mexico	18.0	33.0	3.6
Brazil	27.0	20.9	3.1
Great Britain	3.3	121.6	9.6
Germany	5.0	85.8	7.6
Denmark	12.3	77.1	7.8
Norway	8.2	73.8	8.0
Sweden	6.0	79.2	15.3
Belgium	5.5	123.6	8.0
The Netherlands	8.3	133.7	9.2
Greece	25.6	48.5	3.4
Israel	13.5	84.9	11.4
India	51.3	35.2	1.7
Malaysia	28.3	23.6	3.0
Japan	14.3	111.4	5.5
The Philippines	32.4	. .	3.3
Nigeria	55.6	4.95	2.4
Ghana	33.7	23.15	2.2
Kenya	34.6	4.75	1.2
Uganda	59.4	5.45	1.3
N. Rhodesia	. .	2.95	. .
New Zealand	. .	147.3	10.2

Source: Col. (2): United Nations (1968), Vol. I. Col. (3): Harbison and Myers (1964), p. 33. Col. (4): International Labour Office (1967), Government of Kenya (1965), pp. 4—7, and Smyth and Bennet (1967), p. 31.

TABLE G.2

REGRESSION RESULTS

Constant term	Educational level	Per capita income	Percentage of agriculture in GDP	Harbison and Myers index	Percentage of professional workers in the labour force	R^2
31.689	−6.314** (1.986)	−0.002 (0.002)				0.19
28.359	−6.469** (1.944)		0.090 (0.091)			0.19
32.028	−6.291** (1.956)			−0.033 (0.028)		0.20
32.339	−6.577** (1.959)				−0.291 (0.408)	0.19

Notes: Dependent variable in all regressions is the rate of return of a given educational level in a given country.

Numbers in parenthesis are standard errors.

Appendix H. Additional Tables

This appendix presents the educational investment—output ratios, labour force participation rates and rates of growth of output used in the accounting of the sources of growth in Chapter 7. It also contains absolute and relative enrolments by educational level as well as international migration data which were used in explaining the brain drain in Chapter 9.

TABLE H.1

EDUCATIONAL INVESTMENT—OUTPUT RATIOS AND LABOUR FORCE PARTICIPATION RATES, BY COUNTRY

Country	Educational investment as a fraction of output $\dfrac{I_H}{Y}$	Labour force participation rate π
(1)	(2)	(3)
United States	0.115	56.2
Mexico	0.070	55.3
Venezuela	0.033	55.6
Colombia	0.086	52.6
Chile	0.056	52.8
Great Britain	0.099	61.9
Norway	0.090	52.8
The Netherlands	0.073	52.0
Israel	0.093	52.3
India	0.098	67.2
Malaysia	0.135	59.7
The Philippines	0.075	54.5
S. Korea	0.221	52.0
Nigeria	0.070	57.7
Ghana	0.080	73.0
Kenya	0.062	73.0
New Zealand	0.093	56.8

Source: Col. (2): Enrolments in each education level from UNESCO *Statistical Yearbook* (1968), times total social costs per student year from Table D.3, divided by Gross Domestic Product from United Nations *Yearbook of National Accounts Statistics* (1968).
Col. (3): from International Labour Office (1968).

Note: The Kenyan labour force labour force participation rate is assumed to be equal to that of Ghana.

TABLE H.2

GROSS DOMESTIC PRODUCT AND RATE OF GROWTH OF OUTPUT, BY COUNTRY

Country (1)	GDP (in million US $) (2)	Rate of growth or GDP (per cent) (3)
United States	489,100	4.9
Canada	38,112	5.7
Puerto Rico	1,699	8.3
Mexico	14,928	6.4
Venezuela	7,115	5.2
Colombia	5,354	4.8
Chile	4,673	5.0
Brazil	11,575	4.2
Great Britain	91,289	3.4
Norway	6,931	5.4
Sweden	21,649	5.4
Denmark	8,722	5.1
The Netherlands	17,210	5.1
Belgium	16,962	5.3
Germany	89,815	5.0
Greece	4,527	7.7
Israel	1,409	10.0
India	31,749	3.3
Malaysia	2,346	5.8
The Philippines	7,140	4.8
Japan	51,501	10.1
S. Korea	4,349	6.8
Thailand	5,051	7.0
Hawaii	1,582	5.2
Nigeria	4,496	4.7
Ghana	1,870	3.8
Kenya	1,206	6.9
Uganda	654	4.4
Rhodesia	1,173	5.8
New Zealand	5,132	5.1

Source: Col. (2): United Nations *Yearbook of National Accounts Statistics* (1966 and 1969). United Nations *Statistical Yearbook* (1958 to 1963 and 1966).

Col. (3): United Nations *Yearbook of National Accounts Statistics* (1969). Hawaii from Psacharopoulos (1969a), p. 29.

Notes: GDP refers to year which corresponds to the rate of return study, or the nearest to it.
Rates of growth refer to the 1960—65 period, except for Kenya (1964—68), and Hawaii (1950—60).

TABLE H.3

ABSOLUTE AND RELATIVE ENROLMENTS BY EDUCATIONAL LEVEL AND COUNTRY

Country	Absolute enrolments			Relative enrolments	
	Primary	Secondary	Higher	Secondary/ primary	Higher/ secondary
(1)	(2)	(3)	(4)	(5)	(6)
United States	29,965,000	9,600,000	3,582,726	0.32	0.37
Canada	3,168,857	994,000	142,050	0.31	0.14
Puerto Rico	523,483	195,000	26,038	0.37	0.13
Mexico	6,916,204	891,000	133,374	0.15	0.37
Venezuela	646,795	64,000	7,664	0.10	0.12
Colombia	2,408,489	508,000	49,930	0.21	0.10
Chile	1,173,845	228,000	25,452	0.19	0.11
Brazil	7,477,053	1,177,000	95,691	0.16	0.08
Great Britain	5,364,116	3,605,000	371,178	0.67	0.10
Norway	407,055	277,000	21,001	0.68	0.08
Sweden	622,336	610,000	84,262	0.98	0.14
Denmark	519,279	313,000	47,826	0.60	0.15
The Netherlands	1,409,017	1,096,000	148,590	0.78	0.14
Belgium	963,100	311,000	84,000	0.32	0.27
Germany	5,562,061	3,673,000	343,014	0.66	0.09
Greece	965,782	456,000	58,000	0.47	0.13
Israel	403,279	68,000	15,595	0.17	0.23
India	32,459,000	10,833,000	1,093,641	0.33	0.10
Malaysia	1,423,983	393,000	12,850	0.28	0.03
The Philippines	5,577,901	1,037,000	450,000	0.19	0.43
Japan	12,590,680	9,138,000	699,446	0.72	0.08
S. Korea	4,941,345	1,201,000	141,635	0.24	0.12
Thailand	4,811,933	389,000	50,722	0.08	0.13
Hawaii	109,957	40,703	7,921	0.37	0.19
Nigeria	3,025,981	257,000	10,976	0.08	0.04
Ghana	1,292,213	202,000	4,478	0.16	0.02
Kenya	1,043,416	70,000	3,814	0.07	0.05
Uganda	564,190	97,000	1,580	0.17	0.02
N. Rhodesia	287,536	5,000	..	0.02	..
New Zealand	485,342	163,159	29,553	0.34	0.18

Source: Col. (2), (3) and (4): UNESCO *Statistical Yearbook* (1968); Hawaii from Psacharopoulos (1969c).
Col. (5): = Col. (3) : Col. (2)
Col. (6): = Col. (4) : Col. (3)

TABLE H.4

DISTRIBUTION OF ENROLMENTS BY EDUCATIONAL LEVEL AND COUNTRY (per cent)

Country	Primary	Secondary	Higher	Total
United States	70	22	8	100
Canada	74	23	3	100
Puerto Rico	71	26	3	100
Mexico	87	11	2	100
Venezuela	90	9	1	100
Colombia	81	17	2	100
Chile	82	16	2	100
Brazil	86	13	1	100
Great Britain	57	39	4	100
Norway	58	39	3	100
Sweden	48	46	6	100
Denmark	59	36	5	100
The Netherlands	53	41	6	100
Belgium	71	23	6	100
Germany	58	38	4	100
Greece	65	31	4	100
Israel	83	14	3	100
India	74	24	2	100
Malaysia	78	21	1	100
The Philippines	79	15	6	100
Japan	56	41	3	100
S. Korea	79	19	2	100
Thailand	92	7	1	100
Hawaii	69	26	5	100
Nigeria	92	7.8	0.3	100
Ghana	86.2	13.5	0.3	100
Kenya	93.4	6.3	0.3	100
Uganda	85.2	14.6	0.2	100
N. Rhodesia	..	..	..	..
New Zealand	72	24	4	100

Source: Table H.3.

TABLE H.5

PROFESSIONAL, TECHNICAL AND RELATED WORKERS ADMITTED AS IMMIGRANTS TO THE UNITED STATES, 1958–69 BY COUNTRY OF ORIGIN (numbers)

Country	1958	1959	1960	1961	1962	1963	1964	1965	1966	1967	1968	1969	Average per year
Canada	3,564	3,157	3,545	3,541	3,532	4,047	4,376	4,629	3,703	3,401	3,823	2,431	3,646
Mexico	423	379	583	542	700	627	442	569	593	697	669	484	559
Venezuela	—	39	36	50	57	73	86	74	67	45	63	40	57
Colombia	414	334	340	355	455	631	924	799	723	392	729	647	562
Brazil	—	—	166	149	186	243	281	370	268	191	228	157	224
Chile	—	—	—	—	127	145	169	208	141	122	176	116	150
Great Britain	3,328	2,734	3,187	3,036	3,284	3,917	4,344	4,228	3,921	4,726	5,420	2,513	3,720
Norway	289	299	310	265	232	259	292	299	280	299	330	134	274
Sweden	386	318	393	313	288	353	380	454	355	449	423	153	355
Denmark	185	157	213	177	220	236	218	218	211	262	347	126	214
The Netherlands	383	405	425	405	439	407	407	473	362	366	455	221	396
Belgium	118	110	116	139	157	161	186	159	150	158	147	73	139
Germany	2,051	1,905	1,837	1,728	1,723	1,821	1,965	2,020	1,465	1,467	1,934	924	1,737
Greece	273	218	225	201	261	364	268	212	374	589	512	585	340
Israel	123	125	100	108	129	196	137	145	219	375	425	383	205
India	208	163	118	139	167	595	220	198	1,424	2,474	2,189	2,857	896
Japan	150	122	113	89	131	322	177	139	296	525	432	400	241
The Philippines	303	232	330	318	360	631	277	312	1,041	2,800	5,224	7,138	1,580
New Zealand	—	—	53	46	55	59	57	54	63	115	119	108	73

Source: United States Department of Justice, Immigration and Naturalization Service, *Annual Report* of the respective years.

Appendix I. Glossary of Symbols

This appendix contains a list of the *most frequently* used symbols in this book. When there is a duplication, because of expository simplicity, the alternative meaning of the symbol is explained in the text.

Symbol	*Meaning*
.	Not applicable
. .	Not available
—	Nil or negligible
*	Statistically significant at the 90 per cent level of probability
* *	Statistically significant at the 95 per cent level of probability.
α	The "alpha coefficient", or the part of the gross earnings differential attributable to education alone.
C	The direct cost per student year in the subscripted educational level
Δ	A discrete difference operator
E	Number of students enrolled in the subscripted educational level
g	The annual rate of growth of the subscripted variable
I	Investment in the subscripted form of capital
h (subscript)	Refers to the higher educational level
K_H	The human capital stock
K_M	The physical capital stock
$\dfrac{K_H}{L}$	Human capital per member of the labour force

$\dfrac{K_M}{L}$	Physical capital per member of the labour force
L	Persons in the labour force. If subscripted, persons in the labour force with the subscripted educational level
$\log(\ )$	The natural logarithm of the variable in parenthesis
o (subscript)	Refers to zero years of schooling
op (subscript)	Refers to the "primary or less" educational level
P	Population
p (subscript)	Refers to the primary educational level
r	The internal rate of return to investment in a form of capital
r_H	The overall rate of return to investment in human capital
r_M	The rate of return to investment in physical capital
r_p	The rate of return to investment in the primary educational level
r_s	The rate of return to investment in the secondary educational level
r_h	The rate of return to investment in the higher educational level
r_c	The private cross rate of return to international migration
s	The share of labour with the subscripted educational level in total income
s (subscript)	Refers to the secondary educational level
σ	The elasticity of substitution between the subscripted types of educated labour
t	Time in years
Y	National income
$\dfrac{Y}{L}$	Income per member of the labour force
$\dfrac{Y}{P}$	Per capita income

References

Aarrestad, J. (1969). *Om Utbyttet av å Investere i Utdanning i Norge.* Bergen: Norges Handelshøyskole, Samfunnsøkonomisk Institutt.

Abramovitz, M. (1956). *Resources and Output Trends in the United States since 1870.* Occasional Paper No. 52. New York: National Bureau of Economic Research.

AlBukhari, N. M. A. (1968). Issues in Occupational Education and Training: A Case Study in Jordan. Unpublished Ph.D. dissertation, Stanford University.

Allen, R. G. D. (1938). *Mathematical Analysis for Economists.* London: Macmillan.

Ashenfelter, O. and Mooney, J. D. (1969). Some evidence on the private returns to graduate education. *Southern Economic Journal,* 35 (3).

Bailey, M. J. (1959). Formal criteria for investment decisions. *Journal of Political Economy* (October).

Baldwin, R. E. (1966). *Economic Development and Export Growth.* Berkeley: University of California Press.

Balogh, T. and Streeten, P. O. (1963). The coefficient of ignorance. *Bulletin Oxford University Institute of Economics and Statistics* (May).

Becker, G. S. (1960). Underinvestment in college education. *American Economic Review* (May).

Becker, G. S. (1964). *Human Capital.* Princeton: Princeton University Press.

Becker, G. S. (1967). *Human Capital and the Personal Distribution of Income: An Analytical Approach.* Ann Arbor: University of Michigan Press.

Becker, G. S. and Chiswick, B. R. (1966). Schooling and the distribution of earnings. *American Economic Review* (May).

Bennett, N. (1967). *High Level Manpower Survey, 1967 and Analyses of Requirements, 1967—1981.* Uganda: Manpower Planning Division.

Berry, R. A. and Soligo, R. (1969). Some welfare aspects of international migration. *Journal of Political Economy* (October).

Bertram, G. W. (1966). *The Contribution of Education to Economic Growth,* Staff Study No. 12. Ottawa: Economic Council of Canada.

Blandy, R. (1967). Marshall on human capital: a note: *Journal of Political Economy* (December).

Blaug, M. (1965). The rate of return on investment in education in Great Britain. *The Manchester School* (September).

Blaug, M. (1966). An economic interpretation of the private demand for education. *Economica* (May).

Blaug, M. (1966 and 1970). *Economics of Education: A Selected Annotated Bibliography.* Oxford: Pergamon Press.

Blaug, M. (1967). The private and social returns on investment in education: some results for Great Britain. *Journal of Human Resources*, II (3).

Blaug, M. (1970). *An Introduction to the Economics of Education*. London: Allen Lane The Penguin Press.

Blaug, M. (1971). *The Rate of Return to Investment in Education in Thailand*, A Report to the National Planning Committee on the Third Educational Development Plan, Bangkok: National Education Council.

Blaug, M., Peston, M. H. and Ziderman, A. (1967). *The Utilization of Educated Manpower in Industry* London: Oliver and Boyd.

Blaug, M., Layard, P. R. G. and Woodhall, M. (1969). *The Causes of Graduate Unemployment in India.* London: Allen Lane The Penguin Press.

Bowles, S. (1967a). Sources of growth in the Greek economy, 1952–1961. The Center for International Affairs, Harvard University (mimeo).

Bowles, S. (1967b). The efficient allocation of resources in education. *Quarterly Journal of Economics* (May).

Bowles, S. (1969). *Planning Educational Systems for Economic Growth.* Cambridge, Mass.: Harvard University Press.

Bowles, S. (1970). Aggregation of labor inputs in the economics of growth and planning: experiments with a two-level C.E.S. function. *Journal of Political Economy* (January).

Bowman, M. J. (1964). Schultz, Denison and the contribution of "Eds" to national income growth. *Journal of Political Economy*, (October).

Bowman, M. J. (1966). The human investment revolution in economic thought. *Sociology of Education,* XXXIX (Spring).

Bowman, M. J. (1970). Mass elites at the threshold of the seventies. *Comparative Education* (London).

Bowman, M. J. (1971). Education and economic growth. In *Economic Factors Affecting the Financing of Education,* ed. Jolius *et al.*, Gainesville, Fla.: National Educational Finance Project.

Calcott, D. (1968). Some trends and problems of education in Western Nigeria 1955–66, Part II *West African Journal of Education,* XII (1).

Carnoy, M. (1964). The Cost and Returns to Schooling in Mexico: A Case Study. Unpublished Ph.D. dissertation, University of Chicago.

Carnoy, M. (1967a). Earnings and schooling in Mexico. *Economic Development and Cultural Change* (July).

Carnoy, M. (1967b). Rates of return to schooling in Latin America. *Journal of Human Resources,* II (Summer).

Carnoy, M. (1970). The Rate of Return to Schooling and the Increase in Human Resources in Puerto Rico. Stanford University, Department of Education (mimeo).

Carroll, A. B. and Ihnen, A. I. (1967). Costs and returns for two years of post secondary technical schooling: a pilot study. *Journal of Political Economy* (December).

Castro, C. de M. (1970). Investment in Education in Brazil: A Study of Two Industrial Communities. Ph.D. dissertation, Department of Economics, Vanderbilt University.

Chenery, H. B. and Taylor, L. (1968). Development patterns among countries and over time. *Review of Economics and Statistics* (November).

Chiswick, B. R. (1971). Earnings inequality and economic development. *Quarterly Journal of Economics* (February).

200

Clark, D. H. and Fong, P. E. (1970). Returns to schooling and training in Singapore. *Malayan Economic Review* (October).

Correa, H. (1970). Sources of economic growth in Latin America. *Southern Economic Journal* (July).

Danielsen, A. N. and Okachi, J. (1971). Private rates of return to schooling in Japan. *Journal of Human Resources* (Summer).

Denison, E. F. (1962). *The Sources of Economic Growth in the U.S. and the Alternatives before Us*, Supplementary Paper No. 13. New York: Committee for Economic Development.

Denison, E. F. (1961). Measuring the contribution of education to economic growth. In: *The Residual Factor and Economic Growth*. Paris: OECD.

Denison, E. F. (1967). *Why Growth Rates Differ: Post-War Experience in Nine Western Countries*. Washington, D.C.: The Brookings Institution.

Desaeyere, W. (1969). *Een Onderwijsmodel voor Belgie*. Leuven: Katholieke Universiteit te Leuven, Centrum voor Economische Studien.

Devoretz, D. (1969). Alternative planning models for Philippine educational investment. *The Philippine Economic Journal*, 16.

Dougherty, C. R. S. (1971a). The optimal allocation of investment in education. In: *Studies in Development Planning*, ed. H. B. Chenery. Cambridge, Mass.: Harvard University Press.

Dougherty, C. R. S. (1971b). Estimates of Labour Aggregation Functions. Cambridge, Mass.: Harvard University, Center for International Affairs, Economic Development Report No. 190 *Journal of Political Economy* (forthcoming).

Education and World Affairs (1967). *Nigerian Human Resource Development and Utilization*. New York: Committee on Education and Human Resource Development.

Fabricant, S. (1959). *Basic Facts on Productivity*, Occasional Paper No. 63. New York: National Bureau of Economic Research.

Franco, G. (1964). Rendimiento de la Inversión en Educación en Colombia. Bogotá: CEPE, Universidad de los Andes (July).

Friedman, M. (1962). *Price Theory*. Chicago: Aldine.

Glick, P. C. and Miller, H. P. (1956). Educational level and potential income. *American Sociological Review*, 21.

Goldberger, A. (1964). *Econometric Theory*. New York: John Wiley.

Government of Kenya, (1965). *High-level Manpower, 1964—1970*. Nairobi: Ministry of Economic Planning and Development.

Greenwood, M. J. (1969). An analysis of the determinants of geographic labor mobility in the United States. *Review of Economics and Statistics* (May).

Griliches, Z. (1963). The sources of measured productivity growth: U.S. Agriculture, 1940- 1960. *Journal of Political Economy* (August).

Griliches, Z. (1969). Capital-skill complementarity. *Review of Economics and Statistics* (November).

Griliches, Z. (1970). Notes on the role of education in production functions and growth accounting. In *Education, Income and Human Capital*, W. L. Hansen. New York: National Bureau of Economic Research.

Grubel, H. G. and Scott, A. D. (1966). The international flow of human capital. *American Economic Review* (May).

Hanoch, G. (1965). Personal Earnings and Investment in Schooling. Unpublished Ph.D. dissertation, University of Chicago.

Hanoch, G. (1967). An economic analysis of earnings and schooling. *Journal of Human Resources*, II (3).

Hansen, N. B. (1966). Uddannelsesinvesteringernes rentabilitet. *National-φnonomisk Tidsskrift*, 5- 6, Copenhagen.

Hansen, W. L. (1963). Total and private returns to investment in schooling. *Journal of Political Economy* (April).

Hansen, W. L. (1970). Patterns of rates of return to investment in education: some international comparisons. In *Conference on Policies for Educational Growth*. Paris: OECD (mimeo, DAS/EID/70.3).

Harberger, A. C. (1965). Investment in men versus investment in machines: the case of India. In *Education and Economic Development* ed. C. A. Anderson and M. J. Bowman. Chicago: Aldine.

Harberger, A. and Selowsky, M. (1966). Key Factors in the Economic Growth of Chile (mimeo), presented to the Conference at Cornell University on "The Next Decade of Latin American Development" (20—22 April).

Harbison, F. and Myers, C. A. (1964). *Education, Manpower and Economic Growth*. New York: McGraw-Hill.

Hayami, Y. and Ruttan, V. W. (1970a) Factor prices and technical changes in agricultural development: The United States and Japan, 1880—1960. *Journal of Political Economy* (November).

Hayami, Y. and Ruttan, V. W. (1970b). Agricultural productivity differences among countries. *American Economic Review* (December).

Hewlett, S. A. (1970). Rate of return analysis: its role in determining the significance of education in the development of Brazil (mimeo).

Hinchliffe, K. (1969). Educational Planning Techniques for Developing Countries with Special Reference to Ghana and Nigeria. Unpublished M.Phil. dissertation (University of Leicester).

Hinchliffe, K. (1971). The Rate of Return to Education in Ghana. *Economic Bulletin of Ghana* (June).

Hines, F., Tweeten, L. and Redfern, M. (1970). Social and private rates of return to investment in schooling by race—sex groups and regions. *Journal of Human Resources*, V (3).

Hirshleifer, J. (1958). On the theory of optimal investment decision. *Journal of Political Economy* (August).

Hoerr, O. D. (1970). *Education, Income and Equity in Malaysia*. Harvard Center for International Affairs, Economic Development Report No. 176, (June).

Houthakker, H. S. (1959). Education and income. *Review of Economics and Statistics* (February).

Hunt, S. J. (1963). Income determinants for college graduates and the return to educational investment. *Yale Economic Essays* (Fall).

Husén, T. (1968). Ability, opportunity and career, a 26 years follow up. *Educational Research* (June).

Instituto Brasileiro de Estatistica (1960). *Censos Demografico de 1960*. International Labour Office. *Yearbook of Labour Statistics* (Annual) (Geneva).

International Labour Office, *Yearbook of Labour Statistics* (Annual). Geneva.

Johnson, H. (1964). Towards a generalized capital accumulation approach to economic development. In *The Residual Factor and Economic Growth*. Paris: OECD.

Johnson, H. (1967). Some economic aspects of the brain drain. *Pakistan Development Review* (Autumn).

Jolly, R. (1965). Planning Education in Developing Countries. Unpublished Ph.D. dissertation (Yale University).

Jorgenson, D. W. and Griliches, Z. (1967). The explanation of productivity change. *Review of Economic Studies* (July).

Kiker, B. F. (1966). The historical roots of the concept of human capital. *Journal of Political Economy* (October).

Kiker, B. F. (1968). Marshall on human capital: comment. *Journal of Political Economy* (September).

Killich, A. (1966). In *A Study of Contemporary Ghana*, ed. W. Birmingham, E. Neustadt, E. N. Omaboe, Vol. 1, Chapter V, Section 2. London: Allen and Unwin.

Kim Kwang Suk (1968). Rates of Return on Education in Korea. USAID, mimeo (September).

Klinov-Malul, R. (1966). *The Profitability of Investment in Education in Israel.* Jerusalem: The Maurice Falk Institute for Economic Research in Israel.

Kothari, V. N. (1967). Returns to education in India. *Education as Investment*, ed. B. Singh, Meerut, India: Meenakshi Prakashan.

Kothari, V. N. (1970). Disparities in relative earnings among different countries. *Economic Journal* (September).

Krueger, A. O. (1968). Factor endowments and per capita income differences among countries. *Economic Journal* (September).

Krueger, A. O. (1971). Turkish Education and Manpower Development: Some Impressions. Department of Economics, University of Minnesota (mimeo).

Lassiter, R. L. (1965). The association of income and education for males by region, race and age. *Southern Economic Journal* (July).

Lassiter, R. L. (1966). *The Association of Income and Educational Achievement.* Gainesville: University of Florida Press.

Layard, R., King, J. and Moser, C. (1969). *The Impact of Robbins.* London: Penguin Press.

Layard, P. R. G., Sargan, J. D., Ager, M. E. and Jones, D. J. (1971). *Qualified Manpower and Economic Performance.* London: Allen Lane The Penguin Press.

Layard, P. R. G. (1971). Economic theories of educational planning. In *Essays in Honour of Lionel Robbins*, ed. M. H. Peston and B. A. Corry. London: Weidenfeld and Nicolson.

Leibenstein, H. (1967). *Rates of Return to Education in Greece.* Harvard University, Center for International Affairs, Economic Development Report No. 94, September.

Leite, M. F., Lynch, P., Norris, K., Sheehan, J. and Vaizey, J. (1969). *The Economics of Educational Costing — Inter Country and Inter Regional Comparisons.* Lisbon: Centro de Economia e Financas.

Lerner, M. O. (1970). Determinants of Educational Attainment in Brazil, 1960. Unpublished Ph.D. dissertation, University of California, Berkeley.

Lydall, H. B. (1968). *The Structure of Earnings.* Oxford: Clarendon Press.

McFadden, D. (1963). Further results on CES production functions. *Review of Economic Studies* (June).

Maddison, A. (1963). Facts and observations on labour productivity in Western Europe, N. America and Japan. *Productivity Measurement Review*, (May).

Maglen, L. and Layard, R. (1970). How profitable is engineering education? *Higher Education Review*, II (2).

Magnusson, L. (1970). Samhällsekonomiska Aspekter på den Högre Utbildingen. University of Stockholm, Department of Economics, May (mimeo).

Marshall, A. C. (1920). *Principles of Economics*, 8th ed. London: Macmillan.

Miller, H. P. (1960). Annual and lifetime income in relation to education: 1939–59. *American Economic Review* (December).

Mincer, J. (1962). On the job training: costs, returns and some implications. *Journal of Political Economy* (supplement) (October).

Minhas, B. S. (1963). *An International Comparison of Factor Costs and Factor Use*. Amsterdam: North-Holland.

Ministry of Labour (1967). *Ministry of Labour Gazette*. London. (August).

Moreh, J. (1971). Human capital and economic growth. *Economic and Social Review* (October).

Morgan, J. and David, M. (1963). Education and income. *Quarterly Journal of Economics* (August).

Morgan, J. and Sirageldin, I. (1968). A note on the quality dimension in education. *Journal of Political Economy* (October).

Morris, V. and Ziderman, A. (1971). The economic return on investment in higher education in England and Wales. *Economic Trends*, (May).

Nalla Gounden, A. M. (1967). Investment in education in India. *Journal of Human Resources* (Summer).

Nigeria Manpower Board (1964). *Nigeria's High-level Manpower, 1963—1970*. Apapa: Nigerian National Press.

Nelson, R. R. (1968). A diffusion model of international productivity differences in manufacturing industry. *American Economic Review* (December).

New Zealand Department of Statistics (1969). *Census of Population and Dwellings 1966*. Wellington: Government Printing Office.

O.E.C.D. (1962). *Forecasting Educational Needs for Economic and Social Development*. Paris.

O.E.C.D. (1964). *The Residual Factor and Economic Growth*. Paris: O.E.C.D.

O.E.C.D. (1965). *Mediterranean Regional Project, Greece*. Paris: O.E.C.D.

O.E.C.D. (1967). *Educational Policy and Planning: Sweden*. Paris: O.E.C.D.

O.E.C.D. (1969). *Statistics of the Occupational and Educational Structure of the Labour Force in 53 Countries*. Paris: O.E.C.D.

Ogilvy, B. J. (1968). Investment in New Zealand Education and its Economic Value, 1951—1966. Unpublished M.Com. thesis, University of Auckland.

Ogilvy, B. J. (1970). A cost-benefit study of education in New Zealand. *The New Zealand Journal of Educational Studies* (May).

Parai, L. (1965). *Immigration and Emigration of Professional and Skilled Manpower During the Post-war Period*. Ottawa: Economic Council of Canada, Special Study No. 1.

Patinkin, D. (1968). A "nationalist" model. In *The Brain Drain*, ed. W. Adams. New York: Macmillan.

Pesek, B. P. and Saving, T. R. (1967). *Money, Wealth and Economic Theory.* New York: Macmillan.

Podoluk, J. R. (1965). *Earnings and Education.* Canada: Dominion Bureau of Statistics.

Psacharopoulos, G. (1968). An Economic Analysis of Labor Skill Requirements in Greece, 1954–1965. Unpublished Ph.D. dissertation, University of Chicago.

Psacharopoulos, G. (1969a). *The Anatomy of a Rate of Growth: The Case of Hawaii, 1950—1960.* Honolulu: University of Hawaii, Economic Research Center.

Psacharopoulos, G. (1969b). *The Rate of Return to Investment in Education at the Regional Level: Estimates for the State of Hawaii.* Honolulu: University of Hawaii, Economic Research Center.

Psacharopoulos, G. (1969c). *Enrolment Projections for Higher Education in the State of Hawaii 1969—1980.* Honolulu: University of Hawaii Management Systems Office.

Psacharopoulos, G. (1970). Estimating shadow rates of return to investment in education. *Journal of Human Resources* (Winter).

Psacharopoulos, G. (1971). On some positive aspects of the economics of the brain drain. *Minerva* (April).

Psacharopoulos, G. (forthcoming a). The marginal contribution of education to economic growth. *Economic Development and Cultural Change.*

Psacharopoulos, G. (forthcoming b). The profitability of higher education: a comparison of the experience in Britain and the United States. In *Higher Education in the Seventies,* ed. H. J. Butcher and E. Rudd. New York: McGraw-Hill.

Ramsey, James B. (1970). The marginal efficiency of capital, the internal rate of return, and net present value: an analysis of investment criteria. *Journal of Political Economy* (September).

Renshaw, E. F. (1960). Estimating the returns to education. *The Review of Economics and Statistics* (August).

Richardson, V. A. (1969). The Problems of Manpower and Educational Planning: Analysis and Appraisal of Alternative Techniques, Illustrated by Some Empirical Models. Unpublished Ph.D. dissertation, University of Manchester.

Robinson, S. (1969). Aggregate Production Functions and Growth Models in Economic Development: A Cross-Section Study. Unpublished Ph.D. dissertation, Harvard University.

Rogers III, A. J. (1969). Professional Incomes and Rates of Return to Higher Education in Brazil. Unpublished Ph.D. dissertation, Michigan State University.

Rogers, D. (1969). Private rates of return to education in the United States: a case study. *Yale Economic Essays* (Spring).

Rogers, D. (1972). Student loan programs and the returns to investment in higher levels of education in Kenya. *Economic Development and Cultural Change* (January).

Sahota, G. S. (1968). An economic analysis of internal migration in Brazil. *Journal of Political Economy* (March).

Sato, K. (1967). A two-level C.E.S. production function. *Review of Economic Studies* (April).

Schmidt, K. D. and Baumgarten, Peter (1967). Berufliche Ausbildung und Einkommen. In *Theoretische und Empirische Beiträge zur Wirtschaftsforschung*, ed. A. E. Ott. Tübingen: Mohr.

Schultz, T. P. (1968). Returns to Education in Bogota, Colombia. The Rand Corporation, Memorandum RM-5645-RC/AID (September).

Schultz, T. W. (1961). Education and economic growth. In *Social Forces Influencing American Education*, Chicago: National Society for the Study of Education.

Schultz, T. W. (1963). *The Economic Value of Education*. New York: Columbia University Press.

Schultz, T. W. (1967). The rate of return in allocating investment resources to education. *Journal of Human Resources* (Summer).

Schultz, T. W. (1971). *Investment in Human Capital*. New York: Free Press.

Schwartzman, D. (1968). Education and the quality of labour 1929—1963. *American Economic Review* (June).

Scott, A. D. (1970). The brain drain — is a human capital approach justified? In *Education, Income and Human Capital*, ed. W. L. Hansen. New York: National Bureau of Economic Research.

Selby Smith, C. (1970). Costs and benefits in further education: some evidence from a pilot study. *Economic Journal* (September).

Selowsky, M. (1967). Education and Economic Growth: Some International Comparisons. Unpublished Ph.D. dissertation, University of Chicago.

Selowsky, M. (1968). *The Effect of Unemployment and Growth on the Rate of Return to Education: The Case of Colombia*. Cambridge, Mass: Harvard University, Centre for International Affairs, Report No. 116.

Selowsky, M. (1969). On the measurement of education's contribution to growth. *Quarterly Journal of Economics* (August).

Shoup, C. (1959). *The Fiscal System of Venezuela*. Baltimore: John Hopkins Press.

Smyth, J. A. and Bennett, N. L. (1967). Rates of return on investment in education: a tool for short-term educational planning, illustrated with Ugandan data. In *The World Yearbook of Education*. London: Evans Brothers.

Solomon, E. and Laya, J. C. (1966). Measurement of company profitability: some systematic errors in the accounting rate of return. In *Financial Research and its Implications for Management Decisions*, ed. A. A. Robichek. New York: Wiley.

Solow, R. M. (1957). Technical change and the aggregate production function. *Review of Economics and Statistics* (August).

Solow, R. M. (1963). *Capital Theory and the Rate of Return*. Amsterdam: North-Holland.

Thias, H. H. and Carnoy, M. (1969). Cost-benefit analysis in education: a case study on Kenya. International Bank for Reconstruction and Development, Economics Department, Report EC-173, (November).

Thomas, B. (1954). *Migration and Economic Growth: A Study of Great Britain and the Atlantic Economy*. Cambridge: University Press, National Institute of Economic and Social Research, Economic and Social Studies 12.

Thomas, B. (1967). The international circulation of human capital. *Minerva* (Summer).

Uganda Manpower Planning Division (1967). *High Level Manpower Survey 1967 and Analyses of Requirements, 1967—1981.*
UNESCO. *Statistical Yearbook* (Annual). Paris.
United Nations (1968). *Monthly Bulletin of Statistics.* Geneva.
United Nations. *Statistical Yearbook* (Annual). Geneva.
United Nations. *Demographic Yearbook* (Annual). New York.
United Nations. *Yearbook of National Accounts Statistics* (Annual). New York.
United States Bureau of the Census (1962). *Statistical Abstract of the United States.* Washington, D.C.
United States Department of Justice *Annual Report of the Immigration and Naturalization Service* (Annual). Washington, D.C.

Vaizey, J. (1962). *The Economics of Education.* London: Faber and Faber.
Valdes, A. (1971). Wages and schooling of agricultural workers in Chile. *Economic Development and Cultural Change* (January).

Watanabe, S. (1969). The brain drain from developing to developed countries. *International Labour Review* (April).
Weisbrod, B. A. (1964). *External Benefits of Public Education.* Princeton; Industrial Relations Section, Princeton University.
Weisbrod, B. A. and Karpoff, P. (1968). Monetary returns to college education, student ability and college quality. *Review of Economics and Statistics* (November).
Welch, F. (1970). Education in production. *Journal of Political Economy* (January).
Wilkinson, B. W. (1966). Present values of lifetime earnings for different occupations. *Journal of Political Economy* (December).
Williamson, J. and Devoretz, D. (1967). Education as an asset in the Philippine economy. Second Conference on Population, 27—29 November 1967. Manila, The Philippines (mimeo).
Wolff,P. de and Ruiter, R. (1968). *De Economie van het Onderwijs.* 's Gravenhage: Martinus Nijhoff.
Woodhall, M. (1969). The Use of Cost-Benefit Analysis as a Guide to Resource Allocation in Education: A Case Study on India. International Institute for Educational Planning (mimeo).
Woodhall, M. (1971). *Student Loans: Review of Experience in Scandinavia and Elsewhere.* London: George Harrap.
Woodhall, M. (forthcoming). Investment in women: a reappraisal of the concept of human capital. *International Review of Education.*

Ziderman, A. (1971). Incremental Rates of Return on Investment in Education: Recent Results for Britain. Queen Mary College, University of London (mimeo).

List of Figures

1.1. The private and social rate of return to investment in education by level of education, 6

1.2. The social rate of return to physical and human capital by level of economic development, 8

1.3. A rate of return to investment in education — level of economic development pattern, 9

1.4. A rate of return to investment in higher and secondary education — relative enrolments pattern, 10

1.5. The relationship between human and physical capital by level of economic development, 11

1.6. The relationship between actual and shadow wages by educational level of labour force, 12

1.7. The contribution of education to growth by level of economic development, 13

1.8. The cost of higher education relative to primary by level of economic development, 14

1.9. Earnings differentials between educated labour by level of economic development, 14

1.10. The elasticity of substitution between different kinds of educated labour, 15

2.1. A cost-benefit comparison, 21

5.1. An optimum schooling investment decision, 77

5.2. A demand schedule for schooling, 78

5.3. A demand schedule for schooling when the marginal productivity and cost of financing are positively correlated, 79

6.1. The relationship between the rate of return to investment in education, per capita income and level of educational development, 89

6.2. Differences between the observed and true rate of return — per capita — income relationship because of the *ceteris paribus* assumption, 90

6.3. Overall social rate of return to investment in education and the level of economic development, 92

6.4. An illustrative human capital accumulation model, 108

9.1. The relationship between relative wages and relative quantities of educated labour, 137

9.2. Widening of the wage differential due to the increase in the capital intensity of production, 142

List of Tables

4.1. Social and private rates of return by educational level and country, 62
4.2. Average rates of return by educational level, 65
4.3. Ranking within countries of the social rates of return by educational level, 66
4.4. Differences between private and social rates of return in developed and developing countries, 67
4.5. Rates of return by educational level and sex in certain countries, 69
4.6. Average rates of return by educational level and sex, 69
4.7. Rates of return to secondary general and secondary technical education in certain countries, 70
4.8. Rates of return to postgraduate education in certain countries, 71
4.9. Social rates of return to higher education by subject in certain countries, 72
5.1. Rates of return to investment in physical capital in certain countries, 82
5.2. Overall social rate of return and per capita income, by country, 85
5.3. The returns to alternative forms of capital by level of economic development, 86
6.1. Average rates of return by educational level and per capita income, 91
6.2. Overall social rate of return by the level of development, 93
6.3. Rates of return and relative enrolments by educational level, 96
6.4. Per capita income, physical and educational capital per member of the labour force in certain countries, 100
6.5. Actual versus shadow·shares of labour by educational level, 106
6.6. Actual versus shadow wage rates by educational level, 107
7.1. The contribution of education to economic growth according to alternative accounting schemes, by country, 116
7.2. The contribution of education to economic growth by level of per capita income, 117
7.3. The contribution of education to economic growth by educational level and country, 119
7.4. Income shares of labour by educational level and country, 120
7.5. Cross-sectional Denison-type growth accounting, 123
8.1. Foregone earnings as percentage of total social cost per student year by educational level and country, 126
8.2. Ratios of direct and total costs per student year, by educational level and country, 127
8.3. Distribution of total resources devoted to education by level and country, 129
8.4. Ratios of average annual earnings of labour by educational level and country, 123
9.1. Domestic and cross-rates of return by country of origin, 147
9.2. Proportions of qualified manpower emigrating to the United States by country of origin and other factors, 151

A.1. An actual net age-earnings profile: Higher education over secondary school graduates, Canada 1961, 156
A.2. Rate of return estimates according to alternative assumptions, 156
D.1. Social unit costs per student year by educational level in national currencies, 173
D.2. Value of 1 US$ in national currencies, 176
D.3. Social unit costs per student year by educational level and country, 177
E.1. Educational capital per member of the labour force, by country, 180
E.2. Physical capital per member of the labour force, by country, 181
E.3. Alternative measures of educational development, by country, 182
F.1. Distribution of the labour force by educational level and country, 183
F.2. Average annual wages by educational level and country, 185
G.1. Economic and education development indicators, by country, 189
G.2. Regression results, 190
H.1. Educational investment — output ratios and labour force participation rates, by country, 192
H.2. Gross domestic product and rate of growth of output, by country, 193
H.3. Absolute and relative enrolments by educational level and country, 194
H.4. Distribution of enrolments by educational level and country, 195
H.5. Professional, technical and related workers admitted as immigrants to the United States, 1958—69, by country of origin, 196

Subject Index

α, see alpha coefficient
Ability, 28*ff*, 39, 49*ff*, 59, 79; *see also*
   adjustment of rate of return; earnings standardization
Adjustment of rate of return 28—34,
   67, 159—165
   sensitivity to 155—157
   types of, 159*ff*
     labour force participation, 30
     mortality, 30
     productivity growth, 30—1, 48
     risk and uncertainty, 33
     taxation, 31
     wastage, 33—4;
   see also earnings standardization
Age-earnings profiles, 27
   shape of 155—7; *see also* earnings
Agriculture, share in GDP, 189
Allocation of resources to education,
   2, 75*ff*, 129
Alpha coefficient, 28*ff*
   and earnings functions, 59
   and socio-economic background,
   40; *see also* adjustment of rate of
   return

Benefit-cost analysis, *see* rate of return
Benefits from education, 2
   consumption, 31—2
   external, 32; *see also* earnings
Brain drain, 15—6, 144—153, 196
   determinants, 148*ff*
   returns to, 147; *see also* cross-rate
   of return

C_i, 83—4, 127, 173, 177
Capital; *see* human capital; physical
   capital
Capital market, 78, 80
Chi-square test, 66

Complimentarity, physical and human
   capital, 142—3
Cost
   direct, 127, 173
   by educational level, 13*ff*, 125*ff*
   indirect; *see* earnings foregone
   and per capita income, 14, 125—9
Cross-rate of return
   defined, 145
   estimates, 147; *see also* brain drain

E_i, 194
Earnings
   age profiles, 27
   foregone, 14, 34, 126, 173
   economic development and,
   129—134,142
   educational level and, 13*ff*, 125*ff*,
   132*ff*, 185
   elasticity of substitution, 137*ff*,
   143
   income versus, 25—6
   inequality, 134—5, 142, 144; *see*
   also income distribution
   per capita income and, 14—5
   rate of return and, 27
   marginal product of labour, 26
   standardization, 29, 40; *see also*
   rate of return adjustments
   types of, 25*ff*, 159*ff*
     annual versus hourly, 27—8
     cross-sectional versus longitudi-
     nal, 27
     shadow, 26, 43, 51
Earnings functions, 29, 38, 39, 42, 59
Economic development
   and human capital accumulation,
   87*ff*
   and rate of return, 87*ff*, 107*ff*
Economics of education, 1

Education
   costs of, *see* cost
   contribution to growth, *see* growth
      accounting
   demand for, 77*ff*, 108*ff*
   earnings and, *see* earnings
   investment or consumption, 32
   supply, 108*ff*
Educational capital
   per member of the labour force,
      100, 178—182
   in production functions, 103*ff*
Educational finance, 58, 68
Educational investment
   in growth accounting, 111—123
   as a percentage of GDP, 192
   returns, *see* rate of return
Educational resources, 128*ff*
Emigration, *see* brain drain
Enrolments
   by educational level, 194—5
   and rates of return, 93—7
Exchange rate, 182
External benefits, 32

Factor endowments, 101*ff*
Foregone earnings, *see* earnings foregone

g_y, 112*ff*
G.D.P., 187, 193
   rate of growth, 193; *see also* in-
      come
G.N.P., 101, 178; *see also* income
General secondary, returns to, 70
Growth accounting, 12—3, 111*ff*
   Denison-type, 112, 116·
      cross-sectional, 118*ff*, 123
   estimates, 116, 119, 123
   Schultz-type, 114—5, 116

Harbison and Myers index, *see* index
   of educational development
Human capital
   and economic development, 10—1
   investment in, 79*ff*, 107—110
      returns to, 2, 7—8, 85—6
   per member of the labour force,
      100, 178*ff*, 180, 182

I_H, 112*ff*

$\dfrac{I_H}{Y}$, 192

I_M, 112*ff*

I.C.O.R., 178, 181
Immigration, *see* brain drain
Income, 2, 25—6, 36
   distribution, 144
   median versus mean, 26
   per capita, 85
   and rate of return, 91*ff*
   shares, 120; *see also* earnings;
      G.D.P.; G.N.P.
Index of educational development
   cost-based, 97—9
   Harbison and Myers, 89, 93, 97*ff*,
      179, 182, 188*ff*
Internal rate of return, *see* rate of
   return
Investment
   in human capital, *see* human capital
   in physical capital, *see* physical
      capital
   profitability of, *see* rate of return

K_H, 88, 103*ff*, 180

$\dfrac{K}{L}$, 141*ff*

$\dfrac{K_H}{L}$, 88, 100, 180, 182

K_M, 103*ff*, 181

$\dfrac{K_M}{L}$, 88, 100, 181

·L, 88, 180, 181
L_i, 105, 108*ff*, 183

$\dfrac{L_i}{L_j}$, 138*ff*

Labour force
   by educational level, 183
   participation rate, 30, 192
   wages, *see* earnings

Marginal productivity of schooling,
   77*ff*
Migration, *see* brain drain

212

On-the-job training, 24—5
Opportunity cost, 125; *see also* earnings foregone

π, 115, 192

Patterns of rate of return, 61*ff*; *see also* rate of return
Physical capital
  and economic development, 10—1
  investment in, 79*ff*, 107—110, 101
  per member of the labour force 99—100, 178*ff*, 181
  returns to, 2, 7—8, 82, 86
Production function
  estimates, 104—5
  meta-, 103—4
  rate of return and, 88*ff*
Productivity, 30—1
Professional workers, 189
  emigrating to the U.S., 196
Profitability, *see* rate of return

r_c, 145*ff*, 147, 153
r_H, 75, 83, 85, 86, 89, 93, 112*ff*
r_i, 62, 75, 83, 108*ff*
r_M, 75, 82, 86, 112*ff*
Rate of return
  adjustments, *see* adjustments of rate of return
  allocative efficiency and, 75—6
  defined, 20
  and economic development, 187*ff*
  by educational level, 5—7, 62*ff*, 66
  and enrolments, 9—10, 95—7
  to graduate study, 71
  to investment in human capital; *see* human capital
  to investment in physical capital; *see* physical capital
  and on-the-job training, 24—5
  patterns, 61—73
  and per capita income, 8—9
  present value, versus, 19
  ranking, 66
  sensitivity, 155—7
  by sex, 24, 68—9, 159*ff*
  standard deviation, 65
  by subject, 72
  timing assumptions, 33

by type of secondary school, 70
types, 20*ff*, 85
  average and marginal, 22*ff*
  cross, 145*ff*
  ex post and ex ante, 23*ff*
  overall, 83—4, 93
  private and social, 20*ff*, 31, 66*ff*, 77*ff*, 84—5
Residual, 1
Risk and uncertainty, 33

σ, 138

s_L, 112*ff*, 120*ff*
Salaries, *see* earnings
Shadow wages, 11—2, 26
  estimates, 107; *see also* earnings
Share of labour
  actual, 106, 120
  by educational level, 120
  growth accounting, 112*ff*
  shadow, 106
Substitution, elasticity of, 15, 137—144
  earnings and, 137*ff*
  educational planning and, 137*ff*
  estimates, 139*ff*
  labour force structure and, 137*ff*

Taxation, 21—2, 31
Technical change, 1
Technical secondary, returns to, 70
Timing assumptions, 33

Unemployment, 29—30
Utility maximization, 77, 78

W_i, 95, 185
$\dfrac{W_i}{W_j}$, 132, 138*ff*, 185

Wages, *see* earnings
Wastage, 33—4

Y, 88, 108*ff*, 181
$\dfrac{Y}{L}$, 88
$\dfrac{Y}{P}$, 100

213

Author Index

Aarrestad, J., 47, 168
Abramovitz, M., 1
Allen, R. G. D., 138
Albukhari, N. M. A., 52
Ashenfelter, O., 29

Bailey, M. J., 19
Baldwin, R. E., 60, 172
Balogh, T., 1
Baumgarten, P., 50, 169
Becker, G. S., 29, 36ff, 37, 77, 94, 135
Bennett, N., 59, 172
Berry, R. A., 145
Blandy, R., 1
Blaug, M., 28ff, 31ff, 45ff, 53, 56, 78, 81, 98, 103, 143, 169, 171, 188
Bowles, S., 43, 57, 140, 143ff
Bowman, M. J., 1, 55, 111, 114, 170

Calcott, D., 57
Carnoy, M., 29, 39ff, 44, 49, 59, 61, 65, 118, 131, 166ff, 171
Carroll, A. B., 29
Castro, C. de M., 45
Chenery, H. B., 187
Chiswick, B. R., 135
Clark, D. H., 54, 170
Correa, H., 118

David, M., 28ff
Denison, E. F., 1, 29, 81, 83, 103, 111ff, 130ff, 144
Desayere, W., 50, 169
Devoretz, D., 55, 170
Dougherty, C. R. S., 26ff, 43, 140, 142ff
Danielsen, A. N., 56

Fabricant, S., 1

Fong, P. E., 54, 170
Friedman, M., 110
Glick, P. C., 36
Goldberger, A., 103
Greenwood, M. J., 145
Griliches, Z., 1ff, 111, 142
Grubel, H. G., 145

Hanoch, G., 29, 34, 37, 39, 77, 146
Hansen, N. B., 49, 168
Hansen, W. Lee, 37, 61
Harberger, A. C., 44, 53, 79, 167
Harbison, F., 89, 97ff
Hayami, Y., 103, 119
Henderson-Stewart, D., 45
Hewlett, S. A., 44, 167
Hinchliffe, K., 57ff, 171
Hines, F., 2, 39, 61, 67, 94, 166
Hirshleifer, J., 19
Hoerr, O. D., 54, 170
Houthaker, H. S., 36
Hunt, S. J., 29
Husen, T., 49

Ihnen, A. I., 29
International Labour Office, 146

Johnson, H. G., 107, 145

Karpoff, B., 29
Kiker, B. F., 1
Kim, K. S., 56, 170
Klinov-Malul, R., 52, 169
Kothari, V. N., 53
Krueger, A. O., 52, 102ff, 169

Lassiter, R. L., 38
Laya, J. C., 81
Layard, P. R. G., 27, 33, 46, 71ff, 103, 105, 139, 144, 168

Leibenstein, H., 50, 169
Leite, M. F., 19
Lerner, M. O., 45
Lydall, H. B., 135

McFadden, D., 138
Maddison, A., 81
Maglen, L., 46
Magnusson, L, 48, 168
Marshall, A., 18
Miller, H. P., 38
Mincer, J., 25
Minhas, B. S., 81
Ministry of Labour, 131
Mooney, J. D., 29
Morgan, J., 28ff
Morris, V., 47
Myers, C. A., 89, 97

Nalla Gounden, A. M., 53
Nelson, R. R., 103

O.E.C.D., 1, 51, 98, 143, 183
Ogilvy, B. J., 60, 172
Okachi, K., 56

Parai, L., 150
Patinkin, D., 145
Pesek, B. P., 81
Podoluk, J. R., 39, 166
Psacharopoulos, G., 26ff, 50ff, 56, 64,
    107, 114, 143, 146, 171

Ramsey, J. B., 19, 89
Renshaw, E. F., 26
Richardson, V. A., 46
Robinson, S., 101
Rogers, III, A. J., 45
Rogers, D., 27, 29, 58
Ruiter, P., 49, 168
Ruttan, V. W., 103, 119

Sahota, G. S., 145
Sato, K., 144
Saving, T. R., 81
Schmidt, K—D., 50, 169
Schultz, T. P., 41, 42
Schultz, T. W., 1ff, 28, 32, 34, 37,
    102, 111ff, 114
Schwartzman, D., 28

Scott, A. D., 145
Selby Smith, C., 47
Selowsky, M., 26ff, 43, 44, 53, 101,
    111, 118, 131, 167
Shoup C., 41, 167
Sirageldin, I., 29
Smyth, J. A., 59, 172
Soligo, R., 145
Solomon, E., 81
Solow, R. M., 1ff, 111
Streeten, P. O., 1

Thias, H. H., 29, 41, 59, 118, 171
Thomas, B., 144, 145

United Nations, 146
United States Department of Justice,
    149

Vaizey, J., 32, 125
Valdes, A., 44

Watanabe, S., 150
Weisbrod, B. A., 29, 32
Welch, F., 94, 142
Wilkinson, B. W., 39
Williamson, J., 55
Wolff, P. de, 49, 168
Woodhall, M., 53, 68, 80

Ziderman, A., 47

215

Country Index

Belgium, 50, 169
Brazil, 44*ff*, 68, 149, 167

Canada, 39, 63, 80, 81, 83, 147,
    149*ff*, 155, 166
Chile, 44, 83, 101, 118, 131, 133, 167
Colombia, 6, 41—4, 63*ff*, 67, 70, 117,
    131, 133, 167

Denmark, 49, 168

France, 130*ff*

Germany, 50, 85, 93, 147*ff*, 169
Ghana, 58, 64, 117, 126, 130*ff*, 134,
    171, 178
Great Britain, 7, 12, 45—8, 63, 71*ff*
    83, 117*ff*, 121, 126, 128, 131, 149,
    168
Greece, 50—1, 64, 131, 133, 169

India, 53—4, 72, 81, 99, 101*ff*, 130,
    134, 149*ff*, 152, 169—170
Israel, 52, 63, 133, 169, 178

Hawaii, 56—7, 71, 117*ff*, 171

Japan, 55—6, 81, 83, 98, 170
Jordan, 52

Kenya, 49, 58—9, 68, 80, 82, 118, 133,
    171
Korea, South, 56, 115, 131, 170, 178

Malaysia, 54, 130, 170
Mexico, 39—41, 49, 67, 68, 80, 101*ff*,
    118, 131, 133*ff*, 167

Nigeria, 57, 64, 131, 171
Netherlands, The, 12, 49—50, 83, 115,
    118, 121, 131, 168
New Zealand, 60, 115, 117, 172
Norway, 12, 115, 117*ff*, 130*ff*, 168

Philippines, 55, 96, 121, 128, 131,
    149, 170, 179
Puerto Rico, 39, 166

Rhodesia, Northern, 60, 96, 172

Singapore, 54, 170
Sweden, 48—9, 96, 149, 168

Thailand, 56, 64, 70, 171
Turkey, 52, 169

Uganda, 59—60, 96, 131, 172
U.S.A., 7, 15*ff*, 35—9, 61, 63*ff*, 71,
    94, 99, 101*ff*, 115, 118, 128, 134,
    146, 148*ff*, 166

Venezuela, 41, 64, 80, 93, 115, 117,
    167

Zambia, 60

Books from the
Higher Education Research Unit

Elsevier Scientific Publishing Company — Amsterdam,
Studies on Education'

The Practice of Manpower Forecasting: A Collection of Case Studies by
B. Ahamad, M. Blaug and others (1973)
Returns to Education: An International Comparison by George Psacharopoulos
assisted by Keith Hinchliffe (1973)

In preparation

Demand for Social Scientists
Costs in Universities and Polytechnics
Economic and Social Aspects of the Academic Profession

Published by Allen Lane The Penguin Press
'L.S.E. Studies on Education'

Decision Models for Educational Planning by Peter Armitage, Cyril Smith and
Paul Alper (1969)
The Causes of Graduate Unemployment in India by Mark Blaug, Richard Layard
and Maureen Woodhall (1969)
Paying for Private Schools by Howard Glennerster and Gail Wilson (1970)
Policy and Practice: The Colleges of Advanced Technology by Tyrrell Burgess
and John Pratt (1970)
A Fair Start: The Provision of Pre-school Education by Tessa Blackstone (1971)
*Qualified Manpower and Economic Performance: An Inter-plant Study in the
Electrical Engineering Industry* by P. R. G. Layard, J. D. Sargan, M. E. Ager and
D. J. Jones (1971)

Published by Penguin Books

The Impact of Robbins: Expansion in Higher Education by Richard Layard,
John King and Claus Moser (1969)

Published by Oliver and Boyd

*Graduate School: a Study of Graduate Work at the London School of Eco-
nomics* by H. Glennerster with the assistance of A. Bennett and C. Farrell (1966)
The Utilization of Educated Manpower in Industry by M. Blaug, M. Peston and
A. Ziderman (1967)
Manpower and Educational Development in India (1961—1986) by Tyrrell
Burgess, Richard Layard and Pitambar Pant (1968)
Educational Finance: its Sources and Uses in the United Kingdom by Alan
Peacock, Howard Glennerster and Robert Lavers (1968)
Education and Manpower: Theoretical Models and Empirical Applications by
Tore Thonstad (1969)

Published in collaboration with the
Directorate for Scientific Affairs, O.E.C.D.

*Statistics of the Occupational and Educational Structure of the Labour Force in
53 Countries* (1969)